THE FOREIGN SERVICE
OF THE UNITED STATES

The Foreign Service of the United States

BY

TRACY HOLLINGSWORTH LAY

CONSUL GENERAL OF THE UNITED STATES

Foreword

BY

HON. CHARLES EVANS HUGHES

NEW YORK
PRENTICE-HALL, INC.
1925

FOREWORD

THE new diplomacy is the old art practiced under new conditions. Swift and easy communication multiply the demands upon the human agencies of intercourse. Many questions which the mere lapse of time would solve become insistent because immediately known. The telegraph is burdened with current information and with instructions largely made necessary by the fact that instant communication is possible. With each new facility the total load is made heavier. The enterprise of the press, with its latest equipment, informing, anticipating, conjecturing, warning, the most powerful instrument of popular education, the ready agency of truth and error, with the tremendous leverage of the opinion of the moment, is the force with which diplomacy must daily reckon. But the most important of all developments is the democratization of institutions. The new diplomacy deals formally with governments but actually with the peoples that control governments. The days of intrigue to support dynastic ambitions, to promote the immediate concerns of ruling houses, are over. But democracy is no less keen to safeguard national interests, and the opportunities of prejudice, of passionate devotion to petty ends at the expense of more important national aims, continue. The judgment of peoples must be informed in the midst of the conflicts of partisans and of pseudo-patriotic appeals, and this enlightenment must be achieved by consultations in a house whose doors cannot be closed. We must have our domestic discussions, but everything is borne beyond the three-mile limit. The strident outcries of a minority of unreason may be taken abroad more seriously than at home, while the moderate advice of sober judgment may be regarded elsewhere as evidence of weakness and stimulate excessive demands. Democratization spoils the opportunities of despotic power, of chicane, of secret agreements against the public interest, but it raises its own difficulties when serious controversies creating intense national feeling must be adjusted by reasonable men whose every effort is discounted and may be misinterpreted. Democracy is impatient of the slow processes and mutual concessions which are inevitable in negotiations between equal states. No one is content to wait for the event; uncertainty is unendurable. The event must be anticipated, and the monsters of the imagination must be slain daily.

Peace is more nearly than ever the actual, as it has always been the professed, aim of diplomacy. So long as there are independent and equal states, with divergent interests constantly giving rise to differences which lie outside the field of legal obligation, the agencies of agreement must be the most vital concern of those who seek to promote peace. Given a will to peace, these agencies should secure it; without that disposition, there is little hope in formulas. What is needed is not only the adjustment of grave controversies after they have arisen, but the smoothing out of difficulties so that they do not become serious. Plans for arbitral settlement as an alternative to force are of the utmost importance but they are intended only for those instances where diplomacy fails. Skillful diplomacy is preventive medicine.

In view of the multiplication of international questions and of the interrelation of political and economic problems, it should be apparent that the national interest demands thoroughly trained Foreign Service officers. Increase in the facilities of communication makes personal contacts even more necessary. Information, arguments, demands may be transmitted, but the art of persuasion needs the personal touch. In the harassing multiplicity of things, the direct approach saves time and brings results. No mechanism will ever take the place of interviews of men who respect and trust each other. No business organization in any matter of importance forgets this. Again, there is constantly more to be known, to be analyzed; the affairs of nations are more intricate and special training is needed to deal with them. As an early writer expressed it: "It is rather late to begin digging a well when one feels thirsty."

The new diplomacy requires not the divining of the intent of monarchs, the mere discovery and thwarting of intrigues, but the understanding of peoples. There must be intimate acquaintance with their interests, their problems, the conflicts of parties, the course of opinion. There must be ability to sift; to seize upon what is significant in the mass of news, of rumors, of assertion, of debate; to know the character and particular aims of men who control the action of governments. For this, alertness and general adaptability will not suffice. One must have the equipment of the student of history and politics, and the democratic sympathies and cultural training which enable him to enter into the thoughts of peoples. And while he seeks to do this, he cannot escape giving an impression of the life of his own country. In no slight measure, by his own character and deportment, he determines the reputation of his government.

The Foreign Service of the United States has entered upon a new phase. At last, a competent organization has been achieved on a merit basis, with appropriate promise of career. To hold this service in just esteem, to safe-

guard the gains which have been won so slowly, to perfect the organization, it must be understood by the
American people. This book is adapted to the need.
Democracy with its new diplomacy should be served
expertly and the faithful Foreign Service officer at his
post abroad should have the inspiration and the satisfaction of the assurance that the nature and importance
of his service are appreciated at home.

CONTENTS

INTRODUCTION

THIS book is not an official publication, nor has it been written with a view to giving expression to official opinion. No one in any way shares in the full responsibility of the author for what it contains. Various phases of the same subject have been treated by other authors in works on constitutional and international law and in scattered, descriptive articles, but this appears to be the first time that an intimate analysis of the Foreign Service has been attempted by an officer of that service.

Perhaps the chief characteristics of the work are that it claims to be comprehensive within the scope of its title; that there is little loss of essential material in compressing the subject-matter into a single volume; that it contains the first full description of the reorganized Foreign Service; and that it attempts a number of constructive proposals for the further improvement of the machinery of our foreign relations.

The author is indebted to several of his friends and colleagues for helpful suggestions, and especially to Honorable Charles Evans Hughes for his generous contribution of a valuable Foreword.

THE AUTHOR

CHAPTER I

FOREIGN SERVICE DEVELOPMENT

Scope of this book.—In considering the broad subject of foreign relations, it is of primary importance to establish a clear distinction between policy and instrumentality, or in other words, between those organs of the government which determine the objects to be accomplished, and those the duty of which it is to provide the means of accomplishment. Lord Bryce, in referring to this distinction, which he terms "Ends and Means," points out that "though it exists in all branches of administration, it is less significant in the domestic branches, because in them Ends, if not assumed as generally recognized, are and must be determined by the people through their representatives."[1]

In our system of government, foreign policy[2] may originate in several ways, but its application, or execution, is confided to the President, who acts through the governmental agencies provided him for that purpose. These agencies are the Department of State, and the Foreign Service, which is composed of a diplomatic and a consular branch.[3]

The title of this book, therefore, refers to that part of the established governmental machinery of administration commonly known as the Diplomatic and Consular

[1]James Bryce, "Modern Democracies," vol. II, p. 368.

[2]"Foreign policy," as here employed, refers to the normal, peaceful intercourse of nations, as contrasted with measures involving the use of force.

[3]Sec. 1, Act of May 24, 1924.

1

Service—collectively, the Foreign Service—which comprises our foreign representation. In one sense, the Foreign Service may be described as the eyes, the ears, and the mouth of the Department of State; but in a broader sense, it is an integral part of a vast system for the control of our international relations through which the sovereignty of the nation expresses itself to the foreign world.

Periods of diplomatic importance.—There are two periods in the life of a nation when its foreign affairs, and consequently, its Foreign Service, assume a rôle of almost transcendent importance: in infancy, during its struggle for recognition, for security, and for a permanent international status; and secondly, in maturity, when its social, economic, and political interests have overleaped their domestic boundaries and assumed a world importance. It is natural, then, after a century of adolescence and growth in which the attention of our country has been wrapped in its own national development, that the sudden surge of the United States to the forefront of international prominence should recall to us that earlier, or infant, period in our history when diplomacy was an arm of chief reliance.[4]

The early task of diplomacy.—The first great task of the Foreign Service of the United States was that of

---

[4]"During the Revolution and the Confederation diplomacy was recognized by the intelligent to be as essential to the establishment of our national existence, as arms, diplomats were as carefully chosen as generals; the news of the negotiations of Franklin, Adams, and Jay was as anxiously awaited as that from the army, and their successes brought almost as great a reward of popular acclaim as did those of commanders in the field. * * * * Foreign affairs absorbed attention that was needed for domestic problems, the fate of administrations came to hang upon their foreign policy. Dissertations on diplomatic problems created political reputations. Of the five presidents who succeeded Washington all had had diplomatic experience and four had served as secretaries of state. Practically devoid of a permanent army or navy, we relied for defense upon our diplomats and the ocean."—Fish, "American Diplomacy," pp. 1-2.

winning friends when friends meant all; of effecting
the transition from bondage to freedom of a group of
loosely confederated States, whose bond of unity was
a new theory of government, and whose permanence as
a nation was yet to be proved.

The gravity of international relations in such conditions was obvious. A diplomatic blunder might have
involved a national catastrophe. The situation was too
serious for political tampering with untrained and in-
experienced representatives, where the foremost talent
of the land was required.

Nor was there a dearth of trained diplomatists among
the colonists. The problems of the colonial struggle and
the agitated international relations of ante-revolution-
ary and revolutionary days had afforded an almost un-
rivaled atmosphere for the development of sagacious
diplomatic minds in the school of practical negotiation.[5]

The use of trained diplomatists.—But there is sometimes a tendency to lose from mind the realities of an
historical period, and to draw erroneous lessons from
the record of its achievements. This has proved true
with respect to certain factors in the early successes
of American diplomacy. Thus in the hearings on the
recent foreign service reorganization bill, when the
subject of a trained diplomatic service was under
discussion, Representative John Jacob Rogers of Mas-

[5]"Of men trained in the more essential elements of diplomacy, the
colonies had a greater proportion than any other country of the time. They
had been engaged in continual negotiations, almost independently of Great
Britain, with the Indian tribes, and frequently with the French and
Spaniards. Every colony had had semi-diplomatic disputes with its neigh-
bors, and all had supported agents in England whose functions included
virtually all the elements of a diplomatic mission. Almost continuously
from 1758 to 1774 Benjamin Franklin, as general agent, had occupied a post
in England essentially equivalent to minister to that government. Moreover, the whole movement toward union between the colonies was diplomatic
in its character, and constantly involved the most delicate questions of
management."—*Ibid.*, pp. 21-22.

sachusetts, by way of eliciting instructive testimony, observed:

"We frequently hear Benjamin Franklin mentioned as a pretty good type of the untrained diplomat and as some one whom we should emulate for all time because of his success."

To this, Honorable Hugh Gibson, then United States Minister to Poland, now Minister to Switzerland, replied:

"Benjamin Franklin is frequently cited as an example of a wholly untrained man who made a brilliant success in diplomacy. As a matter of fact, Franklin was one of the best-trained diplomats we ever had. From an early age he concerned himself with political and diplomatic languages, French, Italian, Spanish, and Latin—a remarkably good equipment. In 1757 he was sent to London by the Pennsylvania Assembly to negotiate with the English Government. This was purely a diplomatic mission, involving questions of great importance, and lasted for five years until 1762. From 1764 to 1775, a further period of 11 years, Franklin represented in London not only Pennsylvania, but New Jersey, Georgia, and Massachusetts and handled a wide range of subjects calculated to develop his powers of negotiation and persuasion. He had to develop these powers as he had nothing else to help him achieve success in his mission. These two missions, extending over a period of 16 years, are really Franklin's period of training, although it is the custom to look upon France as his only diplomatic experience. Upon Franklin's return to America at the outbreak of the Revolution, he was entrusted with several diplomatic missions, such as that to Canada to invoke the support of those colonies in the Revolution, and again when he was appointed by the Congress to negotiate terms of peace with Admiral Howe.

"In 1776 Franklin was appointed commissioner to France. He was chosen for this highly important mission precisely because he was the most experienced and successful negotiator who could be found—in other words, because he was our most highly trained diplomat. He was chosen for exactly the same reason we should like to have our men chosen to-day. Franklin remained in France until 1785, a further period of nine years. There is perhaps nobody in our service to-day who had such a good background of experience and training as Franklin had when he went to France, and it is wrong to speak of him as an untrained diplomat." [6]

Foreign affairs under the Articles of Confederation.—Under the Articles of Confederation, the control of foreign relations was vested in the Congress, which had the sole and exclusive right and power of determining on peace and war, of sending and receiving ambassadors, and of entering into treaties and alliances.[7]

There being no central governmental authority other than the Congress, our diplomatic representatives suffered the severe handicap of functioning under the direction of a numerous body which possessed none of those elements of decision, consistency, and continuity of policy so essential to the successful conduct of foreign relations.[8]

---

[6]Hearings before Committee on Foreign Affairs on H.R. 17 and H.R. 6357, 68th Cong., 1st Sess., p. 20.

[7]Art. IX.

[8]"And since the Confederation showed itself so disastrously inefficient in the conduct and direction of foreign affairs, it was natural that the alert and far-seeing foreign secretary should take the lead in seeking a new order of things which should give us a government worthy of the name. There was no more earnest and efficient advocate of Washington's ideal of a strong national government than Jay, especially when speaking from the fulness of his bitter experience as an ill-treated diplomatic agent of

The clumsiness of this arrangement proved to be one of the conspicuous weaknesses of the Confederation, but the unsatisfactory experiences resulting from its operation had the virtue of serving as an instructive lesson to the constitution-builders when a more effective adjustment of powers was undertaken as a basis of permanent union.[9] To the same cause is also due, in large measure, the genius of our present system which links legislative participation with executive control.[10]

Birth of the Diplomatic Service.—The Diplomatic Service was one of the earliest establishments of our Government. It functioned actively during the Confederation, and promptly after the adoption of the Constitution Congress passed an act authorizing the President to draw from the Treasury of the United States a sum not to exceed $40,000 annually to be paid out of the moneys arising from the duties on imports and tonnage for the support of such persons as he might commission to serve the United States in foreign parts, and for the expense incident to the objects on which they might be employed. An outfit was allowed each minister not exceeding the amount of his annual salary and the total of his salary and outfit were not to exceed

Congress abroad, and as the ill-treated foreign secretary of that same incompetent body at home."—Johnson, "America's Foreign Relations," vol. 1, p. 146.

[9]"Under the Articles of Confederation the administration had proved too weak to perform the duties of a national government in maintaining the rights and interests of its citizens among the nations of the world. This failure in diplomacy was one of the causes for the formation of a stronger central authority."—Fish, "American Diplomacy," p. 79.

[10]Alexander Hamilton, during the formative period of the Constitution, wrote in *The Federalist:* "The qualities elsewhere detailed as indispensable in the management of foreign negotiations, point out the executive as the most fit agent in these transactions; while the vast importance of the trust, and the operation of treaties as laws, plead strongly for the participation of the whole or a portion of the legislative body in the office of making them."—Quoted in Johnson, "America's Foreign Relations," vol. I, p. 150.

$9,000 per annum. The compensation of a chargé d'affaires was fifty per cent of that amount.[11]

It should be observed that the appropriations here provided were in the form of a lump sum placed at the disposal of the President with no attempt on the part of Congress to dictate the grades or titles of diplomatic representatives.

While the sum of $40,000 appears modest, even as a start, the true criterion of the diplomatic activity of that period is to be found in the alertness of the Government to international developments, and the energy and despatch with which it responded to the demands of diplomatic exigency. This may be illustrated in two important instances.

Examples of early diplomatic action.—President Washington, on April 22, 1793, issued his epochal proclamation of neutrality in the struggle between Great Britain and France. Immediately there followed the French decree authorizing the seizure of all merchant vessels carrying neutral provisions to a British port [12] but specifically exempting American commerce,[13] to which the British Government responded by an order in council [14] authorizing the seizure of "all ships laden with corn, flour, or meal," without exception. This began the long series of interruptions of American commerce, involving search, seizure and impressment which culminated in the War of 1812.

As a first measure of defensive action, Congress, on March 20, 1794, appropriated one million dollars "to defray any expenses which may be incurred in relation to the intercourse between the United States and for-

---

11Act of July 1, 1790, 1 Stat., p. 128.
12Decree of the National Convention, May 9, 1793.
13Supplemental decree of May 23, 1793.
14June 8, 1793.

eign nations, to be paid out of any monies, which may be in the treasury, not otherwise appropriated, and to be applied, under the direction of the President of the United States, who, if necessary, is hereby authorized to borrow the whole or any part of the said sum of one million dollars; an account of the expenditure whereof, as soon as may be, shall be laid before Congress."

Having thus set the diplomatic stage as an essential preliminary, a Joint Resolution was passed [15] laying an embargo for thirty days on all ships and vessels in the ports of the United States bound for any port or place, and on June 4, 1794, an act was passed authorizing the President to lay an embargo whenever, in his opinion, the public safety should require it.

Again, in the intensity of the struggle to maintain neutral rights at the moment when Napoleon's Berlin decree [16] and the British decrees of blockade and orders in council were imminent, Congress, on February 13, 1806, passed an act, the language of which is so illuminating in its relation to diplomatic history as to merit perusal and reflection.

"Be it enacted * * * That a sum of two millions of dollars be, and the same is hereby appropriated [17] towards defraying any extraordinary expenses which may be incurred in the intercourse between the United States and foreign nations, to be paid out of any money

---

[15] Joint Res. March 26, 1794.

[16] Nov. 21, 1806.

[17] The relative importance of this amount may be judged from the fact that the total expenditures of the government in 1806 were $9,803,617. An appropriation of like proportion to-day would amount to $715,384,473, or about eighty-four times the cost of the entire Foreign Service establishment of the Government, including the Department of State, and the Foreign Service in 1924. The total of governmental expenditures for 1924 was $3,506,677,715.

in the treasury, not otherwise appropriated, and to be applied under the direction of the President of the United States, who shall cause an account thereof to be laid before Congress as soon as may be.

"Sec. 2. And be it further enacted, That the President of the United States be, and hereby is authorized, if necessary, to borrow the said sum, or any part thereof, in behalf of the United States, at a rate of interest not exceeding six per centum, per annum, redeemable at the will of the Congress of the United States. And it shall be lawful for the Bank of the United States to lend the whole, or any part of the same.

"Sec. 3. And be it further enacted, That so much as may be necessary of the surplus of the duties on imports and tonnage, beyond the permanent appropriation heretofore charged upon them, by law, shall be, and hereby is pledged and appropriated for the payment of the interest, and reimbursement of the principal, of all such monies as may be borrowed in pursuance of this act, according to the terms and conditions on which the loan or loans may be effected." [18]

Birth of the Consular Service.—The Consular Service, as a separate agency, was of later development, the United States having at first no consular representation distinct from the Diplomatic Service. The same officers performed both diplomatic and consular functions, reproducing in this respect the history of the consular systems of Europe.[19]

The distinctive status of consuls as agents of international intercourse was expressly recognized in the Constitution, but during the interval of three years before the passage of the first consular law, President

---

[18] Act of Feb. 13, 1806, Stat. 2, pp. 349-350.
[19] Mathews, "The Conduct of American Foreign Relations," p. 97.

Washington, seeing the urgent need of such representation, took the initiative in appointing a number of consuls independently.[20]

The first consular law.—The first enactment relating to the powers and duties of consular officers was the law of April 14, 1792, "for carrying into full effect the convention between the King of the French, and the United States of America, entered into for the purpose of defining and establishing the functions and privileges of their respective consuls and vice consuls."

This act contained a number of general provisions, forming the groundwork of the consular system, and gave authority to consuls to receive protests and declarations; to give copies under the consular seal; to settle the affairs of American citizens dying within the limits of the consulate; to secure property saved from wrecks; to provide for the deposit of the ship's papers; and to afford relief to destitute American seamen.

There was also a provision recognizing the enlarged, or general, powers of consular officers resulting from the nature of their appointments or from any treaty or convention under which they might act.

A supplementary act of February 28, 1803,[21] extended and further defined the duties of consular officers with relation to masters of vessels, and the protection of American seamen and shipping.

The beginning of the spoils system.—After the successful termination of the War of 1812, the attention of the country became absorbed in domestic problems, and matters of international concern were relegated to a position of secondary importance.[22] A long period then

---

[20] *Ibid.*

[21] 2 Stat., 203.

[22] "By 1815 diplomacy had ceased to shape politics; after 1830 politics began to shape diplomacy. With Jackson, 'shirtsleeve' diplomacy began,

ensued in which general neglect and even abuses arose both at home and abroad in the management of the Foreign Service. Appointments to foreign posts were made for internal, partisan reasons, rather than for the fitness, experience, and ability of the persons appointed, while the remuneration, especially of consular officers, was derived from fees collected and retained by them, the amount being largely arbitrary. There were no statutory salaries; consuls were merchants engaged in business at their posts, and no effective system of accounting was required.

By the advent of the Jackson administration such an unsatisfactory state of affairs had developed from these and other practices, that there were evidences of a growing spirit of discontent and even a few tendencies in the direction of general reorganization.

The Livingston report.—No further constructive legislation relating to consular duties having been enacted since 1792, Secretary of State Edward Livingston, on March 2, 1833, rendered a report to President Jackson in which he analyzed the deficiencies of the prevailing system and strongly recommended measures of reform.

But far from any immediate action being taken on these recommendations, the political raid on the service was intensified, while abuses and general inefficiency developed in corresponding proportion. Nevertheless, as the main features of the Livingston report were eventually to be embodied in the basic act of August 18, 1856, they are of interest as foreshadowing the course of important reforms, for which reason the following excerpts are pertinent in this connection:

"To a nation essentially commercial like the United

but it did not reach its zenith till after the Civil War."—Fish, "American Diplomacy," p. 220.

States, the consular functions are highly important, and ought to be strictly defined. They are performed in a foreign country often in collision with the officers of the nation in which they are placed; and therefore, public, as well as private interests, are put in jeopardy by their errors or faults. Frequently, commissioned to reside in countries where there is no public minister of their country, they are forced, in defense of their fellow citizens, to assume, occasionally, diplomatic power, by addressing themselves directly to the Government: without proper instructions given them by law, they may do this unadvisedly, or indiscreetly, and thus involve their country in difficulties and disputes.

"In the various acts they are called on to perform in relation to the commerce of their fellow citizens, they may assume powers injurious to their interests, or refuse to act from ignorance of their duty, where the case would seem to require it. In most of these circumstances, they have no legal adviser, and no rule prescribed by law to guide them in the delicate and important questions that are continually calling for their decision. At home, every officer is surrounded with the means of obtaining information and advice; yet at home, every officer has his duties prescribed and marked out by law. Abroad, an officer is entrusted with the most important function, out of the reach of control or advice, and is left with, comparatively, no written rules for his guidance. * * *

"A more precise designation of the duties of consuls is, therefore, of the first necessity; and if the system of compensation by fees should be persevered in, it would require a more particular table of those which ought to be received. * * *

"The subject of compensation is one that has engaged

my close attention since I have had the direction of the Department, and I have no hesitation in giving a decided opinion, that the exaction of fees has been the source of misundertandings between our Consuls and the Masters of Vessels, injurious to the reputation of the Country,—that it is degrading to the officer who is obliged to wrangle for them,—is unequal in its operations—oppressive to our commerce,—and ought either to be wholly abolished, or so modified as to make the operation of the system more equal, by apportioning the amount to the size of the vessel, or, if possible, to the value of the cargo.

"But I cannot avoid expressing the opinion that these officers, like all others, should be compensated by adequate salaries, and should be prevented from engaging in commerce. According to the present system, our consuls, with very few exceptions, are commission merchants, anxious, like all other merchants, to increase their business and obtain consignments. In many, perhaps in the greater number of cases, the place is sought for chiefly for the advantage and the influence it will give to extend the commercial affairs of the officer. Can it be believed that this official influence will always be properly exercised? When it is, will not contrary suspicions be entertained? This must create jealousy, detraction, and all the arts that rivalship will exercise and provoke, amidst which the dignity of the public officer is degraded, and his influence with the foreign functionaries lost. The Consul at least, therefore, if not the Vice-Consul, ought to be salaried officers. They will never, then, by their countrymen, be suspected of acting towards them as their commercial interest, not as their duty, requires; and their complaints in behalf of their fellow-citizens will be attended to, because they will not be liable to the suspicion of advocating their own interest; consular offices would no longer be held in counting houses, nor the consul himself called, from defending the cause of an injured American citizen, to sell a barrel of sugar, or to despatch the settlement of an account. * * *

"It is not for the sole benefit of the ships which touch at a Consular port that the consular office is created; the whole country is interested in the establishment. The concerns of its general commerce, the protection of its citizens abroad, its reputation is concerned." [23]

Act of March 1, 1855.—On March 1, 1855, Congress enacted a law "to remodel the diplomatic and consular systems of the United States" in which an attempt was made to prescribe grades, posts and salaries, both in the Diplomatic and in the Consular Service. The first section of this law stated "that from and after the thirtieth day of June next, the President of the United States shall, by and with the advice and consent of the Senate, appoint representatives of the grade of envoys extraordinary and ministers plenipotentiary to the following countries, who shall receive an annual compensation for their services not exceeding the amount specified herein for each."

Section 2 adopted the same language for secretaries of legation, and sections 3, 4, and 5 embodied the same mandatory provisions with respect to commissioners and consular officers. It is obvious that Congress in this instance exceeded its authority by attempting to regulate the appointments of the President under his constitutional powers.[24]

---

[23]See Message of President No. 83, page 1, 22nd Cong., 2nd Sess., Foreign Relations, 1832-33.

[24]"After passing, in 1855, an abortive act, some of whose provisions

Attorney General Cushing, in construing the act, largely nullified the operation of its mandatory provisions [25] and it was repealed the following year.[26]

Act of August 18, 1856.—Following more nearly the constitutional guides that had been pointed out by the Attorney General, a law "to regulate the diplomatic and consular systems of the United States" was enacted on August 18, 1856, which contained provisions of far-reaching importance.

It established the basis for the present range of diplomatic salaries as applied to ambassadors, ministers, and chargés d'affaires, without attempting to dictate grades or posts. It also established the position of secretary of legation. In the case of the Consular Service, where the chief abuses had been practiced under the spoils system, it adopted in part the recommendations of Secretary of State Livingston in more precisely defining the duties of consular officers and attempting to place their compensation upon a salary basis. For this latter purpose three schedules were adopted which grouped the consular posts of the service in the order of their respective importance. Consular officers appointed to posts within the first schedule were put upon a salary basis and were prohibited from engaging in private trade. Those appointed to posts of the second schedule likewise received salaries, but were permitted to engage in business. Those of the third schedule remained on a fee basis. An attempt was made to enforce a system of accounting for fees throughout the entire service. A bond was

---

were, in the opinion of Attorney General Cushing, unconstitutional, Congress enacted in the following year an important law carrying out to some extent Livingston's recommendations."—Mathews, "The Conduct of American Foreign Relations," p. 99.

[25]See page 59.

[26]Sec. 33, Act August 18, 1856 (11 Stat., 65).

required of all salaried officers of the first schedule appointed after the passage of the Act.

Consular pupils.—One of its important provisions, which became in later years the entering wedge of the merit system, was the creation of a corps of consular pupils to be appointed by the President and assigned to consulates in the hope that their training in the service might qualify them for promotion to higher grades. A condition to the selection of these young officers was the following: "before the appointment of any such pupil shall be made, satisfactory evidence, by examination or otherwise, shall be furnished of his qualifications and fitness for the office to the Secretary of State, and by him laid before the President." This was the birth of the consular assistant corps which was destined to bring into the service many years afterwards a sufficient number of valuable officers to prove the inherent merit of a trained and non-partisan corps.

Fees and presidential regulations.—The President was authorized to establish a tariff of official fees which it became the duty of all officers to collect and remit to the Treasury. The President was also authorized "to prescribe such regulations and make and issue such orders and instructions, not inconsistent with the Constitution or any law of the United States, in relation to the duties of all diplomatic and consular officers, the transaction of their business, the rendering of accounts and returns, the payment of compensation, the safekeeping of the archives, and public property in the hands of all such officers, the communication of information, and the procurement and transmission of the products of the arts, sciences, manufactures, agriculture, and commerce, from time to time, as he may think conducive to the public interests; and it shall be the duty of all such officers to conform to such regulations, orders and instructions." This provision had the effect of giving the force of law to Executive orders and other regulations of the President, in which regard it has formed the basis of all subsequent consular regulations and instructions to diplomatic officers. There were other less important provisions, many of which remain in force today substantially as first enacted. Reference to these occurs throughout the succeeding chapters.

A period of public indifference.—With the close of the Civil War the United States entered upon another prolonged period of indifference to international affairs, which was a natural consequence of disordered conditions at home and the demands of reconstruction. For nearly half a century no further important legislative action was undertaken towards strengthening and improving the machinery of foreign affairs. This fact has been noted by Rear Admiral Mahan who has pointed out that "an apt illustration of the usual indifference of our American public to international conditions, except for brief moments when some circumstance out of the usual course threatens to involve ourselves, or traverses some of our accepted notions, is to be found in the stationary condition of the organization of the Department of State between the close of the War of Secession and the end of the War with Spain." [27]

Continuance of the spoils system.—Notwithstanding the precautionary measures taken by the act of 1856 to place the service on a salary basis, and to regulate and control the collection of fees, again no adequate system of accounting was provided, and worse still, the list of official fees did not cover all consular activities. Unofficial fees, therefore, became an important source

[27]Mahan, "America's Interest in International Conditions," p. 7.

of irregularity, while the practice of making political appointments grew with each change of administration.

There is, perhaps, no more striking evidence of the disastrous consequences of the old spoils system than that which is contained in the following extract from a statement by William H. Lincoln, who speaks from practical experience with its operations:

"At one time I was president of the New England Ship Owners' Association, president of the Boston Chamber of Commerce four years beginning 1900, president of the Commercial Club of Boston, manager of steamship lines to Europe for 30 years. My experience in shipowning began in 1862 and continued for about 40 years. At one time I was part owner and manager of more than 25 sailing ships which were employed in foreign commerce.

"My experience in regard to our Consular Service (while under the spoils system of appointment) was most unsatisfactory. In many cases the consuls in foreign ports were more desirous of securing benefits for themselves than to protect the interests of American shipowners. * * *

"I consider that the abuses of this system had considerable influence in driving American shipowners out of the business. It was not only vexatious but it involved a large pecuniary loss. The consuls were selected, not for any qualification for the duties, but wholly for political purposes." [28]

The grade of ambassador established.—Although under the Constitution the President had the right to appoint ambassadors, by and with the advice and consent of the Senate, no appointments to that grade were made

---

[28]The statement is quoted in full in the "Report on the Foreign Service," National Civil Service Reform League (1919), pp. 116–118.

prior to the law of March 1, 1893,[29] which was an act making appropriations for the Diplomatic and Consular service, but which contained the following general provision:

"Whenever the President shall be advised that any foreign government is represented, or is about to be represented, in United States by an ambassador, envoy extraordinary, minister plenipotentiary, minister resident, special envoy, or chargé d'affaires, he is authorized, in his discretion, to direct that the representative of United States to such government shall bear the same designation. This provision shall in nowise affect the duties, powers, or salary of such representative."

A year later, June 26, 1894, ambassadors were appointed to Great Britain, France, Russia, and Germany, thus establishing permanently the grade of ambassador in the foreign representation of the United States.

Attempt to establish merit system.—On September 20, 1895, President Cleveland issued an Executive order of historic importance in relation to the evolution of the Foreign Service to a merit basis. It read as follows:

"It being of great importance that the consuls and commercial agents of the United States shall possess the proper qualifications for their respective positions to be ascertained either through a satisfactory record of previous actual service under the Department of State or through an appropriate examination:

"It is hereby ordered that any vacancy in a consulate or commercial agency now or hereafter existing the salary of which is not more than $2,500, nor less than $1,000, or the compensation of which, if derived from

[29] 27 Stat., 497.

official fees, exclusive of notarial and other unofficial receipts, does not exceed $2,500, nor fall below $1,000, shall be filled (a) by a transfer or promotion from some other position under the Department of State of a character tending to qualify the incumbent for the position to be filled; or (b) by appointment of a person not under the Department of State but having previously served thereunder to its satisfaction in a capacity tending to qualify him for the position to be filled; or (c) by the appointment of a person who, having furnished the customary evidence of character, responsibility, and capacity, and being thereupon selected by the President for examination, is found upon such examination to be qualified for the position.

"For the purposes of this order notarial and unofficial fees shall not be regarded, but the compensation of a consulate or commercial agency shall be ascertained, if the office is salaried, by reference to the last preceding appropriation act, and, if the office is not salaried, by reference to the returns of official fees for the last preceding fiscal year.

"The examination herein before provided for shall be by a Board of three persons designated by the Secretary of State who shall also prescribe the subjects to which such examination shall relate and the general mode of conducting the same by the Board.

"A vacancy in a consulate will be filled at discretion only when a suitable appointment cannot be made in, any of the modes indicated in the second paragraph of this order."

Though a promising start seemed to have been made in this initial step, the system was not perpetuated under succeeding administrations, and an interval of twenty years ensued before the notable Act of 1906 laid the final foundation of the present Foreign Service career.

Act of April 5, 1906.—The act of April 5, 1906,[30] dealt only with the Consular Service, which had suffered chief abuse under the irregularities of the spoils system. By its provisions the posts in the Consular Service were classified into nine classes, and consuls general and consuls were graded according to their posts. A corps of five inspectors of consulates, to be designated and commissioned as consuls general at large, was established. Their appointment was to be made by the President, with senatorial confirmation, from among the members of the consular force possessing the requisite qualifications of experience and ability. Each consulate was required to be inspected at least once in every two years.[31]

The subordinate force of the service was Americanized by the provision that "no person who is not an American citizen shall be appointed hereafter in any consulate general or consulate to any clerical position the salary of which is $1,000 a year or more." The prohibition against engaging in business, or legal practice, was extended to all consular officers receiving a salary of more than $1,000 a year and bonds were required of all such officers. Notarial acts, the performance of which had formerly been optional with the consul, were made obligatory. All fees, official and unofficial, were put on an exact accounting basis through the method of attaching adhesive fee stamps to documents.

The points of chief importance in the act were the grading and classifying of the offices, which permitted

---

[30]For full text, see Appendix A.
[31]For duties of consular inspectors, see page 284.

President Roosevelt to take the constructive step of throwing the service under the operation of the civil service law; the creation of inspectors, the requirement of bonds, and the establishment of a definite system of accounting, which put an end to many of the irregularities that had been practiced to the detriment of the nation for almost a century.

The merit system achieved.—Promptly following the passage of the new law, President Roosevelt, on June 27, 1906, issued an Executive order prescribing regulations governing appointments and promotions in the Consular Service.[32] It provided that vacancies in the offices of consul general and consul above class eight should be filled by promotion from the lower grades, based upon ability and efficiency as shown in the service. Vacancies in classes eight and nine were to be filled (a) by the promotion of consular clerks, vice consuls, deputy consuls and consular agents, and (b) by new appointments of candidates passing a satisfactory examination for appointment as consul.

Persons in the service of the State Department, with salaries of $2,000 or upwards, were made eligible for promotion on the basis of ability and efficiency to any grade of the Consular Service above class eight.

The Board of Examiners.—There was constituted a Board of Examiners to formulate rules, to hold examinations, and to pass upon the qualifications of candidates seeking admission to the Consular Service. The composition of the Board was as follows: the Secretary of State or such officer of the Department of State as the President might designate, the Chief of the Consular Bureau, and the Chief Examiner of the Civil

---

[32]For full text see Appendix B.

Service Commission, or some person whom the said Commission might designate.

The examination.—The scope and method of the examinations were to be determined by the Board of Examiners but among the subjects were included at least one modern language other than English; the natural, industrial and commercial resources and the commerce of the United States, especially with reference to the possibilities of increasing and extending the trade of the United States with foreign countries; political economy; elements of international, commercial and maritime law. The President designated candidates between the ages of twenty-one and fifty, who were citizens of the United States, to take the examination.

Whenever a vacancy occurred in the eighth or ninth class of consuls, which the President deemed it expedient to fill, the Secretary of State informed the Board of Examiners, who certified to him the list of those persons eligible for appointment, the certificate being accompanied by a detailed report showing the qualifications as revealed by examination of the persons so certified. The list of names thus submitted was sent to the President for his information.

Appointment and promotion.—No promotions were to be made except for efficiency, as shown by the work accomplished by the officer, the ability, promptness, and diligence displayed by him in the performance of all his official duties, his conduct, and his fitness for the Consular Service.

The last section of the regulations provided that:

"In designations for appointment subject to examination and in appointments after examination, due regard will be had to the rule, that as between candidates of equal merit, appointments should be so made as to secure proportional representation of all the States and Territories in the Consular Service; and neither in the designation for examination or certification or appointment will the political affiliations of the candidate be considered."

It should be remarked in connection with the establishment of the foregoing system, which effectually stabilized the Consular Service, and which has been perpetuated by four successive administrations, that the ability and foresight of Secretary of State Elihu Root is everywhere in evidence.

Spoils system condemned by President Roosevelt.— Following the issuance of his memorable Executive order, President Roosevelt, in defending the merit system as against the old spoils system, made a statement of characteristic vigor in condemnation of the practices which his reform was designed to correct:

"The spoils system of making appointments to and removals from office is so wholly and unmixedly evil; is so emphatically un-American and undemocratic, and is so potent a force for degradation in our public life, that it is difficult to believe that any intelligent man of ordinary decency who has looked into the subject can be its advocate. As a matter of fact, the arguments in favor of the 'merit system' and against the 'spoils system' are not only convincing, but they are absolutely unanswerable.

"In a nutshell, the spoils or patronage theory is that public office is primarily designed for partisan plunder." [33]

---

[33]Quoted in a pamphlet entitled: "American Universities, American Foreign Service and an Adequate Consular Law" (p. 60), issued by The National Business League of America, 1909.

Business interests support merit system.—In 1909 a substantial movement developed in business circles to support the merit system as established under the Roosevelt administration. At first there was a tremor of apprehension lest the incoming administration of President Taft should repeal the Executive order, but this apprehension was short-lived. Secretary Root is quoted as having said that if any one suggested a return to the spoils system to his successor, "Secretary Knox would throw such a man out of the window."

The June issue of the *American Exporter* of New York (1909) contained the following strong declaration in an article entitled "All's Well That Ends Well":

"The business interests of the country will tolerate no 'back track' on this subject, and the President and his Secretary of State may rest assured that they will have the active, organized and vociferous support of those interests in the resistance which we are confident the present administration will present to any or all attempts of the Spoilsmen, in and out of Congress, to regain that foothold in the Consular Service from which they have begun to be dislodged.

"The Consular Service is a 'public trust,' for the extension of American influence and American commerce. It must never again be allowed to degenerate into a public trough, wherein, during each change of administration, the appointees of mere spoilsmen may take their turn, and 'wax fat' at the expense of the American export trade." [34]

The merit system in the Diplomatic Service.—Following the highly successful operation of the Consular Service for three years on the merit basis, President Taft,

---

[34]*Ibid.*, pp. 63-64.

on November 26, 1909, issued an Executive order conferring a similar civil service status upon the Diplomatic Service, applying to positions below grade of minister.

The regulations thus established directed the Secretary of State to report from time to time to the President, along with his recommendations, the names of those secretaries of the higher grades in the Diplomatic Service who by reason of efficient service had demonstrated special capacity for promotion to the rank of chiefs of mission.

It was provided that a careful efficiency record of every officer of the Diplomatic Service should be kept in order that there might be no promotion except upon well established efficiency as shown in the service, and that retention in the service might be conditioned upon the officers maintaining a degree of efficiency well up to the average high standard which the interests of the service demanded.

Initial appointments from outside the service were to be made only to the class of third secretary of embassy, or, in case of higher existent vacancies, to second secretary of legation, or secretary of legation at a post having but one secretary. Vacancies in the higher classes were to be filled by promotion from the lower grades of the service based upon efficiency and ability as shown in the service.

The Board of Examiners.—A Board of Examiners was created, consisting of the Third Assistant Secretary of State, the Solicitor of the Department of State, the Chief of the Diplomatic Bureau, the Chief of the Bureau of Appointments, and the Chief Examiner of the Civil Service Commission, or such persons as might be designated by the Secretary of State and the Commissioner President of the Civil Service Commission, respectively, to serve in their stead. It was the duty of the Board to determine, from among the persons designated by the President for examination, those who were fitted for possible appointment as secretaries of embassy or legation.

The examination.—Examinations were to be held in Washington at such times as the needs of the service required. These examinations were both oral and written, embracing the following subjects: international law, diplomatic usage, and a knowledge of at least one modern language other than English, to wit, French, German, or Spanish; also the natural, industrial, and commercial resources and the commerce of the United States, especially with reference to the possibilities of increasing and extending the trade of the United States with foreign countries; American history, government, and institutions; the modern history since 1850 of Europe, Latin America, and the Far East. The object of the oral examination was to determine the candidate's alertness, his general contemporary information and his natural fitness for the service, including mental, moral, and physical qualifications, character, address, general education, and good command of English.

Determination of ratings.—In the determination of the final rating, the written and oral ratings were given equal weight. A supplemental physical examination was also required. Examination papers were rated on a scale of 100 and no person with a general rating of less than 80 was to be certified as eligible. All candidates had to be citizens of the United States between the ages of 21 and 35. Those attaining the required mark were certified by the Board as eligible for appointment and their names placed on an eligible list where they remained for two years except in case of appointment or withdrawal.

The office of Director of the Consular Service.—At this juncture there was an important development in the creation of the office of Director of the Consular Service under authority contained in the urgent deficiency appropriation act of August 5, 1909.[35] This position was given to Mr. Wilbur J. Carr, who had served in the Department of State for seventeen years, holding respectively the positions of confidential clerk to the Secretary, Chief of the Consular Bureau, a member of the Board of Examiners for the Consular Service, a member of a Board to formulate a plan for the examinations for the Consular Service, a member of the Committee on business methods in the Department of State, and Chief Clerk of the Department. Mr. Carr had been charged with the direction of the Consular Service since August 15, 1907.

The establishment of the position of Director gave purpose and continuity to the administration of the service under the newly established system. It proved to be one of the chief factors in promoting efficiency in consular activities and in developing the scope and usefulness of modern consular functions.

Clamor for an adequate consular law.—In the course of practical administration it became apparent that the system adopted in 1906 was entirely too inflexible to allow for mobility of personnel, or even for a systematic adherence to the principle of promotion on merit. Posts were classified, and salaries were regulated by the classification of posts, as attaching to the post and not to the officer. An officer derived both his grade and his

---

[35]36 Stat., 119.

compensation from the post which he occupied. Naturally, in order to promote an officer on the basis of his demonstrated efficiency at a given post, it became necessary to transfer him to a post of a higher grade, which in many instances was contrary to the best interests of the service and not infrequently negatived the chief usefulness of the officer himself.

Furthermore, there was as yet no recognition in statutory form of the merit principle as established in the Executive orders of Presidents Roosevelt and Taft. A clamor arose to make the system permanent by some form of legislative enactment which, without encroaching upon the powers of the Executive, would assure him of the support and the cooperation of Congress in maintaining a stable service.

Act of February 5, 1915.—The result of this demand was the enactment of the law of February 5, 1915, designed to meet both these requirements. The first section of the act provided: "That hereafter all appointments of secretaries in the diplomatic service and of consuls general and consuls shall be by commission to the offices of secretary of embassy or legation, consul general, or consuls, and not by commission to any particular post, and that such officers shall be assigned to posts and transferred from one post to another by order of the President as the interests of the service may require."

Classification of officers.—Section 2 established a new classification for diplomatic and consular officers as follows:

"That secretaries in the Diplomatic Service and consuls general and consuls shall hereafter be graded and classified as follows, with the salaries of each class herein affixed thereto.

Secretaries

Secretary of class one $3,000
Secretary of class two 2,625
Secretary of class three 2,000
Secretary of class four 1,500
Secretary of class five 1,200

Consuls General

Consul general of class one $12,000
Consul general of class two 8,000
Consul general of class three 6,000
Consul general of class four 5,500
Consul general of class five 4,500

Consuls

Consul of class one $8,000
Consul of class two   6,000
Consul of class three 5,000
Consul of class four 4,500
Consul of class five 4,000
Consul of class six 3,500
Consul of class seven 3,000
Consul of class eight 2,500
Consul of class nine .... 2,000"

Promotions and transfers.—By way of giving effect to the civil service status as contained in the Executive orders, recognition of the principle of promotion on merit was established in the following provision:

"Sec. 5. That the Secretary of State is directed to report from time to time to the President, along with his recommendations for promotion or for transfer between the department and the foreign service, the names of those secretaries in the Diplomatic Service and the names of those consular officers or departmental officers or employees who by reason of efficient service, an accurate record of which shall be kept in the Department of State, have demonstrated special efficiency, and also the names of persons found upon examination to have fitness for appointment to the lower grades of the service."

Assignment to the Department of State.—Another important provision authorized the assignment to duty in the Department of State without the loss of grade, class or salary of any diplomatic secretary, consul general or consul, such assignment to be for a period of not more than three years unless the public interest should demand further service, when the assignment might be extended for a period of not to exceed one year.[36]

Minor provisions.—Minor provisions were also included, relating to the compensation of chargés d'affaires ad interim, and vice consuls in charge; the payment of subsistence expenses for officers on special detail; the extension of the prohibition against engaging in business to all officers in the foreign service; and a definition of consular titles.

The foreign service in post-war conditions.—If the desirability of suitable foreign representation had long been recognized before the war, the necessity for a strong foreign service presented itself as an imperative demand in the complicated condition of world affairs following that event. The relative position of nations had shifted like men on a chessboard and the United States had leaped suddenly to a place of international prominence quite without precedent in the history of modern times.

---

[36]As to the effect of this provision see page 88.

Honorable John Jacob Rogers of Massachusetts, having introduced three bills [37] for the reorganization and improvement of the Foreign Service and having requested an expression of the views of the Secretary of State as to their merits, Secretary Lansing replied, surveying the international situation as follows:

The state of international affairs.—"As a result of the war the entire adjustment of the world has altered, and through no design of our own the United States has come naturally into a position of economic preponderance quite comparable to that which was coveted by Germany and which she sought to attain by means of aggression and force. This relative position of dominance under normal conditions of peace and plenty would not necessarily involve those grave responsibilities of which we are now so keenly conscious. The fact that the greater portion of the world now finds its financial structure seriously weakened, its stocks exhausted, its productive forces impaired and its inhabitants agitated by political unrest and feelings of insecurity, imposes upon us a responsibility towards other nations and grave duties towards ourselves of a magnitude wholly out of proportion to anything that we could predicate upon past experience. Irrespective of the degree of our voluntary participation in world affairs, every movement made by the United States has come to affect the interests of others in a manner so vital that the tremendous forces which we possess and ought to direct wisely must be harmonized with deliberate and well-conceived policies and exercised with constructive ends in view.

"The world's equilibrium in the various spheres of

---

[37] H.R. 2709, H.R. 10587, 66th Cong., 2nd Sess., and H.R. 11058, 66th Cong., 3rd Sess.

human endeavor is broken. The measure of value has shifted position and values themselves have lost their former proportion; wealth has disappeared or been transferred to new owners, and national power has passed to different hands. In political circles statecraft is being directed by those who are dealing with fresh and unfamiliar factors in the shaping of novel and untried policies. There has been devastation of territory, displacement of frontiers, disruption of institutions, and disintegration of empires. The commercial treaty structure has been laid waste; tariff agreements abrogated; tariff policies altered or become obsolete; lines of communication suspended; and routes of trade transformed.

"In their efforts toward reconstitution nations are resorting to artificial stimulation through ingenious devices in which the old idea of stability familiar to past generations has largely disappeared.

"Considerations of national security have so extended to every domain of human activity that economic questions are to-day surcharged with political elements by which they are largely dominated. Thus, in many nations we find all pivotal economic interests being artificially diverted in the direction of general expediency, and expediency finding its application through such international groupings and affiliations as appear to subserve the ends of national ambition or national greed. We are in the midst of an era of transition and transformation in which the future adjustment of the world will be largely determined by the alignments and associations resulting from this empirical employment of forces.

"The position of the United States must be kept clear and its activities directed towards those ends and those ideals which we have so definitely declared.

"The machinery of government now provided for dealing with our foreign relations is in need of complete repair and reorganization. As adequate as it may have been when the old order prevailed and the affairs of the world were free from the present perplexities, it has ceased to be responsive to present needs. The confusion of political and economic issues and the bearings of these on the formulation of policies have made of the whole a composite problem which can not be solved by the application of formulae which are obsolete and ineffective.

War surprised the United States.—"The history of the world is one of recurrent crises in international affairs. Every step from this time onward must be interpreted in its bearings upon the next critical period when the world's structure, or that of our own country, may again be put to the test. The European war came upon the United States in 1914 as a surprise chiefly because its Department of State through inadequate equipment had been unable to gather information and interpret it in a manner which would reveal the hidden purposes of the governments by which hostilities were precipitated. Possibly no blame can be imputed to this Government for this laxity in view of the general confidence in the supremacy of international justice; but to-day, after the experiences through which we have passed, no reasonable effort must be spared to make a similar surprise impossible in the future.

"Necessity is forcing new nations and even the older ones to incur obligations and form political affiliations having a decisive, if not a supreme, bearing on the course of future events. International movements of such import can only be correctly judged through an accurate knowledge of causes and influences and a complete un-

derstanding of the methods and motives involved.
American agents in the foreign field must broaden the
scope and intensify the nature of their work in order
that the Department of State may have at its disposal
knowledge of the actual facts of every development or
turn of events. Any degree of conjecture is fraught
with the gravest danger. Heretofore we have confronted the world with scattered forces. If we are to
profit by the lessons of the war, has not the time now
arrived for us to establish a unity of command?

"Chief among the results to be achieved is a higher
coordination of political and economic data, so that the
two may be considered jointly in their relation to each
other and utilized on the basis of the results attained
through their linking together. Political deduction has
become hazardous without the use of supporting economic data, and commercial intelligence is frequently
misleading and devoid of real value unless viewed in
its proper political setting."

Reorganization recommended.—After recommending
the reorganization and improvement of the Department
of State, Secretary Lansing said in regard to the Foreign Service:

"The diplomatic career is closed to many of our most
talented men because of the failure of the Government
to provide salaries sufficient to enable those of moderate
means to adopt a standard of living abroad appropriate
to the dignity of their positions. The time has come
when we must correct such flagrant defects by combining a new and much greater scale of salaries with a more
extensive program for the purchase of embassies and
legations at foreign capitals. The same grave error
of inadequate salaries applies likewise to diplomatic
secretaries, and the department is frequently much em-

barrassed to find the character of material required for this important work in the limited field of selection which these money exigencies impose. * * *

"It is greatly to be desired that our Diplomatic and Consular Services should be brought closer together and given an interchangeable character. Some steps have already been taken along these lines by administrative practice, but the department finds itself restricted in this regard because of the disproportion between the salaries of consular officers and those of secretaries of corresponding grades in the Diplomatic Service. In order to establish an interchangeable system it is indispensable that the scale of salaries of diplomatic secretaries be revised.

"The broad distinction, which now seems an unwise distinction, between the political interests of the Diplomatic Service and the commercial interests of the Consular Service have heretofore kept the two widely separated, so that embassies and legations have had little knowledge of the work of consular officers in the commercial field, and consular officers have had practically no knowledge of either the political or the economic policies and aims of their own Government."

In the concluding paragraph of the letter he stated:

"From the tenor of the foregoing observations it should be clear that I consider remedial and constructive legislation of an appropriate character not only desirable but imperative." [38]

The original Rogers Bill.—With the beginning of the new Congress, Representative Rogers introduced an elaborate bill,[39] which laid the basis of future reorganization legislation. In accordance with the wishes of Rep-

---

[38]Letter to Hon. Stephen G. Porter, Jan. 21, 1920.
[39]H.R. 17, 67th Cong., 1st Sess.

resentative Rogers, the measure was revised and condensed in the Department of State and submitted in its final draft to President Harding who gave it his hearty endorsement.[40] It was later endorsed by President Coolidge.

The eventual enactment of this measure constitutes the greatest single advance that the foreign service has ever made. Under its provisions a complete reorganization became effective July 1, 1924. The succeeding chapters of this book deal extensively with the purpose and the scope of this reform.

Statement of Honorable Wilbur J. Carr.—Honorable Wilbur J. Carr, Director of the Consular Service,[41] in concluding his testimony on the bill before the Committee on Foreign Affairs, gave the following interesting and dependable appraisal of its merits:

"In my judgment there have been two really fundamental measures in the entire history of this country for the improvement of the foreign service. The first was in 1856, when a bill was passed, * * * which gave form to the diplomatic and consular organization. * * * It was not until 1906 that there was another bill which pretended to improve the service, and that bill related wholly to the Consular Service and was a very excellent measure, and without which this bill could probably not

---

[40]A brief history of the so-called "Rogers bill" is as follows: Introduced by Hon. John Jacob Rogers of Massachusetts as H.R. 17, 1st Sess., 67th Cong.; revised in the Department of State and reintroduced upon the recommendation of President Harding as H.R. 12543; passed the House of Representatives by a vote of 203 to 27; reported unanimously by the Committee on Foreign Relations of the Senate, but failed of passage in the closing days of the Congress. In the 68th Congress the bill was again introduced as H.R. 17, reported from the Committee on Foreign Affairs, as amended, under the number H.R. 6357; passed the House May 1, 1924, by a vote of 134 to 27; passed the Senate by unanimous consent May 15, 1924; approved May 24, 1924.

[41]Now Assistant Secretary of State.

be considered now. But the second measure in all the history of this country in relation to the foreign service, and by far the most important and most far-reaching, is this measure which you have before you. There has not been anything like it since the Government began to exist. In my judgment, if you enact it, you have a bill which will furnish the basic structure of the organization for your foreign service for 50 years, a bill on which you can build any kind of a foreign service you please, a bill on which you can provide for ministers and ambassadors, secretaries, and consuls in the light of what you believe to be responsive to the opinion of the country. I do not think I can stress too much the importance of this bill being enacted into law." [42]

Bibliography.

Bryce, James (Viscount): "Modern Democracies" (vol. II); Macmillan, New York, 1921.

Fish, Carl Russell: "American Diplomacy"; Henry Holt & Co., New York, 1919.

"Foreign Relations of the United States," 1832-33.

Foster, John Watson: "A Century of American Diplomacy, 1776-1876"; Boston, 1900.

Hearings before the Committee on Foreign Affairs, H. of R., on H. R. 17 and H. R. 6357, 68th Cong., 1st Sess., for the reorganization and improvement of the foreign service; Gov. Printing Office, Washington.

Johnson, Willis Fletcher: "America's Foreign Relations"; Century Co., New York, 1916.

Lyman, Theodore: "Diplomacy of the United States, Being an Account of the Foreign Relations of the Country from the First Treaty with France in 1778"; Sec. Ed., Boston, 1828.

Mahan, A. T.: "The Interest of America in International Conditions"; Little, Brown & Co., Boston, 1910.

---

[42] Hearings on H.R. 17 and H.R. 6357 before the Committee on Foreign Affairs, pp. 138, 139.

Mathews, John Mabry: "The Conduct of American Foreign Relations"; Century Co., New York, 1922.

National Business League of America: "American Universities, American Foreign Service, and an Adequate Consular Law"; Chicago, 1909.

National Civil Service Reform League: "Report on the Foreign Service"; New York, 1919.

Trescot, William Henry: "Diplomatic History of the American Revolution; An Historical Study"; New York, 1852.

Wharton, Francis: "Revolutionary Diplomatic Correspondence of the United States"; 6 vols., Washington, 1889.

CHAPTER II

THE CONTROL OF FOREIGN RELATIONS

The Constitution.—A comprehensive analysis of the Foreign Service involves a consideration of the powers from which it draws its attributes under the constitution, and the manner in which these powers are exercised by the coordinate agencies of the government to which they are entrusted.

The specific provisions of the Constitution relating to foreign affairs divide its powers among three branches of the Federal Government: the President, the Senate, and Congress.

Powers of the President and the Senate. — The powers of the President and those of the Senate are contained in the following:

"The executive power shall be vested in a President of the United States of America;[1] * * * The President shall be Commander-in-Chief of the Army and Navy of the United States, and of the militia of the several States when called into the actual service of the United States; * * * He shall have power, by and with the advice and consent of the Senate, to make treaties, provided two-thirds of the Senators present concur; and he shall nominate, and, by and with the advice and consent of the Senate, shall appoint ambassadors, other public ministers and consuls; * * * The President shall have power to fill up all vacancies that may happen during

---

[1]Art. II, Sec. 1.

the recess of the Senate, by granting commissions which shall expire at the end of their next session; * * * [2] He shall receive ambassadors and other public ministers; he shall take care that the laws be faithfully executed, and shall commission all the officers of the United States." [3]

Powers of Congress.—The provisions establishing the authority of Congress are as follows:

"The Congress shall have power to lay and collect taxes, duties, imposts, and excises, to pay the debts and provide for the common defense and general welfare of the United States; * * * to regulate commerce with foreign nations; * * * to establish a uniform rule of naturalization; * * * to define and punish piracies and felonies committed on the high seas and offenses against the law of nations; to declare war, grant letters of marque and reprisal, and make rules concerning captures on land and water; to raise and support armies * * * to provide and maintain a navy * * * to make all laws which shall be necessary and proper for carrying into execution the foregoing powers, and all other powers vested by this Constitution in the Government of the United States, or in any department or officer thereof." [4]

"No State shall enter into any Treaty, Alliance, or Confederation" [5];

"No State shall, without the Consent of Congress, * * * enter into any Agreement or Compact with another State, or with a foreign Power." [6]

Treaties the supreme law of the land.—Authority of law is conferred upon the formal acts resulting from

---

[2] Art. II, Sec. 2.
[3] Art. II, Sec. 3.
[4] Art. I, Sec. 8.
[5] Art. I, Sec. 10, par. 1.
[6] Art. I, Sec. 10, par. 3.

the exercise of the foregoing powers, in the following
general provision:

"This Constitution, and the laws of the United States
which shall be made in pursuance thereof, and all
treaties made, or which shall be made, under the authority of the United States, shall be the supreme law of
the land; and the judges in every State shall be bound
thereby, anything in the Constitution or laws of any
State to the contrary notwithstanding."[7]

Constitutional provisions meager.—Many important
issues and, at times, embarrassing conflicts, have arisen
with respect to the distribution and the limitation of
powers under the foregoing provisions. Perhaps no
part of the Constitution has given rise to a greater
divergency of views, although many of the more difficult
points have come to be understood and accepted as a
result of construction and experience. The authority of
the President in relation to that of Congress is a prolific
source of controversy, due to the insufficiency of the
treatment accorded their respective functional domains.

The President.—The President is the dominant
authority in the conduct of foreign relations, his acts
being less subject to the detailed direction of Congress
than in the administration of domestic affairs. Thomas
Jefferson in 1793, referred to him as the only channel of
communication between the United States and foreign
nations, stating that it is from him alone "that foreign
nations or their agents are to learn what is or has been
the will of the nation"; that whatever he communicated
as such, they had a right and were bound to consider
"as the expression of the nation"; and that no foreign
agent could be "allowed to question it," or "to interpose

---

[7] Art. VI, par. 2.

between him and any other branch of government, under the pretext of either's transgressing their functions."[8] The views thus expressed, having been judicially confirmed[9] and widely established in practice, are now of common acceptation.[10]

It has been seen that the Constitution expressly confers upon the President, subject to the control of the Senate, the power to make treaties; to appoint all foreign representatives of the United States; and, without such senatorial control, to receive ambassadors and other public ministers, which, combined with the power to send diplomatic representatives, constitutes the power of recognition of foreign governments.

The presidential initiative.—From the sum total of these powers there results a still greater power; that of the presidential initiative, which operates as an actuating mainspring for the entire governmental system through which our foreign relations are carried on. It is mainly through the exercise of this initiative that foreign policies are evolved and given effect.

Initiative in foreign policy, however, is not exclusively reserved to the Executive, and it not infrequently happens that Congress may assert its jurisdiction with corresponding vigor, either by urging a particular course of action upon the President, or by seeking to

---

[8]Moore, "Digest of International Law," vol. 4, p. 680.

[9]"As the Executive head of the nation, the President is made the only legitimate organ of the General Government, to open and carry on correspondence or negotiations with foreign nations, in matters concerning the interests of the country or of its citizens."—Nelson, J., v. Hollins, 4 Blatch. 451, 454.

[10]"The Executive is the sole mouthpiece of the nation in communication with foreign sovereignties."—Senate Committee on Foreign Relations, 54th Cong., 2nd Sess., Sen. Doc. No. 56, p. 21.

"In short, the entire diplomatic relations between this and other countries are under the control of the executive; and the action of the executive in such matters is binding upon Congress, the courts, and all federal and state officers."—McClain, "Constitutional Law," p. 214.

divert him from a line of procedure upon which he has already embarked. In the main, the President initiates, directs, and concludes, in matters of major importance, checked by the advisory and the veto powers of the Senate in the case of permanent international agreements, and by the restrictive powers of Congress in matters involving appropriations, or requiring the joint action of the two houses.

Dual responsibility of the President.—As the central figure in dealing with foreign affairs the President is charged with the double responsibility of safeguarding the limitations set up by the Constitution and, at the same time, of discharging the international obligations of the nation. Whatever course of action he may determine upon must, therefore, be governed on the one hand by the requirements of constitutional law and, on the other, by those of international law; his powers emanating from the one, his responsibilities from the other. Conflicts may, and do, occur in the application of these two laws.[11]

As he must discharge his functions ordinarily through agencies provided by Congress, which has the power of controlling expenditures and largely of shaping such agencies into conformity with its own views, he is far from having a free hand to enforce his will, except in extraordinary emergencies, or when the course of action to which he is committed has won the approval and the active support of public opinion. His position may therefore be described as strong, but not autocratic.

Appointments.—In the appointment of ambassadors,

---

[11]"Nations usually adopt the international point of view in discussing the powers and responsibilities of other nations, the constitutional point of view in discussing their own powers and responsibilities."—Wright, "The Control of American Foreign Relations," p. 5.

other public ministers and consuls, the authority of the President is subject to two distinct constitutional limitations: his nominations must be confirmed by the Senate, and all appropriations which may be required to defray expenses must be made by Congress.[12]

The President is free to select his own appointees, and to designate their grades.

"The Senate has no right to require the President to nominate any particular individual, and the President has no right to require the Senate to confirm any particular nomination." [13]

The use of secret agents.—There is, however, a category of foreign representatives commonly known as "secret agents," who are appointed and commissioned by the President without reference to the Senate for confirmation, and whose compensation and expenses are paid from the contingent fund without necessitating recourse to Congress for specific appropriations. Frequent controversies have arisen over this seeming evasion of constitutional obligations, but such appointments have generally been justified on the grounds that the power to negotiate and conclude treaties entitles the Executive to complete freedom in the selection of agencies for the purpose.

Such representatives are not, in the constitutional sense, public ministers, although they have frequently exercised the powers of an ambassador or minister. They may become an essential instrument for the car-

---

[12]"The President, under the Constitution, has power to appoint diplomatic agents of any rank, at any place, and at any time, subject to the constitutional limitations in respect to the Senate. The authority to make such appointments is not derived from, and cannot be limited by, any act of Congress, except in so far as appropriations of money are required to provide for the expenses of this branch of the public service."—Moore, "Digest of International Law," vol. 4, p. 451.

[13]Sen. Doc. 231, 56th Cong., 2nd Sess., part 4, p. 33.

rying through of negotiations in which the element of secrecy is a factor of success.

The fact is generally recognized that "the employment of such agencies is a necessary part of the proper exercise of the diplomatic power which is entrusted by the Constitution with the President. Without such authority our foreign relations would be so embarrassed with difficulties that it would be impossible to conduct them with safety or success. The precedents also show that the Senate, though in session, need not be consulted as to the appointment of such agents, or as to the instructions which the President may give them." [14]

The secret fund.—There is placed at the disposal of the President by Congress a contingent allowance from which he is authorized to make extraordinary expenditures. Recognizing that these cannot always be accounted for with propriety, as they may involve transactions of the utmost delicacy, the statutes provide a convenient method of settlement as follows:

"Whenever any sum of money has been or shall be issued, from the Treasury, for the purposes of intercourse or treaty with foreign nations, in pursuance of any law, the President is authorized to cause the same to be duly settled annually with the proper accounting officers of the Treasury, by causing the same to be accounted for, specifically, if the expenditure may, in his judgment, be made public; and by making or causing the Secretary of State to make a certificate of the amount of such expenditure as he may think it advisable not to specify; and every such certificate shall be deemed a sufficient voucher for the sum therein expressed to have been expended." [15]

---

[14]Sen. Doc. 231, 56th Cong., 2nd Sess., part 6, p. 387.
[15]R.S. 291.

Conflicts of power.—If frequent resort to the use of "secret agents," or "personal representatives," as a substitute for the regularly appointed diplomatic representatives has appeared sometimes to ignore the rights of the Senate, Congress, on the other hand, has shown no hesitancy in making use of its own powers to limit by statute the constitutional authority of the President both in the matter of selection and of grade. The manner in which this has been attempted, and in some instances accomplished, appears under the heading in relation to the powers of Congress.

This, with other evidences of friction between the Executive and the Legislative authority, has been widely deplored by commentators and on occasions has aroused a considerable degree of public resentment.

Some authorities claim to see in its results a gradual augmentation of the powers of the President, while others seem able to detect precisely the opposite tendency as manifested through the steady encroachments of Congress upon the constitutional domain of the Executive.

Viscount Grey is accredited with the criticism that the American Constitution "not only makes possible, but, under certain conditions, renders inevitable conflict between the Executive and the Legislature." [16]

The importance of such conflicts may easily be exaggerated. Most of them are in the nature of "little tiffs," as Lord Bryce describes them,[17] and do not involve issues of fundamental import in the national or the international sense, nor distort the constitutional balance.

They are attributable, as a very natural result, to the

---

[16]Letter to the *Times*, Jan. 31, 1920, cited in Wright, "The Control of American Foreign Relations," p. 361.

[17]Bryce, "The American Commonwealth", vol. I, p. 111.

interplay of the forces of initiative and control. It is worthy of note that the President never fails finally to obtain full authority for meeting all the obligations for which he bears responsibility as the nation's chief executive, while neither Congress nor the Senate feels that it has suffered a loss of prestige or power in providing him with the means.

The Senate.—The Senate, as distinguished from Congress, possesses two distinct executive functions [18] which are expressly conferred upon it by the Constitution: to advise and consent to treaties, a two-thirds vote of those present being essential to affirmative action; and to confirm, by simple majority vote, the nominations of the President to the position of ambassador, or other public minister, or consul. In each of these cases it exercises a veto power over the proposals of the Executive. Thus the participation of the Senate in the control of foreign affairs is direct, and its relation to the President is organic with respect to two of his most important functions.

Secret sessions.—Consideration by the Senate of matters dealing with foreign relations is customarily conducted in secret session which enables it to avoid the hazards and inconveniences of premature publicity.

"But within recent years an agitation has arisen in favor of considering them (treaties) in open executive session, and this has been done in a few cases, the most conspicuous instance being that of the peace treaty with Germany, including the Covenant of the League of Nations. The experience in this case, however, cannot be said to show this method to be wholly satisfactory. It

---

[18]Bryce, "The American Commonwealth," vol. I, pp. 98, 107.

seemed to render compromise between the various factions in the Senate more difficult." [19]

Lord Bryce points out with respect to the rôle of the Senate and the use of the secret session: "This control of foreign policy by the Senate does something to meet the difficulties which popular governments find in dealing with foreign Powers. If each step to be taken must be previously submitted to the ruling assembly, the nation is forced to show its whole hand, and precious opportunities of winning an ally or striking a bargain may be lost. If on the other hand the executive is permitted to conduct negotiations in secret, there is always the risk, either that the assembly may disavow what has been done, a risk which makes foreign states legitimately suspicious and unwilling to negotiate, or that the nation may have to ratify, because it feels bound in honour by the act of its executive agents, arrangements which its judgment condemns." [20]

A point of criticism.—A criticism which has often been made against the Senate is its lack of international vision, accompanied by a tendency towards vacillation in matters of foreign policy; a most unfortunate element in the conduct of foreign relations where continuity of purpose is a prime requisite.

"The Senate has been mainly guided by its Foreign Relations Committee, a fluctuating body, usually containing a few able men among others who know little of anything outside their own country and may regard the interests of their own State rather than those of the Union. Jealous of its powers, and often impelled by party motives, the Senate has frequently checked the President's action, sometimes with unfortunate re-

---

[19]Mathews, "The Conduct of American Foreign Relations," pp. 161-162.
[20]Bryce, "The American Commonwealth," vol. I, p. 108.

sults. It can debate with closed doors, but this does not ensure secrecy." [21]

Treaties and the Senate.—In dealing with treaties, the Senate takes no official cognizance of the proposed text until a copy thereof is submitted to it by the President as a basis of formal action. Once a treaty is in its possession, however, consent may be given to its ratification without change, or to its ratification with amendments or reservations, or it may be rejected altogether. It may also be killed by an unacceptable amendment designed for that purpose. Generally the Senate is uninformed as to the course of negotiations until they are concluded. [22]

It may request information of the President, but he may refuse to comply if he deems it "incompatible with the public interest."

"The Senate has no right to demand that he (the President) shall unfold to the world or to it, even in executive session, his instructions or the prospect or progress of the negotiation. I said 'right.' I use that word advisedly in order to illustrate what all men who have studied the subject are willing to concede—that under the Constitution, the absolute power of negotiation is in the President and the means of negotiation subject wholly to his will and his judgment." [23]

There are many instances in which the President has withdrawn treaties "from the consideration of the Sen-

---

[21] Bryce, "Modern Democracies," vol. II, pp. 373-374.

[22] "At the outset Washington sought to associate the Senate with himself in the negotiation of treaties, but this method of proceeding went badly and was presently abandoned."—Corwin, "The President's Control of Foreign Relations," p. 85.

[23] Senator Spooner, quoted in Corwin, pp. 171-172.

ate, either to effect changes by negotiation or to terminate proceedings thereon." [24]

An early incident.—An example of a very early incident, involving the relations between the President and the Senate in the matter of negotiations, is drawn from the diary of John Quincy Adams in which he writes:

"Mr. Crawford told twice over the story of President Washington's having at an early period of his administration gone to the Senate with a project of a treaty to be negotiated, and been present at their deliberations upon it. They debated it and proposed alterations so that when Washington left the Senate Chamber he said he would be damned if he ever went there again. And ever since that time treaties have been negotiated by the Executive before submitting them to the consideration of the Senate." [25]

Appointments.—The chief result to be obtained through the senatorial confirmation of appointments is to prevent the abuse of patronage. "It was designed to prevent the President from making himself a tyrant by filling the great offices with his accomplices or tools." [26]

In this way the Senate has acted as a restraining force, while at the same time, instances are not wanting where its influence has been exerted in the interest of senatorial patronage, which may not be different in kind from that which its powers were designed to check.

Under the old spoils system of political appointment which prevailed until 1906, the President and the Sec-

---

[24]Crandall, "Treaties, Their Making and Enforcement," p. 98, cited in Corwin, p. 92.

[25]"Memoirs," 6: p. 427.

[26]Bryce, "The American Commonwealth," vol. I, p. 111.

retary of State often found themselves under embarrassing pressure from all sides, as evidenced by the following amusing notes from "The Life of John Hay": "One of the first annoyances which beset Secretary Hay was the rapacity of office-seekers. When they did not attack him themselves, they worked through their Senators. To say 'no' to the local statesman of Pumpkin Four Corners, who aspired to be consul general in London, was easy; but to deny his Senator might alienate one whose hostile vote would kill an important treaty. In vain did Hay protest that his predecessor, Judge Day, had swept the shelf clean; in vain did he declare that there were fifty applicants for every vacancy; the swarm gave him no respite. And if Senators slackened, Congressmen redoubled their importunities. At first, the Secretary saw the ludicrousness of this system and discharged its drudgery with a smile; but later, when his health made even pin-pricks unendurable, he turned the business over to Assistant Secretary Loomis." [27]

On the whole, the relations between the Senate and the Executive have been highly satisfactory and "it must be admitted that the participation of the Senate causes in practice less friction and delay than might have been expected from a dual control." [28]

The United States an example.—Lord Bryce comments upon the system of control in the United States, as shared by the Executive and the Senate, in the following striking language:

"Yet different as the circumstances of England are, the day may come when in England the question of limiting the at present wide discretion of the executive

27Thayer, "The Life of John Hay," vol. II, pp. 188-189.
28Bryce, "The American Commonwealth," vol. I, p. 111.

in foreign affairs will have to be dealt with. The example of the American Senate may then be cited." [29]

The British "Union of Democratic Control" in its first pamphlet, "The Morrow of the War" (1914), advocating the democratization of foreign policy, states:

"The nation should insist upon this essential reform, and should seriously apply itself to considering what other steps are needed to ensure some mechanical means whereby a greater national control of foreign policy can be secured: whether by the establishment of a permanent Committee of the House of Commons, by the adaptation to suit our needs of the American system under which a two-thirds majority of one branch of the Legislature is required for the validity of international agreements, or other procedure." [30]

Congress.—The powers of Congress, in dealing with foreign relations, are general in character as contrasted with the specific powers of the President and of the Senate. They are derived principally from the power to regulate foreign commerce and to make all laws necessary and proper for carrying into execution the provisions of the Constitution. A third power, however, and perhaps the most effective, is that which results from the control of appropriations. Through this medium the House of Representatives is frequently enabled to assert itself, and to exercise considerable influence even in relation to matters which otherwise lie beyond its jurisdiction. Its rôle, however, is largely one of control; not of initiative. Against congressional initiative the President holds a veto.

Power to declare war.—The power to declare war is specifically vested in Congress, but the Constitution

---

[29] Ibid., p. 109.
[30] Quoted in Ponsonby, "Democracy and Diplomacy," pp. 20, 21.

is silent as to which branch of the Government shall make peace. A state of war is sometimes precipitated by acts of hostility before any formal declaration of war is made, in which case the power of Congress is largely negatived as an instrument of control.

Indeed, the proclamation of blockade by President Lincoln on April 19, 1861, was promptly accepted by foreign nations as a notification that a state of war existed, and the power of the President thus to proclaim war without authority of Congress was sustained by the Supreme Court. [31]

The termination of war.—War is usually terminated by a treaty of peace, which is negotiated by the President through such agencies as he may elect to employ, and submitted to the Senate for advice and consent as to ratification. As the House of Representatives has no voice in the ratification of treaties, it normally plays no direct part in settling the terms of peace.

The President's power to recognize the termination of war was admitted by the Supreme Court in the case of the Civil War.[32]

"His proclamation or his reception or dispatch of diplomatic representatives from or to a former enemy therefore seems the proper method for recognizing peace in the absence of treaty, though, as in the case of recognizing new States, he is of course free to solicit the advice of Congress, which action would usually be desirable." [33]

Termination of war with Germany.—An interesting situation of this character arose recently through the

---

[31]Prize Cases, 2 Black 635; Moore, Digest 1:190; 7:172; Willoughby, "Constitutional Law," 2:210.

[32]The Protector, 12 Wall. 700; For proclamation of President Johnson see 14 Stat., 811. See also Moore, "Digest," vol. VII, pp. 336-337.

[33]Wright, "The Control of American Foreign Relations," p. 293,

failure of the Senate to ratify the Treaty of Versailles. War with Germany was originally declared by a joint resolution of Congress.[34]

A proclamation announcing a state of peace would doubtless have been sufficient for purposes of international cognizance, but there were important and delicate considerations involved in the matter of preserving acquired rights in the final settlement. Accordingly, after much debate and a delay of several years, it was finally decided that the war should be terminated in the same manner that it was declared; by joint resolution. This was done [35] and a treaty of peace subsequently concluded and submitted to the Senate.

Following the exchange of ratifications,[36] the President issued a proclamation [37] recognizing that war terminated on July 2, 1921, the date of the passage of the joint resolution.

As a joint resolution requires the signature of the President, the usual procedure for reestablishing a state of peace was in this instance completely reversed. The action originated in Congress and became effective through presidential approval, the proclamation being merely the formal announcement of a recognized state of fact.

Recognition of foreign governments.—As has been seen, the Constitution confers upon the President the power to receive ambassadors and other public ministers, and this power, combined with that of sending

---

[34]S. J. Res. 1, Apr. 6, 1917, 40 Stat., 1.

[35]"Resolved by the Senate and House of Representatives of the United States of America in Congress assembled, That the state of war declared to exist between the Imperial German Government and the United States of America by the joint resolution of Congress approved April 6, 1917, is hereby declared at an end."—S.J. Res. 16, July 2, 1921. 42 Stat, 105,

[36]Aug. 25, 1921, 42 Stat., 1939, part 2.

[37]Nov. 14, 1921, Treaty Series No. 658,

diplomatic representatives, constitutes the power of recognition.[38] No mention is made of other governmental agencies in this connection, nor of a substitute procedure in case the presidential initiative is not exercised.[39]

The question as to whether his power is exclusive or whether Congress may confer recognition upon a foreign government under its power to regulate foreign commerce has been widely debated and is still a subject of discussion.[40]

In practice, recognition has always been accorded by authority of the President, but in a few cases he has first sought the approval of Congress or of the Senate.

Attempts at congressional recognition.—In 1896 the Committee on Foreign Relations of the Senate recommended the adoption of a joint resolution declaring "that the independence of the Republic of Cuba be and the same is hereby, acknowledged by the United States of America." [41]

The same day a concurrent resolution was offered declaring: "The question of the recognition by this Government of any people as a free and independent nation

---

[38]See page 43.

[39]"In every case, as it appears, of a new government and of belligerency the question of recognition was determined solely by the Executive."—Moore, "Digest of International Law," vol. I, pp. 243-244.

[40]"Recognition, as it is known to International Law, belongs, it seems clear, to the President alone, or to the President in conjunction with the Senate. * * *

"Furthermore, practical considerations point to the same conclusion. For even if we should admit that Congress, incidentally to discharging some legislative function like that of regulating commerce, might in some sense 'recognize' a new state or government, the question still remains how it would communicate its recognition, having the power neither to dispatch nor to receive diplomatic agents. As was said of the States of the Confederation, Congress is as to other governments 'both deaf and dumb'."—Corwin, "The President's Control of Foreign Relations," p. 82.

[41]Senate Rep. 1160, 54th Cong., 2nd Sess.; Sen. Doc. 231, 56th Cong., 2nd Sess., part 7, p. 64.

is one exclusively for the determination of Congress in its capacity as the lawmaking power." [42]

The following year the Senate Committee on Foreign Relations, after a thorough investigation of the whole subject, came to the conclusion that "the 'recognition' of independence or belligerency of a foreign power, technically speaking, is distinctly a diplomatic matter. * * * Foreign nations communicate only through their respective executive departments. Resolutions of their legislative departments upon diplomatic matters have no status in international law. In the department of international law, therefore, properly speaking, a congressional recognition of belligerency or independence would be a nullity." [43]

The joint resolution as finally passed, although it declared: "the people of the Island of Cuba are, and of right ought to be, free and independent," [44] was not considered as conferring recognition upon Cuba. [45]

A more recent attempt to influence recognition by congressional action was that initiated by Senator Borah in the case of the Russian Soviet Government. [46]

Extensive hearings were held before a sub-committee of the Senate Committee on Foreign Relations, but no final action has been taken on the proposal.

International congresses and conferences.—Congress has sometimes endeavored to limit by statute the freedom of the President in dealing with foreign nations by

---

[42]Cong. Rec., Dec. 21, 1896, vol. 29, p. 357.

[43]Sen. Doc. 56, 54th Cong., 2nd Sess., p. 43. Conclusions reprinted in Corwin, "The President's Control of Foreign Relations," pp. 79-80.

[44]April 20, 1898, 30 Stat., 738.

[45]"The contention that the United States recognized the existence of an established government known as the Republic of Cuba * * * is without merit."—Neely v. Henkel, 180 U. S., 124-5.

[46]"*Resolved,* That the Senate of the United States favors the recognition of the present Soviet Government of Russia." (S. Res. 50, 68th Cong., 1st Sess.)

restricting his participation in international events. Such an attempt was made in 1913 when there was added to a deficiency bill the following extraordinary provision:

"Hereafter the Executive shall not extend or accept any invitation to participate in any international congress, conference, or like event, without first having specific authority of law to do so." [47]

Such an enactment may have practical value in assuring the support by Congress of the policy of the President or of any commitments or obligations resulting therefrom, but it is difficult to see how the authority to participate in an international conference could be reserved to Congress, while the authority to negotiate with foreign nations is committed to the President. The fact that Congress controls the purse strings is in this, as in other cases, a factor of importance, but should the President deem it advisable to undertake such participation upon his own responsibility, he might employ any of his regularly appointed diplomatic representatives, or designate a secret agent, as has often been done.[48]

As another interesting aspect of the issue, Congress, in 1920, on its own initiative, and without a formal recommendation to that effect from the President, appropriated $9,000 for participation in the Pan Pacific Scientific Congress held in Honolulu in August of that year under the auspices of the Pan Pacific Union.

Appointments.—In the matter of diplomatic and

---

[47] Act of March 4, 1913, 37 Stat., 913.

[48] "Congress has undoubtedly gone beyond its powers in thus attempting to control the President's foreign negotiations and the President has ignored the act, notably at the Versailles Peace Congress. The actual influence of Congress in this field depends upon the necessity for appropriations. If international conferences become frequent, this necessity would doubtless be controlling."—Wright, "The Control of American Foreign Relations," p. 328.

consular appointments, there has been a long series of attempts to limit by statute the powers of the President. The first of these was embraced in the act of March 1, 1855, which stipulated that:

"From and after the 30th of June, next, the President of the United States shall, by and with the advice and consent of the Senate, appoint representatives of the grade of envoys extraordinary and ministers plenipotentiary," with a specified annual compensation for each, "to the following countries, etc. * * * The President shall appoint no other than citizens of the United States who are residents thereof, or who shall be abroad in the employment of the Government, at the time of their appointment."

Act of 1855 construed.—Attorney General Cushing, in construing this act, held that it "must be deemed directory or recommendatory only, and not mandatory," stating:

"The limit of the range of selection for the appointment of constitutional officers depends on the Constitution. Congress may refuse to make appropriations to pay a person unless appointed from this or that category; but the President may, in my judgment, employ him, if the public interest requires it, whether he be a citizen or not, and whether or not at the time of appointment he be actually within the United States. * * * For Congress can not by law constitutionally require the President to make removals or appointments of public ministers on a given day, or to make such appointments of a prescribed rank, or to make or not make them at this or that place. He, with the advice of the Senate, enters into treaties; he, with the advice of the Senate, appoints ambassadors and other public ministers. It is a constitutional power to appoint to a constitutional office, not a statute power nor a statute office. Like the power to pardon, it is not limitable by Congress." [49]

There remains on the statute books a provision of law which declares:

"There shall be but one minister resident accredited to Guatemala, Costa Rica, Honduras, Salvador, and Nicaragua; and the President may select the place of residence for the minister in any one of those States. And he shall receive compensation at the rate of ten thousand dollars per annum." [50]

The effect of this enactment has long since been nullified by the appointment of a minister to each of the countries named.

The appointment of ambassadors.—Until 1893 no ambassadors were appointed, although it is clear, under the provisions of the Constitution, that the President had the right to make such appointments by and with the advice and consent of the Senate. In that year the act making appropriations for the Diplomatic and Consular Service contained the following provision:

"Whenever the President shall be advised that any foreign government is represented, or is about to be represented, in United States by an ambassador, envoy extraordinary, minister plenipotentiary, minister resident, special envoy, or chargé d'affaires, he is authorized, in his discretion, to direct that the representative of United States to such government shall bear the same designation. This provision shall in nowise affect the duties, powers, or salary of such representative." [51]

As a consequence of this enactment, which indicated to the President that Congress was ready and willing

---

[49]Cushing, Att. Gen., 7 Op. 215, 217.

[50]R.S. 1682, amended, March 3, 1875, c. 153, 18 Stat., 484.

[51]Act of March 1, 1893, 27 Stat., 497.

to provide the necessary appropriations for the salaries of ambassadors, ambassadorships were created in the following countries: Great Britain, France, Germany, and Russia, 1894; Italy, 1898; Mexico, 1899; Brazil, 1905; Japan and Turkey, 1906.

Authorization of Congress required.—In 1909 the statutory authority of 1893 for the appointment of ambassadors was modified by the following:

"Hereafter no new ambassadorship shall be created unless the same shall be provided for by Act of Congress." [52] The effect of this enactment, however, is not altogether binding. Ambassadorships have been established by special authorization under this provision to Spain in 1913, Argentine and Chile, 1914, Belgium, 1919, and Cuba, 1923. President Wilson established the ambassadorship to Peru in 1919 without such authorization.

Commenting upon this provision, Representative Towner, in a ruling as Chairman of the Committee of the Whole, while diplomatic and consular appropriations were under discussion in 1921, stated:

"Congress in 1909 passed an act to the effect that the President should not appoint ambassadors except upon the authority of Congress. That had no effect upon the constitutional power of the President. He could make such appointments nevertheless." [53]

Limitations by mutual consent.—By far the most important and the most effective legislative enactments of this character are those contained in the series of reorganization acts of April 5, 1906, February 5, 1915, and May 24, 1924, and the presidential Executive orders of June 27, 1906, Nov. 26, 1909, and June 7,

---

[52]March 2, 1909, 35 Stat., 672.
[53]*Cong. Record,* 66th Cong., 3rd Sess., p. 2316.

1924. These laws, establishing what is known as the merit system in the Foreign Service, have been placed on the statute books by mutual consent, with the President taking the lead.

Upon the recommendation of the President, and through his collaboration, the Diplomatic and Consular Services, as regards all positions below the grade of minister, have been placed upon a permanent civil service basis in such a manner as to render these positions of a statutory, rather than a constitutional, character through the creation of the statutory title "Foreign Service officer." This title, which is made to govern the payment of salary, is of statutory creation, and appointments thereto are subject to statutory conditions and limitations. The requirements prescribed for appointment include a competitive examination under rules and regulations made by the President, and a suitable period of probation in an unclassified grade.[54]

The origin of foreign policy.—Foreign policy usually originates with the Executive.[55]

"Not only the language of the Constitution but also the practice of more than a century, establishes the principle that this power rests mainly in the President. Generally, although not invariably, the power of initiative and the power of control go together." [56]

Within the limits of the Constitution, and in harmony with the sentiment of the country, he adopts specific policies with relation to all international questions and proceeds to their execution. He likewise enunciates

---

[54]This development is discussed at greater length on page 258.

[55]"When foreign affairs play a prominent part in the politics and policy of a nation, its Executive must of necessity be its guide; must utter every initial judgment, take every first step of action, supply the information upon which it is to act, suggest and in large measure control its conduct."—Woodrow Wilson, "Congressional Government," pp. xi-xiii.

[56]Mathews, "The Conduct of American Foreign Relations," p. 5.

broad, general principles which may become the fixed and permanent policy of the nation. This was true of the advice contained in Washington's farewell address "to steer clear of permanent alliance with any portion of the foreign world." It was also true of the Monroe Doctrine, which was developed solely on executive initiative, and of the policy of the Open Door, which, since the commitments resulting from the Conference on the Limitation of Armament, must be considered as established.

Executive agreements.—Quite apart from the simple enunciation of a foreign policy, the President is recognized as possessing certain powers of making executive or diplomatic agreements which require no ratification, and which are considered as binding upon his administration, as well as upon succeeding administrations, unless repudiated. Such agreements usually take the form of an exchange of diplomatic notes, and not infrequently give expression to important declarations of foreign policy.

This was true of the Hay Open Door policy of 1899-1900; of the Gentleman's Agreement of 1907 with Japan for the regulation of immigration from that country;[57] of the Root-Takahira agreement of 1908, and of the Lansing-Ishii agreement of 1917, defining the policy of the United States in the Far East.

Congress and foreign policy.—Congress has frequently made declarations of foreign policy in the form of joint resolutions, purporting to shape the course of executive action, which have either been vetoed or ignored by the President as not binding upon him. Other such declarations "have often furnished the President

---

[57]This agreement was nullified by legislative action through the enactment of the immigration law of 1924.

valuable guidance in the shaping of his foreign policy in conformity with public opinion." [58]

By its own declaration, "Congress has a constitutional right to an authoritative voice in declaring and prescribing the foreign policy of the United States." [59] In practice, however, foreign policy has developed largely through executive action and declarations.

Of recent years, congressional declarations of foreign policy have appeared as provisions in appropriation acts which render them fairly immune to veto. Such was true in the case of the Naval Appropriation Act of August 16, 1916,[60] which contains the following:

"It is hereby declared to be the policy of the United States to adjust and settle its international disputes through mediation or arbitration, to the end that war may be honorably avoided. It looks with apprehension and disfavor upon a general increase of armament throughout the world, but it realizes that no single nation can disarm, and that without a common agreement upon the subject every considerable power must maintain a relative standing in military strength."

The same declaration further authorized and requested the President to invite, "at an appropriate time, not later than the close of the war in Europe, all the great Governments of the world to send representatives to a conference which shall be charged with the

---

[58]Corwin, "The President's Control of Foreign Relations," p. 45.

[59]"Congress has a constitutional right to an authoritative voice in declaring and prescribing the foreign policy of the United States, as well in the recognition of new powers as in other matters; and it is the constitutional duty of the executive department to respect that policy, not less in diplomatic negotiations than in the use of national force when authorized by law."—Mathews, "The Conduct of American Foreign Relations," p. 14, citing *Cong. Globe,* 38th Cong. 2nd Sess., Dec. 19, 1864, pp. 66-7, cf. J. M. Callahan, "Evolution of Seward's Mexican Policy," p. 49; Hinds, "Precedents," II, p. 1009.

[60]39 Stat., 618.

duty of formulating a plan for a court of arbitration or other tribunal, to which disputed questions between nations shall be referred for adjudication and peaceful settlement, and to consider the question of disarmament and submit their recommendation to their respective Governments for approval." For this purpose the sum of two hundred thousand dollars was appropriated, and the President was authorized to appoint nine American citizens to represent the United States. No effect was given to the foregoing provisions.

The policy of limiting armament.—The Naval Appropriation Act of July 12, 1921, contains a section which, it has been liberally claimed, influenced the action of the President in calling the Conference on the Limitation of Armament, although negotiations to that end are understood to have been well under way before its final passage. It reads as follows:

"That the President is authorized and requested to invite the Governments of Great Britain and Japan to send representatives to a conference, which shall be charged with the duty of promptly entering into an understanding or agreement by which the naval expenditures and building programs of each of said Governments, to wit, the United States, Great Britain, and Japan, shall be substantially reduced annually during the next five years to such an extent and upon such terms as may be agreed upon, which understanding or agreement is to be reported to the respective Governments for approval."

A similar proposal appears in the Naval Appropriation Act of May 28, 1924,[61] in which the President is requested "to enter into negotiations with the Governments of Great Britain, France, Italy, and Japan and

---

[61] 43 Stat., 204.

such other governments as he may deem proper with the view of reaching an understanding or agreement relative to limiting the construction of all types and sizes of subsurface and surface craft of 10,000 tons standard displacement or less, and of aircraft, and limiting the number of officers and enlisted men."

The immigration policy.—By far the most important recent example of the exercise of congressional initiative in foreign policy was involved in the adoption of the so-called "Japanese exclusion provision" of the Immigration Act of May 26, 1924. The action taken in this case was contrary to the advice of Secretary of State Hughes, who recommended a more moderate course in which diplomacy might have a hand. The President, in approving the law, let it be understood that he would have vetoed this provision had it been possible to separate it from the rest of the act.

Senatorial declaration of policy.—The Senate, aside from its participation in joint action with the House, frequently undertakes to enunciate policy by two means at its disposal: (a) through reservations to treaties; (b) by Senate resolution. "Thus in consenting to the ratification of the conventions adopted at the First and Second Hague Conferences, and at the Algeciras Conference in 1906, the Senate did so on condition that such action should not be so construed as to require the United States to depart from its traditional policy against participation in the settlement of European political questions, nor from its traditional attitude toward purely American questions." [62]

At the time of the Magdalena Bay incident, when it was reported that a Japanese corporation was attempting to secure control of the land at that point in Lower

[62]Mathews, "The Conduct of American Foreign Relations", pp. 16-17.

California, the Senate adopted a resolution declaring:

"That when any harbor or other place in the American continents is so situated that the occupation thereof for naval or military purposes might threaten the communications or the safety of the United States, the Government of the United States could not see without grave concern the possession of such harbor or other place by any corporation or association which has such a relation to another Government, not American, as to give that Government practical power of control for naval or military purposes." [63]

While declarations of this character may accord with the national sentiment, they have no binding effect either upon the President or upon the course of future congressional action.

The declarations of political parties.—Policy sometimes evolves from the crystallization of public sentiment. Responsive thereto, the platforms of political parties make declarations which, in case of victory at the polls, are considered as morally, though not legally binding upon the Executive. Thus the platforms of the two leading parties in the campaign of 1924 declare:

"The Republican Party reaffirms its stand for agreement among the nations to prevent war and preserve peace. As an important step in this direction we endorse the Permanent Court of International Justice and favor the adherence of the United States to this tribunal as recommended by President Coolidge." [64]

"The Democratic Party pledges all its energies to the outlawing of the whole war system," wherefore it asserts that "there is no substitute for the League of Nations as an agency working for peace," and promises

---

[63]*Ibid.*
[64]*N. Y. Times,* June 12, 1924.

an innovation in dealing with the League of Nations issue by submitting it to a referendum election advisory to the Government to be held officially under Act of Congress.[65] A criticism of this proposal points out that "there is neither constitutional basis for a statute nor a statute which provides for a national referendum." [66]

Bibliography.

Baldwin, S. E.: "The Share of the President in a Declaration of War"; *American Journal of International Law,* XII, 1-14, January, 1918.

Barrett, J. F.: "International Agreements Without the Advice and Consent of the Senate"; Yale Law Journal, XV, November, 1905.

Bryce, James: "The American Commonwealth"; Macmillan, New York, 1912.

Carnegie Endowment for International Peace: "American Foreign Policy"; Publication No. 17, Division of Intercourse and Publicity.

Chow, S. R.: *"Controle Parlementaire de la Politique Étrangère";* E. Sagot and Co., Paris, 1920.

Command Papers for 1912, Miscellaneous No. 5: "Treatment of International Questions by Parliament in European countries, the United States, and Japan." London.

Corwin, Edward S.: "The President's Control of Foreign Relations"; Princeton University Press, 1917.

Crandall, S. B.: "Treaties, Their Making and Enforcement"; Sec. Ed., Washington, 1916.

Goebel, Julius, Jr.: "The Recognition Policy of the U. S."; *Columbia University Studies in History, Economics and Public Law,* LXVI, No. 1.

Hyde, Charles Cheney: "International Law"; Little, Brown & Co., Boston, 1922.

Hughes, Charles Evans: "Some Observations on the Conduct of our Foreign Relations"; *American Journal of International Law,* July, 1922.

---

[65]*Ibid.,* June 29, 1924.

[66]*Ibid.,* see remarks of Hon. Newton D. Baker.

Hughes, Charles Evans: "Some Aspects of the Work of the State Department"; *American Journal of International Law,* July, 1922.

Mathews, John Mabry: "The Conduct of American Foreign Relations"; Century Co., New York, 1922.

Myers, Denys P.: "The Control of Foreign Relations"; *American Political Science Review,* February, 1917.

Myers, Denys P.; "Legislatures and Foreign Relations"; *American Political Science Review,* November, 1917.

Moore, John Bassett: "Digest of International Law"; 8 vols., Gov. Printing Office, Washington, 1906.

Moore, John Bassett: "Treaties and Executive Agreements"; *Political Science Quarterly,* XX, 385-420, September, 1905.

Morrell, P.: "The Control of Foreign Affairs"; *Contemporary Review,* November, 1912.

Parliamentary Debates, Commons, 5th Series, 104; 841-902.

Penfield, W. L.: "Recognition of a New State—Is it an Executive Function?"; *American Law Review,* XXXII, 390-408, May-June, 1898.

Ponsonby, Arthur: "Democracy and Diplomacy"; Methuen & Co., Ltd., London, 1915.

Thayer, William Roscoe: "The Life of John Hay"; Houghton, Mifflin Co., Boston, 1915.

Thomas, C. S.: "The Power of Congress to Establish Peace"; *American Law Review,* LV, 86-104, January-February, 1921.

Turner, E. R.: "Control of Diplomacy"; *The Nation,* June 8, 1916.

Wright, Quincy: "The Control of American Foreign Relations"; Macmillan, New York, 1922.

Wriston, H. M.: "Presidential Special Agents in Diplomacy"; *American Political Science Review,* X, 481-499, August, 1916.

Chapter III

THE DEPARTMENT OF STATE

Historical sketch.—The executive department of the government which deals with foreign affairs had its origin in the "Committee of Secret Correspondence," selected by the Continental Congress in Philadelphia, November 29, 1775. It was composed of the following members: Benjamin Franklin, Chairman, Benjamin Harrison of Virginia, John Dickinson of Pennsylvania, Thomas Johnson of Maryland, and John Jay of New York.

On April 17, 1777, the name of the Committee was changed to the "Committee for Foreign Affairs," and in January, 1781, there was laid before Congress "a plan for the Department of Foreign Affairs," the opening paragraph of which stated:

"That the extent and rising power of these United States entitles them to a place among the great potentates of Europe, while our political and commercial interests point out the propriety of cultivating with them a friendly correspondence and connection." [1]

The department was organized in August of the same year, and according to the report of a congressional committee on August 14, 1888, it then occupied two rooms; one for the Secretary, and one for his deputy and clerks.[2]

The first Secretary of Foreign Affairs under the

---

[1] Hunt, "The Department of State of the U. S." (1898), p. 9.
[2] *Ibid.*, p. 11.

Articles of Confederation was Robert R. Livingston of New York, the only other incumbent of this office before the adoption of the Constitution being John Jay.

The Department of Foreign Affairs.—By the act of July 27, 1789, there came into existence, as the first executive department of the Government under the Constitution, the "Department of Foreign Affairs." It was placed under the direction of a Secretary for the Department of Foreign Affairs.

The same year, in adjusting the other executive functions of the Government, it was decided that instead of creating a new department for "Home Affairs," certain additional duties of this character should be entrusted to the Department of Foreign Affairs. Accordingly, by act of September 15, 1789, its functions were thus extended, and by virtue of this assumption of "home duties," its name was changed to the "Department of State," and the title of its directing head became "Secretary of State."

On June 17, 1790, Thomas Jefferson submitted to the Treasury an estimate of expenses for that year from which it appears that the total number of persons then employed was eight, consisting of a Secretary of State, four clerks, one French interpreter, and two messengers.[3]

The total annual expenditures of the department as then estimated were $8,061.

The Secretary of State.—The Secretary of State is regarded as first in rank among the members of the Cabinet, and in the event of vacancy in the office of both President and Vice-President, he succeeds to the position as Acting President.[4] His office is second in impor-

---

[3]Hunt, "The History of the Dept. of State," pp. 148-149.
[4]Act of Jan. 19, 1886, 24 Stat., I.

tance only to the presidency, to which it has frequently been regarded as a stepping-stone.

Thomas Jefferson, James Madison, James Monroe, John Quincy Adams, Martin Van Buren, and James Buchanan were Secretaries of State before they became President. Among other distinguished men who have filled this high office are to be found Edmund Randolph, Timothy Pickering, John Marshall, Henry Clay, Daniel Webster, John C. Calhoun, Edward Everett, William L. Marcy, Lewis Cass, William H. Seward, and James G. Blaine.

Recent Secretaries of State have been Richard Olney, John Sherman, William R. Day, John Hay, Elihu Root, Robert Bacon, Philander C. Knox, William Jennings Bryan, Robert Lansing, Bainbridge Colby, and Charles Evans Hughes.

Duties of the Secretary of State.—Manifestly it is impossible for the President to exercise personally all the powers attributed to him as the central figure in the conduct of foreign relations. It is therefore provided by statute that:

"The Secretary of State shall perform such duties as shall from time to time be enjoined on or intrusted to him by the President relative to correspondences, commissions, or instructions to or with public ministers or consuls from the United States, or to negotiations with public ministers from foreign states or princes, or to memorials or other applications from foreign public ministers or other foreigners, or to such other matters respecting foreign affairs as the President of the United States shall assign to the Department, and he shall conduct the business of the Department in such manner as the President shall direct." [5]

[5] R. S. 202.

The delicate and important nature of the duties thus intrusted to him renders his relations with the President peculiarly close and confidential.

A Secretary of State may, through the strength of his personality and his recognized ability, largely overshadow the President in moments when the intensity of international relations causes the public attention to become focused upon the issues involved.

Contact with foreign representatives.—Although foreign diplomatic representatives are officially received by the President, the President does not, as a rule, hold communication directly with them on official matters. It is the Secretary of State who acts as the medium of communication, conducting all correspondence and negotiations, as well as concluding the action to be taken under the powers and on the responsibility of the President.

Very naturally, in matters of great importance the President is kept currently informed of developments and not infrequently he has taken direct guidance of affairs into his own hands.[6]

Aside from direct contact with foreign diplomatic representatives, and as a part of his "home duties," the Secretary of State is the medium of correspondence

---

[6]"Mr. Hay used to tell his friends that often President McKinley did not send for him once a month on business, but that he saw President Roosevelt every day. That statement illustrates the difference in initiative between the two Presidents; or, at least, the ratio of their interest in foreign relations. From the moment of Mr. Roosevelt's accession, the State Department felt a new impelling force behind it. The Secretary still conducted the negotiations, but the origination and decision of policy came to rest more and more with the President. In no other case was this so true as in that of the Panama Canal. In the earlier stages Mr. Roosevelt gave directions which Mr. Hay carried out; before the end, however, the President took the business into his own hands; and has always frankly assumed entire responsibility for the decisive stroke."——Thayer, "Life of John Hay," p. 297, vol. II.

between the President and the chief executives of the several States of the United States.

Relations with Congress.—The relations of the Secretary of State with Congress are less direct than are those of the minister of foreign affairs under a parliamentary form of government. He may, upon invitation, appear before the committees of Congress and make statements, or furnish information not incompatible with the public interest, but as the powers which he exercises belong to the President, Congress usually addresses its formal requests and recommendations to the Chief Executive, and receives its information through him. Lord Bryce observes that "the President's best policy is to keep the leaders of the senatorial majority, and in particular the Committee on Foreign Relations, informed of the progress of any pending negotiation," and that "much depends upon the confidence which the Senate feels in the judgment of the Secretary of State and on the tact which he shows in his dealings with Senators." [7]

Importance of the position.—The administrative duties of the Secretary of State, as head of the most important department of the Government, and of the Foreign Service as well, are proportional in their delicacy to his larger and more constructive functions. He is, in fact, the pivot of the entire system, with enormous powers sufficiently within his control to give the stamp of his personality to the whole range of transactions to which the nation is a party during his incumbency. Given the transcendent importance, both present and future, of the foreign relations of the United States, it is obvious that this position is one of such special trust

---

[7] Bryce, "The American Commonwealth," vol. I, p. 107.

as to merit the selection only of men of surpassing integrity and ability.

It should never again be possible for a learned critic to observe with justice, as did Lord Bryce, that:

"The President has a Secretary of State to advise him, who is sometimes a man of first-rate gifts, but more frequently only a politician selected because of his party standing, and possessing little knowledge of world affairs. The staff of the office has been small, and too frequently changed." [8]

The Department of State.—The Department of State is peculiarly the administrative instrumentality of the President for the conduct of foreign relations.

It forms, with the Foreign Service (diplomatic and consular), a single system through which the extensive powers of the President are exercised, and his decisions and policies carried into execution. Because of the confidential nature of its work, the Department of State makes no general or regular report to Congress, as is required of the other departments of the government. In fact, its relations with Congress are altogether unique, having no parallel in any other executive agency.

Relations with Congress.—"It is a department which from the beginning the Senate has never assumed the right to direct or control, except as to clearly defined matters relating to duties imposed by statute and not connected with the conduct of foreign relations. We direct all the other heads of departments to transmit to the Senate designated papers or information. We do not address directions to the Secretary of State, nor do we direct requests, even, to the Secretary of State. We direct requests to the real head of that department, the

8Bryce, "Modern Democracies," vol. II, p. 373.

President of the United States, and, as a matter of courtesy, we add the qualifying words: "if in his judgment not incompatible with the public interest.' " [9]

Relations with foreign governments.—The position of the Department of State with relation to foreign governments has been thus described by Secretary of State Seward:

"This Department is the legal organ of communication between the President of the United States and foreign countries. All foreign powers recognize it and transmit their communications to it, through the dispatches of our ministers abroad, or their own diplomatic representatives residing near this Government. These communications are submitted to the President, and, when proper, are replied to under his direction by the Secretary of State. This mutual correspondence is recorded and preserved in the archives of this Department. This is, I believe, the same system which prevails in the governments of civilized states everywhere." [10]

Departmental duties.—Apart from the duties already attributed to the Secretary of State as expressive of his rôle in the conduct of foreign relations, there are many others of importance, though of a more routine character, which, if such a distinction may be made, it seems proper to ascribe to the department rather than to the Secretary, since they are conferred by statute, and not delegated by the President. For the most part, these belong to the category of "home affairs," and are largely of an administrative nature.

---

[9]Remarks of Senator Spooner, Cong. Rec., 59th Cong., 1st Sess., vol. XL, pt. 2, p. 1419, Senate Debate quoted in Reinsch, "Readings in Am. Fed. Govt.," p. 85; Corwin, op. cit., p. 176; Hunt, "The Department of State of the United States," 1914, pp. 84, 105.

[10]Moore, "Digest of International Law," vol. 4, p. 781, citing Mr. Seward, Sec. of State, to Mr. Dayton, min., to France, June 27, 1862, MS. Inst. France, XVI, 189.

The duties include the custody of the great seal of
the United States, the countersigning and affixing of
the seal to all executive proclamations, to various commissions, and to warrants for the extradition of fugi-
tives from justice; the custody of treaties made with
foreign states, and of the laws of the United States;
the granting and the issuance of passports and of exequaturs to foreign consuls in the United States; the
publication of the laws and resolutions of Congress,
amendments to the Constitution, and proclamations declaring the admission of new States into the Union; the
preparation of the volumes of "Foreign Relations of
the United States." In the administration of the immigration law, there results from the duties imposed upon
consular officers a very active function having to do
with the granting of visas and the administration of
the quota system in conjunction with the Department
of Labor.

Departmental organization.—Originally the entire
staff of the department consisted of a Secretary of State
and two clerks. As the work increased in volume and
importance, additional clerks were added, and their
duties separated into administrative units, known to-
day as divisions and bureaus.

Congress provided an Assistant Secretary of State in
1853, a Second Assistant Secretary in 1866 and a Third
Assistant Secretary in 1874. Formerly, the Assistant
Secretary succeeded to the office of Acting Secretary
in the absence of the head of the department, but in
1909 provision was made for a Counselor, whose rank
was established as next in importance to that of the
Secretary.

The same year the position of Director of the Consular Service was created,[11] and an appropriation for a "resident diplomatic officer" provided. Dependent upon an annual appropriation which, in the absence of statutory authorization, was always subject to a point of order, the position of Counselor endured for several years, when the title was changed to that of "Undersecretary of State," which has since been established by permanent enactment.[12]

Recent changes.—The Foreign Service reorganization act of May 24, 1924, carries the following provision relating to the Department of State:

"The titles 'Second Assistant Secretary of State' and 'Third Assistant Secretary of State' shall hereafter be known as 'Assistant Secretary of State' without numerical distinction of rank: but the change of title shall in no way impair the commissions, salaries, and duties of the present incumbents.

"There is hereby established in the Department of State an additional 'Assistant Secretary of State,' who shall be appointed by the President, by and with the advice and consent of the Senate, and shall be entitled to compensation at the rate of $7,500 per annum.

"The position of Director of the Consular Service is abolished and the salary provided for that office is hereby made available for the salary of the additional Assistant Secretary of State herein authorized." [13]

Thus on July 1, 1924, the date on which the act became effective, the former Director of the Consular Service became an Assistant Secretary of State, of which there are now four, all having the same designation.

The position of Assistant Secretary.—The four posi-

---

[11]Act of Aug. 5, 1909, 36 Stat., 119. See also page 28.

[12]Act of Jan. 3, 1923, 42 Stat., 1068.

[13]Sec. 22, Act of May 24, 1924.

tions of Assistant Secretary are regarded as political by virtue of the fact that appointments to them are made by the President, by and with the advice and consent of the Senate. This, however, does not imply that all of them are subject to the whims of purely partisan fancy. Continuity in foreign policy, and consequently, the stability of official personnel, are elements of priceless value, indispensable to the successful handling of diplomatic questions. This fact was long recognized in relation to the position of Second Assistant Secretary of State, which was held continuously by one official, Honorable Alvey A. Adee, through successive administrations for forty-two years, until his death in July, 1924. The memoirs of many prominent men bear striking testimony of the value of his work.

"As Second Assistant Secretary of State, Mr. Adee was then, as he is to-day, the only permanent official of high rank under the executive. Administrations came and went, Adee stayed on. Presidents ignorant of diplomacy and international law felt reasonably safe in appointing as their chief secretaries gentlemen as ignorant as themselves, because they knew that Adee was there to guard against blunders." [14]

The newly created assistant secretaryship, now filled by a permanent official, Honorable Wilbur J. Carr, seems destined to create another strong tradition and to establish two of these important offices on a non-political basis.

During the Harding-Coolidge administration, the Undersecretary of State, and three of the assistant secretaries have been selected from the diplomatic service, which is a practice worthy of perpetuation.

The distribution of functions.—In order to understand

---

[14] See Thayer, "The Life of John Hay," vol. II, pp. 186-187.

the delimitation of functions and the system of supervision and direction, prevailing in the department, a brief description of the duties of the Undersecretary and of the four Assistant Secretaries, together with those of the several divisions and bureaus, seems necessary.[15]

Duties of the Undersecretary of State.—The Undersecretary of State is the principal assistant of the Secretary of State in the discharge of his various functions, aiding in the formulation and execution of the foreign policies of the Government, and in the reception of representatives of foreign governments, and so forth. In matters which do not require the personal attention of the Secretary of State, he acts for the Secretary of State, and in the absence of the Secretary of State he becomes the Acting Secretary of State. The Undersecretary of State is charged with the general direction of the work of the Department of State and of the Foreign Service, and is chairman of the Foreign Service Personnel Board.

Duties of Assistant Secretaries of State.—An Assistant Secretary is charged with all matters pertaining to foreign commercial policy, commercial treaties, transportation and communication, and so forth, and supervises the Office of the Economic Adviser. In the absence of the Secretary of State and the Undersecretary of State, he becomes the Acting Secretary of State.

An Assistant Secretary has supervision over the Division of Passport Control, the Office of Coordination and Review, and the Visa Office. He makes decisions in citizenship and other cases involving complex questions of law and policy, and is consulted by the officers of

---

[15]The distribution of functions is not permanent and may be changed at the will of the Secretary of State.

the department upon matters of diplomatic procedure and general questions of international law and policy, particularly when involving the traditional practice of the Department of State.

An Assistant Secretary is charged with the administration of the department, administrative matters concerning international conferences and commissions, and with matters pertaining to ceremonial and protocol. He has supervision over the office of the chief clerk, the Division of Publications, the Bureau of Accounts, and the Bureau of Indexes and Archives. He is charged further with the presentation to the President of ambassadors and ministers of foreign countries newly accredited to the United States, and is a member of the Foreign Service Personnel Board.

An Assistant Secretary directs the Consular Service and all consular activities in connection with the work of the several bureaus and divisions of the department. His office has charge of the censoring, grading, and criticizing of commercial and economic reports; the drafting of correspondence on consular trade assistance and reporting; and the distribution of commercial and economic reports to the Department of Commerce and such other Government departments and organizations and non-Government organizations as may properly receive them. He is also the Budget officer of the Department of State and is charged with the supervision of the preparation of all estimates of appropriations for the department and for the foreign service and of their presentation to Congress. He furthermore supervises the expenditures made from the appropriation "Emergencies arising in the Diplomatic and Consular Service," and is a member of the Foreign Service Personnel Board.

Office of the Solicitor.—The Office of the Solicitor deals with questions of municipal and international law; handles claims of citizens of the United States against foreign governments and of nationals of foreign countries against the United States; and looks after matters pertaining to international extradition, the protection of interests of American citizens in foreign countries, the rights of aliens in the United States, international arbitrations, and the drafting and interpretation of treaties.

Foreign Service Personnel Board.—The Foreign Service Personnel Board prepares efficiency records of Foreign Service officers, and submits to the Secretary of State the names of Foreign Service officers recommended for advancement in the service, for designation as counselors of embassy or legation, and for promotion to the grade of minister. It recommends to the Secretary of State the assignment of Foreign Service officers to posts and their transfer from one branch of the service to the other, according to the needs of the service; it also makes recommendations to the Secretary of State regarding separations from the service. The office of the executive committee of the Foreign Service Personnel Board is charged with the receipt and custody of all applications for appointment in the Foreign Service and with arranging for examinations for entrance to the Foreign Service. It handles the correspondence relating thereto; prints and distributes blank forms of application for appointment in the Foreign Service and pamphlets regarding requirements for entrance therein.

Office of the Chief Clerk.—The Office of the Chief Clerk has general supervision of the clerks and other employees of the department and of routine departmental matters. It purchases supplies and has custody of the property of the department; supervises and assigns office rooms and space; issues passes, when required, to persons entitled to enter the building; authenticates applications for automobile licenses of foreign diplomatic officers residing in Washington; corresponds on departmental matters; grants leaves of absence and sick leave; and has charge of the preparation and custody of efficiency records of the department. The chief clerk signs authentications and such other papers as the Secretary of State may direct. The appointment section of his office has charge of the receipt and custody of applications for appointment in the departmental service and of the indorsements of applicants; takes care of correspondence relating thereto; prepares nominations to the Senate of Foreign Service officers and other officers commissioned by the Department of State whose appointments are subject to confirmation by the Senate; issues commissions, exequaturs, and warrants of extradition; handles the bonding of foreign service officers and other officers accountable to the department for moneys received or expended; prepares copy for the department register, diplomatic and consular list, and mailing list, editing, proof-reading, and distributing the same; watches civil service and departmental personnel matters; administers oaths of office; and has custody of the seal of the United States.

Division of Far Eastern Affairs.—The Division of Far Eastern Affairs has general supervision, under the secretaries, of relations, diplomatic and consular, political and economic, with China and leased territories, Japan, Siam, the Far Eastern possessions of European nations (in conjunction with the Division of Western

European Affairs), and Siberia (in conjunction with the Division of Eastern European Affairs).

Division of Latin-American Affairs.—The Division of Latin-American Affairs has general supervision, under the secretaries, of relations, diplomatic and consular, political and economic, with Argentina, Bolivia, Brazil, Chile, Colombia, Costa Rica, Cuba, Dominican Republic, Ecuador, Guatemala, Haiti, Honduras, Nicaragua, Panama, Paraguay, Peru, Salvador, Uruguay, and Venezuela.

Division of Western European Affairs.—The Division of Western European Affairs has general supervision, under the secretaries, of relations, diplomatic and consular, political and economic, with Austria, Belgium, British Empire (Canada, the Union of South Africa, British colonies, or protectorates not elsewhere enumerated, and, in conjunction with the Far Eastern Division, Australia, New Zealand, India, and other British or European possessions in the Far East), Czechoslovakia, Denmark, France (Morocco), Germany, Hungary, Italy, Liberia, the Netherlands, Norway, Portugal, Spain, Sweden, and Switzerland.

Division of Near Eastern Affairs.—The Division of Near Eastern Affairs has general supervision, under the secretaries, of relations, diplomatic and consular, political and economic, with Abyssinia, Afghanistan, Albania, Armenia, Azerbaijan, Bulgaria, Egypt, Georgia, Greece, Hedjaz, Mesopotamia, Palestine, Persia, Rumania, Kingdom of the Serbs, Croats, and Slovenes, Syria, and Turkey.

Division of Mexican Affairs.—The Division of Mexican Affairs has general supervision, under the secretaries, of relations, diplomatic and consular, political and economic, with Mexico.

Division of Eastern European Affairs.—The Division of Eastern European Affairs has general supervision, under the secretaries, of matters pertaining to Russia (including Siberia), and of relations, diplomatic and consular, political and economic, with Esthonia, Finland, Latvia, Lithuania, and Poland.

Office of the Economic Adviser.—The Office of the Economic Adviser gives advice and recommendations to the Department on questions of general economic policy; unifies and coordinates economic matters within the department; establishes and maintains *liaison* with the various economic bureaus in other departments; handles economic cases which have no regional character or which overlap geographical divisions; drafts correspondence on matters falling within the following special fields: natural resources, finance, foreign commercial policy, commercial treaties and tariffs, transportation and communications.

Division of Passport Control.—This division has charge of the examination and adjudication of applications for passports and for registration in consulates of the United States as American citizens; issues departmental passports; supervises the department's passport agencies in New York, Chicago, San Francisco, New Orleans, and Seattle; directs the clerks of courts who take passport applications; has custody of applications for passports and registration; handles the correspondence regarding citizenship, passports, registration, and right to protection while abroad; and issues letters of introduction.

Visa Office.—The Visa Office has charge of matters pertaining to the entry of aliens into the United States with respect to the granting or refusal of visas; handles correspondence on matters pertaining to visa work; and

examines visa applications submitted by American consuls abroad.

Division of Publications.—The Division of Publications issues requisitions on the Public Printer and has
general supervision of press work done for the department, of which the chief of the division is the editor;
compiles the session laws, statutes at large of the United
States, papers relating to the foreign relations of the
United States, and other publications; has custody of
the original laws, treaties, proclamations, and Executive
orders; has charge of printing of the slip laws and
printing and distribution of treaties, proclamations, and
Executive orders; also has custody of Indian treaties
and other historical manuscripts, of papers relating to
constitutional amendments and the ascertainment of
electors, and of records of boundary and claims commissions; executes authentications.

Division of Political and Economic Information.—
This division has charge of the collection and coordination of political, ethnological, geographical, social, and
economic information; has custody of the map collection
of the department and the drafting of such special maps
as may be required; and manages the library of the
department.

Division of Current Information.—The Division of
Current Information has charge of the preparation of
news items for the press; receives and replies to inquiries from newspaper correspondents; prepares and
distributes to officials of the department daily press
summaries and special articles; and furnishes officials
with press bulletins, copies of texts, and general information bearing upon foreign relations.

Division of Foreign Service Administration.—This
division is charged with the general administration of

the Foreign Service. It handles matters of appropriations and expenditures, rentals, equipment and supplies, organizations, instruction of diplomatic and consular officers, and so forth. Correspondence relating to the foregoing and to customs courtesies and free entry, letters rogatory, decoration of American citizens by foreign governments, international exchange of publications, diplomatic pouch service between the United States and foreign countries, and the designation of commercial, military, and naval attachés which come within its domain. It is interested further in the whereabouts and welfare of Americans abroad, shipping and seamen, settlement of estates of deceased Americans in foreign countries, consular protection of American interests and, other than commerce, the general work of consular offices, such as immigration, quarantine, notarial acts, protection of the customs revenue, and so forth.

Bureau of Indexes and Archives.—The Bureau of Indexes and Archives records and indexes the correspondence of the department; has custody of the archives; and attends to telegraph, telephone, and cipher communications.

Bureau of Accounts.—The Bureau of Accounts has the custody and disbursement of appropriations and indemnity funds, conducts correspondence relating thereto, and makes an administrative examination of accounts.

Significance of departmental adjustment.—It will be seen that the departmental organization embraces geographical divisions, a legal establishment, an economic establishment, and various administrative divisions, or bureaus. The interrelation of these constitutes a fine mechanism of automatic control, designed to secure balanced judgments and dependable decisions.

The subjects dealt with are generally of such momentous import that all possible consequences, however remote, must be scrupulously examined before a final decision is reached.[16]

The work of the department, therefore, must proceed cautiously, and with due deliberation in each case. Hasty action would destroy its value altogether.

There are four chief factors which commonly enter into the consideration of an international question: the political aspects; the economic aspects; the legal aspects; and any precedent which may be involved. These must be reviewed from two angles: from the American view-point; and from the foreign view-point. It is clear that a proper coordination of these operations, with due regard to expert judgment in each, is the aim of that highly technical organization which seems to present so few complexities in its outward aspects.

The use of field men.—How is one to describe in terms of mechanism the operations of such a system? Perhaps an analysis will serve. In 1909, it has been seen, an appropriation was obtained for the salary of a "resident diplomatic officer," which position, it was intended, should be filled by a man of considerable diplomatic experience, transferred to the department from the Diplomatic Service. In that way the Secretary of State would always have at hand for consultation a man of practical experience in the foreign field. This proved the beginning of an important development.

Elaborating upon the idea of a resident diplomatic

[16] "A wrong step in foreign policy can never be corrected, for it affects not only ourselves but the opinion which others have of us."—Cosmos, "The Basis of Durable Peace," p. 110.

officer, authority was later obtained for the assignment to the department of any diplomatic secretary or consul, without loss of grade, class or salary, for a period of three years, and if the public interest demanded further service, the assignment might be extended for an additional year.[17]

The effect of this enactment was to make immediately available to the department the experience and the expert knowledge of the entire Foreign Service with reference to all important regions of the earth. The latest diplomatic and consular list shows that on July 1, 1924, there were twenty diplomatic secretaries and thirty-two consular officers thus assigned to the department, representing a range of service covering every important section of the world.[18]

Previous authorization had already been obtained for the appointment of a number of "officers to aid in important drafting work," to which positions non-service men were appointed.[19] Officers of both these categories are assigned to the various geographical and administrative divisions and bureaus in such manner as to afford facilities for applying both the American and the foreign view-point to the study of important questions. Again, as the training of diplomatic officers and consular officers differs widely, their distribution in the department takes into account a balancing of those qualities peculiar to each.

Multi-visioned treatment of cases.—Thus we have the type which looks from the purely American view-point; that which looks from a view-point gained through prac-

---

[17]Act of February 5, 1915. See also Act of May 24, 1924, Sec. 14, extending this provision to all foreign service officers.

[18]See a further discussion of this point on page 276.

[19]Act of June 17, 1910, 36 Stat., 484.

tical consular experience, and that which embodies the practical diplomatic experience. The legal aspects of the work which require the application both of international and of municipal law, are confided to a Solicitor, with a staff of eleven assistants to the Solicitor, seven assistant solicitors, six law clerks, and five clerks. Here again there is specialization as to subject-matter and as to region.

The economists of the department are distributed among the geographical divisions, their work being brought to a focus in the office of the Economic Adviser.

Many references back and forth are sometimes necessary in bringing to bear upon a given question these various points of view and in establishing the technical merits of each. Expressions of opinion in such consultations take the form of written memoranda which serve to plot out the course of procedure and to lay the basis of final action. As communications issuing from the department should in all cases measure up as nearly as possible to the form of finished state papers, a document, before being submitted for final signature, receives the initials of all officials concerned in its subject-matter, and of those in supervision over them.

Interchange of personnel.—The practice of assigning diplomatic and consular offices to the Department of State has gained in importance from year to year. At present such men are carefully selected on the basis of their personal qualifications and assigned to definite and highly responsible tasks. Their influence in the department has been wholesome and constructive. It is obvious that to be of greatest value they should, as nearly as possible, represent "the best minds" of the service within their respective spheres of activity.

Former Secretary of State Robert Lansing has questioned one feature of the reorganization act in the following manner:

"If there is a criticism, it is that the Bill failed to include in its general scheme of consolidation certain officers of the Department of State, such as chiefs and assistant chiefs of bureaus and divisions, assistant solicitors, drafting officers, and in fact all officers who do not belong to the clerical force. It would have improved the Bill if such officers had been graded and made eligible for transfer to the Foreign Service, whenever it seemed advisable to send them into the foreign field. It would unquestionably improve the efficiency of the departmental organization and give them a proper standing not only with foreign diplomats but also with the members of our Foreign Service." [20]

The bill as finally passed, contained the following provision:

"That hereafter appointments to the position of Foreign Service officer shall be made after examination and a suitable period of probation in an unclassified grade or, after five years of continuous service in the Department of State, by transfer therefrom under such rules and regulations as the President may prescribe." [21]

The presidential Executive order of June 7, 1924, prescribing administrative regulations for the service, also provides:

"Officers and employees, after five years of continuous service in the Department of State, are eligible for appointment by transfer to any class in the Foreign Service upon the recommendation of the Foreign Service

---

[20]"The Proposed Consolidation of the Diplomatic and Consular Services of the United States," an article in the *American Journal of International Law*, April, 1923.

[21]Sec. 5, Act of May 24, 1924.

Personnel Board and with the approval of the Secretary of State."

It is made the duty of the Foreign Service Personnel Board "From time to time after the Act of May 24, 1924, becomes effective, and as vacancies arise, to submit to the Secretary of State lists of those Foreign Service officers whose records of efficiency entitle them to advancement in the service, and who are therefore recommended for promotion, and the names of those officers and employees in the Department of State who, after five years of continuous service, and because of special ability and merit are recommended for appointment by transfer to the position of Foreign Service officer." [22] This would seem to cover, in effect, the views expressed by Mr. Lansing.

Experience of the British system.—One of the chief points of attack in the British system was its Foreign Office, and the formula of "interchangeability," which was prescribed as a measure of reform, applied in this connection to an amalgamation of the Foreign Office and the field.

Mr. Arthur Ponsonby, M. P., quotes the late Sir R. Morier, for many years British Ambassador at St. Petersburg, as follows:

"It is most important that the Diplomatic Service should be to a certain extent nationalized, and that the Foreign Office should be to a certain extent internationalized." [23] The problem, however, was even more fundamental than is here implied, for it was liberally charged that the system of administration in the Foreign Office had degenerated into a bureaucracy and that the service was being stifled by its sterility. The final result was

---

[22]Executive order of June 7, 1924.
[23]Ponsonby, "Democracy and Diplomacy," p. 65.

a Royal Commission of investigation, a shake-up, and a general reorganization of the entire system with amalgamation and democratization as its aims.

The necessity for a Strong State Department.—It would be futile to build a strong Foreign Service, such as now seems assured, without a Department of State of corresponding strength and dependability.[24] Our foreign representatives act upon instructions, and their whole official life is guided from the executive source in Washington. A weak or inefficient Department of State would nullify their efforts and negative the value of their training and experience. Unless the material which they gather and transmit to Washington is subjected here to a laboratory process of study and analysis, what is to be its practical value towards enlightening the country and guiding the action of the Government?

In 1909 Secretary Root is accredited with having said of his position in the department, that he was like a man trying to conduct the business of a large metropolitan law firm in the office of a village squire.[25]

Ten years later, in 1919, Secretary Lansing served the following warning on Congress in supporting his estimates for appropriations:

"The Government now faces a decision with respect to the conduct of our foreign affairs. It must reorganize and greatly enlarge the Department of State or there will be a breakdown of the most serious character. The department will not function on its present basis under the burden of the new load." [26]

---

[24]"We should never forget that the keynote of foreign service is the personality of those in control; that is, the personnel of the Department of State."—*Report on the Foreign Service,* National Civil Service Reform League (1919), p. 71.

[25]*The Nation,* Sept., 1909, p. 294, cited in Mathews, "The Conduct of American Foreign Relations," p. 47.

[26]Letter to the Secretary of the Treasury, Nov. 10, 1919.

Four years later, Secretary Hughes, in January, 1924, stated in his testimony on the Foreign Service reorganization bill:

"We need in the United States the very best representation abroad that we can get. Instead of getting out of difficulties, I mean international difficulties, they multiply. Whatever the future may be, the present shows a constant increase of important situations, of new interests, of new problems, to which we must address ourselves with all the ability that we have at our command." [27]

Constructive criticisms.—We have seen Lord Bryce's criticism to the effect that "the staff of the office (Department of State) has been small, and too frequently changed" [28] and Secretary Hay's testimonial as to the value of the one permanent official, Second Assistant Secretary Adee. [29] To this should be added another opinion of like character, and of equal force and effect. Ambassador Walter Hines Page wrote:

"All of which means that it is high time we were constructing a Foreign Service. First of all, Congress ought to make it possible to have half a dozen or more permanent foreign under-secretaries—men who, after service in the department, could go out as ministers and ambassadors; it ought generously to reorganize the whole thing. It ought to have a competent study made of the foreign offices of other governments. Of course it ought to get room to work in. Then it ought at once to give its ambassadors and ministers homes and dignified treatment. We've got to play a part in the world whether we wish to or not." [30]

---

[27] Hearings on H.R. 17 and H.R. 6357, 68th Cong., 1st Sess., p. 13.
[28] See page 75.
[29] See page 79.
[30] Hendrick, "Life and Letters of Walter H. Page," vol. I, p. 335, Letter to Colonel Edward M. House, Sept. 22, 1914.

The need of a special legislative status.—The great difficulty in securing proper support for the Department of State lies in the fact that it continues to be assimilated with the other executive departments of the government, whereas its character is quite different. The domestic departments deal with purely internal matters, and some of them might, without altogether calamitous results, be abolished. The scope of their functions and the extent of their activities are optional with each Congress. But the State Department deals with foreign nations, and the demands that are made upon it are limited only by the extent of the external interests of the country. It is in daily competition, or even conflict, with the efficiency and skill of all the foreign offices of the world in the defense and the furtherance of American rights. Its vigilance must be constant.

The whole of our international interests centers there. Furthermore, and of necessity, these are dealt with in such a confidential way that the first evidences of inefficiency in this vital organism may reveal themselves to the country in the most disastrous consequences. One deplorable blunder may easily be more expensive to the nation than the cost of maintaining an efficient foreign establishment for a century.

The Secretary of State underpaid.—The salary of the Secretary of State is entirely inadequate.[31] Even Secretary Bryan, the "Commoner," found this to be true to an extent which forced him to seek other sources of revenue in a manner still fresh in the public mind. The position of the Secretary of State is unlike that of other

---

[31]The Report of the National Civil Service Reform League shows, from a careful statistical study, that the salary of the Secretary of State ($12,000), measured in actual purchasing power as compared with the year 1898 (when his salary was $8,000) bears the following relation: 1898, $8,000; 1918, $4,200. The Secretary of State for Foreign Affairs in Great Britain received $24,300.—*Report on the Foreign Service* (1919), pp. 75-77.

Cabinet officers. He deals personally with the diplomatic officials of other nations, who form a numerous and costly clientele. His official obligations are enormous and compelling. He will fail, to the national detriment and discredit, unless he fulfils them.[32] In many ways his representative character is like that of an ambassador, and the same considerations which have led to the adoption of representation allowances for the Foreign Service should suggest an extension of the same facilities to the Secretary of State. In no other way is this great office ever to be properly filled, except by quasi-millionaires.

Permanent assistant secretaries required.—Secretary Hughes, upon taking office, promptly selected a trained service man of the grade of ambassador, to be Undersecretary of State. The two vacant positions of assistant secretary he filled with other diplomatic officers selected from the career service. Largely through this sagacious move, the chief points of weakness in the departmental structure have been overcome temporarily, but future administrations may hardly be expected to follow this constructive example. Such appointments, therefore, while a splendid expedient, do not establish and maintain continuity.

It has long been recognized that there should be permanent and very capable officials in this department, and that the whole of the establishment should be

---

[32]"Although the Secretary of State is usually considered the leading man in the Cabinet, his salary of $12,000 is no greater than that received by the other members of the Cabinet and is quite insufficient, in view of his living expenses and the social duties incumbent upon him. The outbreak of the European War greatly increased the work and responsibilities of the state department and accentuated the inadequacy of its personnel and financial support. It is only within recent years that either Congress or the country has begun to realize the great importance of the work of the department and the need that it should be adequately supported."— Mathews, "The Conduct of American Foreign Relations," p. 50.

strengthened to the utmost.[33] Must the United States, in the most important international period of its existence, suffer some sad blunder or reversal before a law to that effect is enacted?

The Foreign Service reorganization act carries a provision in the retirement feature which permits Foreign Service officers to retain their retirement status when appointed to an official position in the Department of State.[34] If this provision should be so broadened as to apply as well to salary, the whole of the trained Foreign Service might then be considered as a field of selection for permanent assistant secretaries.

A suggested formula of reform.—The only functions of the Department of State which in any way resemble those of the other executive departments of the Government are the so-called "home functions," which are largely routine in character, and which have no relation to the conduct of foreign affairs. It has been suggested that these should be transferred to some other department and the name of the Department of State changed back to the "Department of Foreign Affairs." In the unique rôle of a foreign office, pure and simple, it would be a small establishment and could, with appropriate discrimination, receive special legislative treatment at the hands of Congress. As matters now stand, it suffers its proportional share of every financial curtailment of the Government, precisely as though its work were dependent upon domestic, instead of foreign, exigencies.

---

[33]"In addition to making provision for adequate salaries it is equally important to perfect the machinery for selecting and promoting those who are ablest among the officers. In the first place political appointments should be limited to the Secretary of State and one other official, who replaces him in his absence."—*Report on the Foreign Service,* National Civil Service Reform League (1919), p. 83.

[34]Sec. 18(o), Act of May 24, 1924.

The four positions of assistant secretary could be rendered non-partisan and permanent by a simple statute declaring them to be so, and requiring, in case of removals, that the President submit to Congress a written statement of the reasons which prompted his action.[35] There is a precedent for this procedure in the position of consular assistant (formerly consular clerk).[36] But, of course, another difficulty would be to find suitable men; men of education, ability, experience, personality, vision, and character, to whom such a permanent trust might reasonably be confided. We have had such men, and we have them in the department now, temporarily. Surely the Foreign Service is capable of supplying the requisite number of additional permanent officials.

Bibliography.

Hughes, Charles Evans: "Some Aspects of the Work of the State Department"; *American Journal of International Law,* July, 1922.

Hughes, Charles Evans: "Some Observations on the Conduct of our Foreign Relations"; *American Journal of International Law,* July, 1922.

Hunt, Gaillard: "The Department of State of the United States; Its History and Functions"; Yale University Press, New Haven, 1914.

Low, Sydney: "Foreign Office Autocracy"; *Fortnightly Review,* January, 1912.

---

[35]The problem here, like that which confronted the Foreign Service for so many years, is a question of securing relief from political pressure. The Report of the National Civil Service Reform League states that "very often one of the Assistant Secretaries of State is a scion of politics, and forced upon the Secretary of State by influential members of Congress."—p. 84.

[36]"And no clerk (consular assistant) so appointed shall be removed from office, except for cause stated in writing, which shall be submitted to Congress at the session first following such removal."—Act of June 20, 1864, R. S. 1705.

Phillips, William: "An Account of the Development of the Geographical Divisions in the Department of State"; *American Consular Bulletin,* Washington, December, 1922.

"Reorganization of the Department of State"; *The Nation,* LXXXIX, 294-5, September 30, 1909.

"Rules and Regulations Governing the Dept. of State"; Sen. Doc. No. 359, 59th Cong., 2nd Sess., 1917.

Sweetser, A.: "Why the Dept. of State should be Reorganized"; *World's Work,* XXXIX, 511-15, March, 1920.

Thayer, William Roscoe: "The Life of John Hay"; Houghton, Mifflin Co., Boston, 1915.

Young, George: "Diplomacy, Old and New"; Harcourt, Brace & Co., New York, 1921.

CHAPTER IV

THE DIPLOMATIC SERVICE

A branch of the Foreign Service.—By way of facilitating analysis, the Diplomatic Service and the Consular Service will first be discussed in separate chapters, and afterwards as a single Foreign Service composed of two coordinate branches which function on a basis of amalgamation and interchangeability as a result of recent reorganization.

Together, these two units, operating abroad under the direction of the Secretary of State, constitute, with the Department of State, the executive machinery for the conduct of foreign relations. They are now administered jointly as the "Foreign Service of the United States." [1]

Diplomatic offices.—Diplomatic offices are created by international law, and by the Constitution; not by act of Congress, nor by the President. [2]

The expression "ambassadors and other public ministers," as used in the Constitution, is understood as comprehending all officers having diplomatic functions, whatever their title or designation. [3]

James Madison, in 1822, clearly showed the nature of diplomatic offices by pointing out, in contrast with views originally held by him:

---

[1] Act of May 24, 1924.

[2] Attorney General Cushing held "that 'public ministers' as a class are created by the Constitution and law of nations, not by act of Congress. No act of Congress created the office of minister * * * to which ministers were sent by President Washington."—7 Op. U. S. Att. Gen., 212.

[3] Moore, "Digest of International Law," vol. IV, p. 439.

"According to my recollection, this subject was on some occasion carefully searched into; and it was found that the practice of government had, from the beginning, been regulated by the idea that the places or offices of public ministers and consuls existed under the law and usages of nations, and were always open to receive appointments as they might be made by competent authorities." [4]

Diplomatic grades.—The Constitution does not attempt to prescribe or enumerate grades of diplomatic officers, all grades being comprehended within the general designation "ambassadors and other public ministers." [5] Although the United States is not a party to the established international rules governing the relative rank of diplomatic representatives, the Department of State, in determining diplomatic grades and questions of precedence, follows the rule of Vienna, as modified by the Congress of Aix-la-Chapelle, [6] whereby four grades of such representation are recognized: ambassador, minister plenipotentiary, minister resident, and chargé d'affaires.

The Revised Statutes, in defining the official designations of diplomatic officers, state that " 'Diplomatic officer' shall be deemed to include ambassadors, envoys extraordinary, ministers plenipotentiary, ministers resident, commissioners, chargés d'affaires, agents, counselors [7] and secretaries of legation, and none others." [8]

---

[4] *Ibid.*, p. 451, quoting from 3 Madison's Works, 267, 268.

[5] "Ambassadors and other public ministers" means "all possible diplomatic agents which any foreign power may accredit to the U. S."—7 Op. U. S. Att. Gen. 209.

[6] Moore, "Digest of International Law," vol. IV, pp. 430-431 and 732-733.

[7] "The President may, whenever he considers it advisable so to do, designate and assign any Foreign Service officer as counselor of embassy or legation."—Act of May 24, 1924, Sec. 16.

[8] R.S. 1674.

Ambassadors. — Ambassadors, or ambassadors extraordinary and plenipotentiary, are accredited to sovereigns, and constitute diplomatic representatives of the first class. There are fourteen ambassadors of the United States who receive salaries of $17,500 per annum. They are accredited to the following countries: Argentina, Belgium,[9] Brazil, Chile, Cuba, France, Germany, Great Britain, Italy, Japan, Mexico, Peru, Spain, Turkey.

Ministers.—Ministers of the United States are entitled "envoy extraordinary and minister plenipotentiary." They are accredited to sovereigns, and constitute diplomatic representatives of the second class. There are thirty-five ministers of the United States, two of whom receive salaries of $12,000 per annum, being accredited to China and The Netherlands. The remaining thirty-three receive salaries of $10,000 per annum and are accredited as follows: Albania, Austria, Bolivia, Bulgaria, Czechoslovakia, Colombia, Costa Rica, Denmark, Dominican Republic, Ecuador, Egypt, Finland, Greece, Guatemala, Haiti, Honduras, Hungary, Nicaragua, Norway, Panama, Paraguay, Persia, Poland, Portugal, Rumania, Salvador, Siam, Sweden, Switzerland, Uruguay, Venezuela, the Kingdom of Serbs, Croats and Slovenes, and one minister accredited to Esthonia, Latvia, and Lithuania.

Minister resident.—A minister resident is a diplomatic representative of the intermediate class. The diplomatic representative of the United States to Liberia is a "Minister Resident and Consul General," the consular office being superadded. The salary of the Minister Resident to Liberia is $5,000 per annum. There is no other post of this title in the service.

---

[9]The Ambassador to Belgium is also Minister to Luxemburg.

Commissioners.—"The rank of 'commissaire' (commissioner) is not mentioned in the rules of Vienna and Aix-la-Chapelle. In the practice of this Government commissioners have often, from the foundation of the Government, borne commissions signed by the head of the Government and have been accredited and received as full envoys. Other commissioners, however, have been at times appointed on the certification of the Secretary of State and without diplomatic capacity. The title is vague, and only the language and purport of the incumbent's commission and credential letters can determine whether it possesses a diplomatic character; and the government to which he is accredited usually assigns his rank by the formality of acceptance." [10] A commissioner appointed to any country receives 75 per centum of the salary of the ambassador or minister to such country. A Foreign Service officer appointed to act as commissioner retains his statutory salary as Foreign Service officer. [11] There is at present a United States Commissioner to Turkey. The office of commissioner usually disappears upon the establishment of full diplomatic relations.

Chargés d'affaires.—Chargés d'affaires are diplomatic representatives of the third class. They are commissioned by the President and accredited by the Secretary of State to the minister of foreign affairs of the government to which they are sent.

A chargé d'affaires receives 50 per centum of the

---

[10] Mr. Foster, Sec. of State, to Mr. Heard, No. 151, dip. series, Oct. 81, 1892, MS. inst. Korea I, 414, quoted in Moore, vol. IV, p. 440.

[11] "That within the discretion of the President, any Foreign Service officer may be appointed to act as commissioner, chargé d'affaires, minister resident, or diplomatic agent for such period as the public interests may require without loss of grade, class or salary: Provided, however, That no such officer shall receive more than one salary."—Act of May 24, 1924, Sec, 17,

salary of a minister or minister resident to the country to which he is accredited. A Foreign Service officer appointed to act as chargé d'affaires retains his statutory salary as a Foreign Service officer, but in case such salary is less than one-half the salary of a minister, he receives enough additional compensation to make up the difference.[12] There is no chargé d'affaires of the United States as distinguished from chargé d'affaires ad interim, at present.

Chargé d'affaires ad interim.—In the absence of the head of the mission, the counselor, or secretary, acts ex-officio as chargé d'affaires ad interim and needs no special letter of credence. In the absence, however, of a counselor or secretary, the Secretary of State may designate any competent person to act ad interim, in which case he is specifically accredited by letter to the minister of foreign affairs. A chargé d'affaires ad interim is compensated in the same manner as a chargé d'affaires.

Agents.—An agent, in the practice of the United States, is a diplomatic representative accredited to the minister of foreign affairs of a dependent state. There is only one such grade now in the service, that of "Agent and Consul General" to Morocco, the consular office being superadded. He receives $7,500 per annum.

---

[12]"That section 1685 of the Revised Statutes as amended by the Act entitled 'An Act for the improvement of the Foreign Service, approved February 5, 1915,' is hereby amended to read as follows:

" 'Sec. 1685. That for such time as any Foreign Service officer shall be lawfully authorized to act as *chargé d'affaires ad interim* or to assume charge of a consulate general or consulate during the absence of the principal officer at the post to which he shall have been assigned, he shall, if his salary is less than one-half that of such principal officer, receive in addition to his salary as Foreign Service officer compensation equal to the difference between such salary and one-half of the salary provided by law for the ambassador, minister, or principal consular officer, as the case may be.' "—Act of May 24, 1924, Sec. 17.

Counselors.—A counselor of embassy or legation is next in rank to the chief of mission under whom he serves. Counselors are designated by the President from among Foreign Service officers, and receive the statutory salary of their class. There are twelve counselors of embassy who, as Foreign Service officers, class one, receive $9,000 per annum, and three counselors of legation who, as Foreign Service officers of class two, receive $8,000 per annum.

Secretaries.—"A secretary of a mission is according to admitted principles of international law, a 'public minister.' His personal privileges, immunities, domiciliary privileges, and exemptions are generally those of the diplomatic representative of whose official household he forms a part." [13] "As long as the head of the mission is present, the secretary is not recognized by any foreign government as being authorized to perform a single official act other than as directed by the head of the mission." [14]

Prior to the reorganization act which became effective on July 1, 1924, there were four classes of diplomatic secretaries receiving, respectively, $4,000, $3,625, $3,000, and $2,500. [15]

The numerical classification of the position of secretary is now abolished, and distinction in rank is established through the classification of Foreign Service officers. Diplomatic secretaries have all been recommissioned as Foreign Service officers, and their salaries adjusted to the new scale of compensation in the following manner:

Secretaries of class one designated as counselors of

---

[13]*Instructions to Diplomatic Officers of the United States*, 1897, p. 20.
[14]*Ibid.*, p. 13.
[15]Act of Feb. 5, 1915, as amended by Act of June 4, 1920, 41 Stat., 740.

embassy were recommissioned as Foreign Service officers, class one, $9,000; secretaries of class one desig-
nated as counselors of legation, as Foreign Service
officers, class two, $8,000; secretaries of class one not
designated as counselors, as Foreign Service officers,
class three, $7,000; secretaries of class two, as Foreign
Service officers, class four, $6,000; secretaries of class
three, as Foreign Service officers, class six, $4,000; and
secretaries of class four, as Foreign Service officers,
class eight, $3,500.

There were 121 secretaries in the service on the date
of the reclassification.[16]

Superadded consular office.—"When the office of
consul general is added to that of envoy extraordinary
and minister plenipotentiary, minister resident, chargé
d'affaires, or secretary of legation, the diplomatic rank
is regarded as superior to and independent of the consular rank. In the possible case of objection, by the
government of the country of residence, to a diplomatic
officer who is also a consular officer performing the functions of both offices, the vice consul, if there be one,
may be put in charge of the business of the consulate
general or consulate." [17]

Mode of appointment.—All diplomatic officers are appointed by the President, by and with the advice and
consent of the Senate, except counselors of embassy and
legation who are merely designated by the President
from among Foreign Service officers thus appointed.
The positions of ambassador and minister are considered as political in character and appointments to these
grades are generally made on that basis. On the other
hand, the classified service below the grade of minister

---

[16]For table see page 263.
[17]*Instructions to Diplomatic Officers of the United States*, 1897.

is administered in accordance with civil service principles, and is rigidly non-partisan.

All officers in the Foreign Service hold their appointments "at the pleasure of the President," which means that he may at any moment "recall" or replace them.

"A recall is usually accomplished at the pleasure of the President, during a session of the Senate, by sending to that body the nomination of the officer's successor. Upon the confirmation and commission of his successor the original incumbent's office ceases." [18]

Coincidental with a change of administration, ambassadors and ministers usually tender their resignations, and a number of changes in these positions are effected by the incoming régime. There are, however, certain of these positions which have come to be considered as non-political through having been filled by the promotion on merit of trained men from the career service where no political motive was involved. Such promotions are generally considered as differing widely from those of the purely political category, and tradition is rapidly establishing them as permanent. [19]

The advent of the merit system.—Formerly, under the spoils system, diplomatic secretaries were appointed for political reasons, as ambassadors and ministers are to-day. But in 1909, three years following the stabilization of the Consular Service, President Taft, by Executive order, placed the Diplomatic Service below the grade of minister on a civil service basis, requiring a competitive

---

[18]*Instructions to Diplomatic Officers of the United States,* quoted in Moore, Digest of International Law, vol. IV, p. 470.

[19]The relative merits of the two modes of appointment are discussed at length in the chapter entitled: "Defects in the Old Foreign Service Organization."

examination for determining the qualifications of candidates.[20]

The regulations thus established remained in force until July 1, 1924, the date of the general reorganization, when they were superseded by new regulations combining the requirements for the Diplomatic Service with those for the Consular Service as applied to the new position of Foreign Service officer.[21]

Diplomatic duties.—It is difficult to give an adequate description of the duties of diplomatic representatives, as these duties vary with the nature of the problems and the circumstances which call their initiative into play. Broadly speaking, however, the Diplomatic Service is charged with promoting, safeguarding and defending the interests and the good name of the United States in foreign countries. Each of these three categories of activity imposes definite responsibilities requiring the exercise of constant vigilance and calling for the highest qualities of individual ability.

In the matter of promoting the national interests, there is, first of all, the duty of cultivating friendly relations, which is far from being an indefinite or nebulous function as the popular mind is sometimes prone to conceive it. The relations of one nation with another are governed by substantial factors of common interest; not by platitudes or the staging of subtle effects.

Finding and developing this basis of common interest, then, is the first task of the diplomatist, for it underlies all his other activities, and in no small degree sets the limit of his possible achievements. The treaty structure is of immediate importance in this connection, especially commercial treaties, or those having a bearing upon

---

[20]See page 25 and Appendix C.
[21]Executive order of June 7, 1924. See Appendix F.

economic matters. Where a basis of mutually profitable intercourse does not exist, it is the function of diplomacy to create one; where it does exist, then the corresponding duty of fostering and protecting it arises. The negotiation of commercial treaties is an essential instrument in laying the foundation of broader relations.

Under the second category of duties, namely, that of safeguarding the national interests, diplomatic officers are watchful of economic and political developments which may either directly or indirectly affect the interests of the United States; they urge the favorable interpretation of treaties, keep the channels of trade clear of discriminations, and assure the security of American property interests and the rights of travel and peaceful intercourse.

In defending the national interest and good name, they are on guard against propaganda and political agitations of a foreign nationalistic or anti-American character; they protest treaty violations and insist upon justice for Americans in the courts; they urge the full measure of international privilege in all domains of activity; they apprehend international alliances and the menace of militaristic or other movements tending to impair the security of the United States.

Finally, the Diplomatic Service is an instrumentality for giving effect abroad to American foreign policy. As Mr. George Young has aptly expressed it: "You can best succeed nowadays as a democratic diplomatist; that is, by making most of the other side want what you want, and by making the best of what they want." [22]

The nature of diplomatic functions.—Lord Bryce has described the scope and character of diplomatic functions as follows:

---

[22] Young, "Diplomacy Old and New," p. 87.

"The duties of a diplomatic envoy in quiet times consist chiefly in the adjustment of comparatively petty questions relating to business matters, and especially to favors asked or grievances complained of by the citizens of the country he represents, with the transmission of similar requests or complaints made by the government to which he is accredited on behalf of its own citizens. Such time as remains over from current business of this kind is usefully devoted to following the politics of the country in which he resides and reporting to his own government on passing events and the movements of public opinion. In this respect the functions of envoys have undergone great changes in recent times. It is not with sovereigns and courts that envoys are to-day chiefly concerned; more important is it that they should observe and study the wider circles of politicians who sit in legislatures and of journalists who address and profess to represent public sentiment. The British traveller, who fifty years ago in vacation journeys through Europe used to pay his respects to the ambassadors and ministers of those days, was often surprised at the slender knowledge they seemed to possess of political parties and of popular feeling in the countries where they resided. Nowadays these are the things an envoy most needs to regard. He ought to have his eyes everywhere and on everything. The accounts he transmits to his government at home may be of great service to them in explaining the situation they have to deal with, in pointing out to what extent words may be discounted which have been said publicly for the purpose of producing political effect, and also in the way of explaining unavowed motives, of indicating hidden dangers. The things which his Foreign Office at home cannot be expected to understand, and particularly the ebbs and flows of popular sentiment, are the things he must carefully report and explain. So far as his own direct action is concerned, his aim will be not merely to straighten out difficulties, but to prevent differences from passing into disputes. It is always better to keep controversies from arising than to be driven to argue and settle them, probably by compromise, after they have begun to be troublesome." [23]

Another representative view.—Honorable John W. Davis in his testimony before the Committee on Foreign Affairs in 1922, brought out the following important points:

"The function of the diplomatic officer nowadays is to let his Government know who the man is at the other end of the wire and what sort of influences are working on him that will make him amenable to this suggestion or make him disposed to refuse that. A diplomatic officer of to-day who is receiving by wire correspondence for transmittal to the Government to which he is accredited, even where it comes as it frequently does in the shape of a formal note, prepared in the State Department, must feel it his duty to examine that note in the light of his acquaintanceship with the men on the ground. If he finds anything in it which his knowledge convinces him is inexpedient, it is his duty to advise his Government that in that respect the note ought to be corrected to meet the particular situation. We can no more get along without that sort of personal contact than a business man can sell his goods by mail without drummers, who know his individual customers, their tastes, and how far they can be accommodated." [24]

By way of contrast.—Sir Park Goff, in a debate in

---

[23]Bryce, "International Relations," pp. 152-153.
[24]Hearings on H.R. 17 and H.R. 6357, 68th Congress, 1st Session, p. 207.

the House of Commons May 21, 1919, painted a striking contrast to the foregoing sketch of modern diplomatic functions by stating: "It was different in the Middle Ages, when an ambassador was sent abroad to persuade some Royalty for reasons of State to marry a lady with a hump or with the face of an angel and a Satanic temper, or when Earls of Holland and Carlisle went to Paris to arrange the marriage of Charles and Henrietta and to conclude that treaty." [25]

Operation of the Diplomatic Service.—As has been shown, the Diplomatic Service operates under the Department of State through the immediate direction of the Secretary of State, acting upon the instructions of the President.[26]

The jurisdiction of an ambassador, minister, or other chief of a diplomatic mission abroad extends to the entire country to which he is accredited. The embassy or legation is established in the capital immediately accessible to the government and the sources of political information. It exercises supervisory powers over all other representatives of the United States, including the Consular Service, within the territorial limits of the country.

The chief of mission is in supreme authority, no other member of his official household being considered as having any powers that do not emanate from him. Counselors of embassy or legation and diplomatic secretaries, together with the other employees of the diplomatic establishment, are subordinate to the chief of mission and act upon his instructions.

Duties of the counselor.—The counselor is the principal assistant and technical adviser in matters of inter-

[25]*Parliamentary Debates*, Official Report, vol. 116, p. 296.
[26]See page 75.

national law and diplomatic practice. He exercises general administrative supervision over the work of the chancery, including that of the diplomatic secretaries and clerks. He familiarizes himself with the history, language, and culture of the country and with its political, economic and social conditions; prepares important correspondence for transmission to the Foreign Office and to the Department of State; and signs all such as does not require the signature of the chief of mission. He receives visitors, confers with foreign governmental officials, establishes personal relations and business contacts with important personages as a source of information, and handles, largely on his own responsibility, many questions of current importance. He also prepares reports on political, economic, and other subjects for the Department of State and makes analyses and briefs for the aid of the chief of mission. The counselor acts as chargé d'affaires ad interim in the absence of the chief of mission.

Duties of diplomatic secretaries.—The duties of secretaries are similar in type to those of a counselor, though differing widely in scope and in the degree of their importance. They gather material, make reports, analyze cases, receive visitors and establish contacts in much the same fashion, being guided in their activities by the advice and immediate supervision of the counselor.

Consular collaboration.—Scattered throughout the country the local consular establishments are likewise engaged in watching developments and reporting to the mission all important matters which by their nature may become the subject of diplomatic action.[27]

_____

[27]"One of the most important agencies for the protection of citizens abroad is the consular service. While the consul has no diplomatic or

Instructions to diplomatic officers.—Congress rarely undertakes, and then only in general terms, to give instructions to diplomatic officers through measures of legislation. When enacted, such measures usually partake of the nature of prohibitions against certain forms of activity, as that diplomatic officers shall not engage in business or practice as lawyers in the countries to which they are accredited, or correspond independently with any private person, newspaper or other periodical regarding the public affairs of any foreign government.[28]

The act of August 18, 1856, authorized the President "to prescribe such rules and regulations, and make and issue such orders and instructions, not inconsistent with the Constitution or any law of the United States, in relation to the duties of all diplomatic and consular officers. * * * It shall be the duty of all such officers to

---

representative character, and his political functions are limited, the considerable number of consuls and their location in the more important commercial centers results in a closer relation between a consul and his fellow citizens abroad than is possible for a diplomatic officer. Treaties and custom, therefore, confide to the consul a wide range of protective functions, short of the presentation of diplomatic claims or the making of representations to the central government."—Borchard, "Diplomatic Protection of Citizens Abroad," pp. 435-436.

[28]"That no ambassador, minister, minister resident, diplomatic agent, or secretary in the Diplomatic Service of any grade or class shall, while he holds his office, be interested in or transact any business as a merchant, factor, broker, or other trader, or as an agent for any such person to, from, or within the country or countries to which he or the chief of his mission, as the case may be, is accredited, either in his own name or in the name or through the agency of any other person, nor shall he, in such country or countries, practice as a lawyer for compensation or be interested in the fees or compensation of any lawyer so practicing."—Act of Feb. 5, 1915, Sec. 7, 88 Stat., 807.

"No diplomatic or consular officer shall correspond in regard to the public affairs of any foreign government with any private person, newspaper, or other periodical, or otherwise than with the proper officers of the United States, nor recommend any person, at home or abroad, for any employment of trust or profit under the government of the country in which he is located; nor ask or accept, for himself or any other person, any present, emolument, pecuniary favor, office, or title of any kind, from any such government."—R.S. 1751.

conform to such regulations, orders and instructions." [29]

By virtue of this authorization, a set of diplomatic regulations was issued in 1897 under the title "Instructions to Diplomatic Officers of the United States." These are regulatory in character and do not go beyond the establishment of general principles which are subject to modification from time to time by Executive order.

Other important directions given to diplomatic officers in relation to the transaction of current affairs are either general in character, as applying to the entire service, or special, as applying to a particular mission. These are issued by the Secretary of State. Congress has frequently requested the President to transmit for its consideration, copies of instructions to diplomatic officers relating to particular negotiations or to the duties of a particular mission. In some instances the President has complied in full; in others, certain matter of a confidential character has been deleted; while not infrequently the President has declined to make known his instructions. An instructive instance of this character arose during the administration of President Polk in relation to the negotiation of a treaty with Mexico. In explaining his position, the President stated:

"I avail myself of this occasion to observe that, as a general rule applicable to all our important negotiations with foreign powers, it could not fail to be prejudicial to the public interest to publish the instructions to our ministers until some time had elapsed after the conclusion of such negotiations." [30]

The value of a trained service.—It is extraordinary that there should remain to-day a question in any one's

---

[29]11 Stat., 65; R.S. 1752.

[30]Richardson, "Messages and Papers of the Presidents," IV, 602; Hinds, *Precedents* II, 988.

mind as to the value of expert training in the practice of diplomacy.[31] No phase of governmental activity, or indeed, of human relations, is more vast or intricate than that which deals with the relations of peoples whose geographical remoteness is as a mere incident compared with their fundamental differences of race, language, religion, laws, customs, and ideals.

One of the chief aims of the career service is to develop trained diplomatists to fill the positions of ambassador and minister, but its usefulness is by no means limited to this hopeful prospect. In fact, a trained corps of diplomatic secretaries is all the more necessary where the chief of mission is not himself a man of extensive diplomatic experience. Honorable John W. Davis brought out this point very clearly in his testimony before the Committee on Foreign Affairs when the reorganization bill was under consideration. He stated:

"I do not think the importance of such a service can be exaggerated. You may send abroad, if you choose, as ambassadors and ministers, men who have the gifts of angels. They land in the foreign country, most of them, a country with which they have not been previously largely acquainted. There are a great many routine methods of doing things with other governments which these have built up around themselves. They must depend upon their secretaries, who should be men of experience, who know what the methods of operation are. They must depend largely upon their secretaries

---

[31]"We require four years' study in a special school before we allow a doctor to diagnose a disease, for fear one man may decline or die unnecessarily. But apparently we consider anyone should be able to practise unprepared on the diseases and developments of peoples; though failure may mean not the death of one man but of millions."—George Young, "Diplomacy Old and New," p. 97.

also to bring them the current information upon which they depend. You have got to have a staff of secretaries persona grata at the foreign offices with individual contacts there not only for the information they bring you but to check up the information you get yourself. You can not always believe the first story you hear, and these men are really your eyes and ears. They can not be too good." [32]

In somewhat similar terms, Secretary of State Hughes emphasized the importance of the work performed by the career service, as follows:

"The United States Government is entitled to the very best representation it can have. But if we could have in our posts as diplomatic representatives, ambassadors, and ministers, the ablest men the country provided, still they would go to their posts under the absolute necessity of depending upon a trained staff. You can not get along without a staff in any line of important work. It is not that the members of the staff can supply the exact experience, the judgment, or wide vision, or personal acquaintance that the head of the mission may have, but it is that the head of the mission, if he is to do his work, must have men at his call who are fully equipped with information, able to take his instructions and transmute them into actual contacts with others in foreign offices, able to give his energy, his force, his point of view, a trained and expert presentation." [33]

The utilization of the trained service.—It is appropriate at this juncture to point out a discouraging and shortsighted administrative practice which in the past

[32]Hearings on H.R. 17 and H.R. 6357, before the Committee on Foreign Affairs, 68th Cong., 1st Sess., pp. 209-210.
[33]Ibid., p. 13.

has operated to the detriment of the service. Within the range of international relations there arise many important occasions calling for the services of trained men in connection with particular negotiations or special missions. Too often the regular Foreign Service establishment has been overlooked on these occasions, with the result that the national interest has suffered a threefold loss: first, through failure to utilize the professional capabilities of its own officers; secondly, through the neglect of valuable opportunities to train and develop these men for the assumption of broad responsibilities; and finally, through the discouragement which such a practice brings to the serious efforts of all within the service.[34]

Within recent years, and especially under the administration of Secretary Hughes, a great improvement has been shown in the utilization of the officers of the regular establishment, justifying the hope that the new Foreign Service is destined to share more liberally in the affairs of its immediate concern.

The social factor.—Among the influences exerted by the war to change the nature of diplomatic functions, two are to be especially noted as affecting both the type and the qualifications of foreign representatives: the declining importance of the social factor, and the increasing importance of the economic factor.

Formerly the work of the Diplomatic Service was considered to be purely political. Its contact was lim-

[34]"One of the worst abuses in the conduct of our foreign affairs is our habit of appointing 'lame ducks,' second-rate politicians and other incompetents, to important positions of international commissions or as delegates to international conferences. The other civilized nations as a rule appoint their governmental expert and diplomatic and consular representatives to these positions, with the consequence that their representatives grow in wisdom and acquire a larger confidence and recognition from their fellow citizens."—"Report on the Foreign Service," by the National Civil Service Reform League (1919), p. 65.

ited to a small circle of society centering around a court of official personages whose dealings with foreign relations were largely secret, personal, and autocratic. A diplomatic mission, operating within this restricted realm, drew its chief substance from its social relations.[35]

But "the triumph of democracy marks the definite shifting of these sources of power from the aristrocratic individuals of a ruling family and class, to the mass organizations, and their leaders, which, taken together, form the country's sovereign public opinion. Most diplomats are aware, in the abstract, of this fundamental transference of power, but too many have been tardy in deducing all the consequences, especially as affecting their own ways and methods." [36]

It is not alone in the shifting of sources and the transference of power that vital changes have occurred, but in the very substance and nature of diplomatic data, and in the broadened range of observation which the new order imposes.

The economic factor.—International problems have changed character. The interdependence of nations has forced the economic factor to the fore, and questions which but yesterday were dealt with as of purely political concern are now recognized as having their genesis in economic laws and their repercussions in the remotest ranks of society. Conversely, many of our most intimate domestic issues have taken on an international, or a' diplomatic character. Our rates of taxation, the status

---

[35]"There may have been some justification for this idea in former times, when diplomatic intrigue was confined to courts and high society, and when all countries were governed by aristocrats or autocrats. But to-day, when high society is to a large extent divorced from Government in most countries, the qualification becomes an anachronism. Moreover, neither birth nor wealth is a necessary accessory of good manners, still less of ability."— Ponsonby, "Democracy and Diplomacy," pp. 63-64.

[36]Paul Scott Mowrer, "Our Foreign Affairs," p. 215.

of our loans, the distress of agriculture, the industrial outlook, all are now seen to share in the phenomenon of international interdependence and to have become the immediate concern of those who deal with foreign relations.

As applied to the Foreign Service, Mr. Robert Lansing, former Secretary of State, recently discussed the influence of these changes as follows:

"Formerly diplomacy was confined almost exclusively to political and legal subjects and the training of the members of the Diplomatic Service was devoted to that branch of international intercourse. To-day our embassies and legations are dealing more and more with commercial, financial and industrial questions, of which the average diplomatic secretary has little knowledge and for which he has even less aptitude. We must presume that our future relations with other nations will be chiefly economic, and the men serving this country in a diplomatic capacity should be trained in these subjects as our consular officers are at the present time. Formerly the line between business and politics in foreign affairs was clear and distinct, but now that line has very largely disappeared. The Rogers Bill recognized this and obliterated the old distinction between the Diplomatic and Consular Services." [37]

As here implied, one of the basic considerations involved in the Foreign Service reorganization plan was the coordination of the political and the economic factors of diplomacy through the amalgamation of the Diplomatic and the Consular Services on an interchangeable basis. Other nations, mindful of the same impelling conditions, have made haste to reorganize their foreign

[37]An article entitled "The Proposed Consolidation of the Diplomatic and Consular Services of the United States," published in the *American Journal of International Law* for April, 1923.

establishments along similar lines. In the British service the lack of equipment to handle the current problems of diplomacy has been thus pointed out by Mr. George Young:

"When, as of late, some commercial work, such as concession hunting and commercial negotiation, has been required from diplomats, it has generally had to be entrusted to experts from Big Business, or the Board of Trade, with much prejudice to our interests." [38]

Again, it was observed by Sir Park Goff in the House of Commons:

"One reason why diplomats are at a great and serious disadvantage is that they live and move in such a narrow circle, and are therefore ignorant of current events, whereas a Consul can know everything without loss of dignity and can gain an enormous amount of valuable information." [39]

Even as this page is being written there appears in the morning paper an important article from Geneva under the heading: "Warning by Briand, Economic Reasons May Bring On War," in which the former French premier, speaking before the League of Nations Assembly, emphasized the important rôle which economic considerations are destined to play in future international relations. He is quoted as stating:

"Men may say that economic wars are possible because the interests of nations may be swayed by the same considerations as the interests of selfish individuals, and that under influence of selfish interests the ideal and duty may be obscured or mutilated. To-morrow, therefore, having now settled political questions, the League of Nations must settle completely the diffi-

---

[38] "Diplomacy Old and New," p. 35.
[39] "Parliamentary Debates, Official Report," vol. 116, p. 295.

cult economic problems. But France will be ever ready to help in their solution." [40]

The interests of the United States in international affairs are transcendently economic. If we are likewise to help in the solution of these problems, or even protect our interests therein, the machinery of our foreign relations must be adequately and appropriately adjusted to the task.

It is obvious that the diplomatist of the future must add to his former qualifications a type of training not heretofore considered essential in his educational curriculum. Diplomacy has struck a basis of substance, calling for the analytical rather than the synthetic faculty and stressing ability, as in an applied science, rather than talent, as in a subtle art.[41]

The hope of developing a new type of foreign representative to meet these important demands lies in combining in a single officer the complementary advantages of the diplomatic and of the consular experience and in broadening the training afforded by these to the limits of dependable vision.

Bibliography.

Borchard, Edwin M.: "The Diplomatic Protection of Citizens Abroad"; Banks Law Pub. Co., New York, 1915.

Bernard, Mountague: "Lectures on Diplomacy"; Macmillan, New York, 1922.

---

[40] *The Washington Post,* October 2, 1924.

[41] "During recent years our Consular Service has been greatly improved and reflects credit upon our Nation, but there is room for further improvement. I advocate, in the selection of Consuls, that due consideration be given to their qualifications for future service in the Diplomatic Corps, so ambassadors be chosen from men who have attained distinction in the Consular Service. We need business men and men of affairs rather than parlor-knights in our diplomatic service."—Honorable John Hays Hammond, "The Issues of 1916," published in *The Forum* for July, 1916.

Bryce, James (Viscount): "International Relations"; Macmillan, New York, 1922.

Foster, John Watson: "The Practice of Diplomacy as Illustrated in the Foreign Relations of the U. S."; Houghton, Mifflin & Co., Boston, 1906.

Hart, Albert Bushnell: "The Foundations of American Foreign Policy"; New York, 1901.

Heatley, David Playfair: "Diplomacy and the Study of International Relations"; Oxford, Clarendon Press, 1919.

Hyde, Charles Cheney: "International Law"; Little, Brown & Co., Boston, 1922.

Johnston, Sir Harry: "Common Sense in Foreign Policy"; London, 1913.

Munz, Sigmund: "Our Diplomats"; *Contemporary Review,* March, 1922.

Moore, John Bassett: "Principles of American Diplomacy"; New York, 1918.

Moore, John Bassett: "Digest of International Law" (vol. IV); Government Printing Office, Washington, 1906.

Poole, DeWitt C.: "The Conduct of Foreign Relations Under Modern Democratic Conditions"; Yale University Press, New Haven, Conn., 1924.

Satow, Sir Ernest Mason: "A Guide to Diplomatic Practice"; Longmans Green & Co., New York, 1917.

Thayer, William Roscoe: "The Life of John Hay"; Houghton, Mifflin Co., Boston, 1915.

Woolsey, Theodore Salisbury: "America's Foreign Policy: Essays and Addresses"; New York, 1898, Century Co.

CHAPTER V

THE CONSULAR SERVICE

A branch of the Foreign Service.—The Consular Service forms, with the Diplomatic Service, what is known under the statutes as the "Foreign Service of the United States." The two are coordinate branches of a single Foreign Service, operating under the immediate direction of the Secretary of State. Together they afford those faculties of perception, of observation and of speech which give to the Department of State, and through it, to the President, the power of intelligent decision and of action in matters involving American interests at places remote from our own frontiers.

Historical sketch.—The origin of consular functions antedates the development of diplomatic intercourse.

"Early in the history of commerce it became necessary for commercial states to establish a jurisdiction over seamen, vessels, and merchandise. And as the operations of commerce in foreign ports might involve national interests, as well as the individual interests of merchants and seamen, it became equally necessary that this jurisdiction should be exercised by a national agent. Hence we find among the commercial states of antiquity commercial magistrates with functions similar to those vested in the consuls of modern times, though much more extensive. * * *

"During the Middle Ages consuls were quasi-public ministers, who watched over the interests of their countrymen, deciding their disputes, protecting their commerce, and exercising large judicial and commercial powers, independent of the local law." [1]

When public ministers, in name and in fact, came to be established, the consular office lost its representative character, and with it much of its former dignity and importance. The growth of world commerce and the intensification of international relations in our own time have had the effect of broadening again the scope of consular functions by placing upon these representatives numerous duties of an entirely modern character.

Nature of the consular office.—Modern consular officers are commercial, or business, representatives of their country, stationed at foreign capitals and at important ports and trade centers, or at other points where the national interests require the support or the protection of the government.

Consular offices, as has been seen, exist "under the law and usages of nations"; therefore, under international law, and under the Constitution.[2] They are not created by act of Congress, nor by the President.

Recognizing the international character of consular functions, the first law enacted in the United States, establishing the powers and duties of consuls, expressly provided:

"That the specification of certain powers and duties, in this act, to be exercised or performed by the consuls and vice consuls of the United States, shall not be construed to the exclusion of others, resulting from the nature of their appointments, or any treaty or convention under which they may act." [3]

Consuls are not public ministers.—The Constitution, in expressly enumerating "consuls," apart from "ambassa-

---

[1] U. S. Consular Regulations (1896), pp. 1-2.
[2] See page 100.
[3] Act of April 14, 1792, Sec. 9, 1 Stat., 257.

dors and other public ministers," recognizes that consular officers are not public ministers, which fact is amply supported by international law and the practice of nations.[4]

"A consular officer in civilized countries now has, under public law, no acknowledged representative or diplomatic character as regards the country to which he is accredited. He has, however, a certain representative character as affecting the commercial interests of the country from which he receives his appointment; and there may be circumstances, as, for example, in the absence of a diplomatic representative, which, apart from usage, make it proper for him to address the local government upon subjects which relate to the duties and rights of his office, and which are usually dealt with through a legation." [5]

"Although consuls have no right to claim the privileges and immunities of diplomatic representatives, they are under the special protection of international law, and are regarded as the officers both of the state which appoints and the state which receives them." [6]

"Consuls are to be considered as distinguished foreigners, dignified by a commission from their sovereign, and specially recommended by him to the respect of the nation with whom they reside. They are subject to the laws of the land indeed precisely as other foreigners are * * * but if, at any time, their conduct should render it necessary to assert the authority of the laws over

---

[4]"Consuls are not public ministers. Whatever protection they may be entitled to in the discharge of their official duties, and whatever special privileges may be conferred upon them by the local laws and usages, or by international compact, they are not entitled, by the general law of nations, to the peculiar immunities of ambassadors."—Wheaton's International Law, Dana's ed. p. 324, Moore, vol. V, p. 32.

[5]U. S. Consular Regulations (1896), p. 27.

[6]*Ibid.*

them, the rigor of those laws should be tempered by our respect for their sovereign, as far as the case will admit." [7]

By way of establishing a definite delimitation between the functions of consular officers and those of diplomatic officers, the law provides that "no consular officer shall exercise diplomatic functions, or hold any diplomatic correspondence or relation on the part of the United States, in, with, or to the government or country to which he is appointed, or any other country or government, when there is in such country any officer of the United States authorized to perform diplomatic functions therein; nor in any case, unless expressly authorized by the President so to do." [8]

Under the Constitution the Supreme Court has original jurisdiction in all cases affecting consuls in the United States.

Consular grades.—The term "consul," as used in the Constitution, denotes any principal consular officer or any person invested by the United States with the functions of a consul general or consul. As ordinarily used, in a specific sense, it denotes a particular grade of consular officer, but is sometimes used, in a generic sense, to embrace all consular officers. [9]

The term "consular officer" includes consuls general, consuls, vice consuls, interpreters in consular offices, student interpreters and consular agents. [10]

Consuls general and consuls are full, principal, and permanent consular officers as distinguished from subordinates and substitutes. [11]

---

[7] Jefferson, Sec. for Foreign Affairs, to Mr. Newton, Sept. 8, 1791, 4 MS. Am. Let. 283, cited in Moore, vol. V, pp. 33-34.

[8] R. S. 1738.

[9] 15 C. Cls. R. 74.

[10] Act of Feb. 5, 1915, Sec. 6. 38 Stat., 806.

[11] *Ibid.*

A vice consul is a subordinate officer but also has the character of a substitute officer in that he assumes charge of a consular post when the principal officer is absent.

Consuls general.—The grade of consul general is superior in importance to that of consul and differs from it principally by the addition of supervisory powers over the work of other consular officers within a given jurisdiction. The grade of consul general is susceptible of division into three categories according to the nature of the duties performed by these officers:

1. Those who exercise supervisory authority over a given territory, as for example, the Consul General at London, who supervises the work of all consular officers throughout the British Isles. The same applies to Paris, Berlin, and other prominent capitals, or commercial centers.

2. Those who perform semi-diplomatic functions, as for example, the Consul General at Ottawa, Canada; Calcutta, India; Melbourne, Australia; Cape Town, South Africa; and so forth, being important capitals of self-governing dominions in which there is no diplomatic mission of the United States.

3. Those who occupy important posts within the supervisory jurisdiction of a more important office, as for example, Liverpool, England, which is a consulate general because of its commercial importance, requiring an officer of high rank. It exercises no supervision over other offices, but on the contrary, is under the supervisory jurisdiction of London. The same applies to Munich, Bavaria, which is under the supervision of Berlin, and Rome, Italy, which is under the supervision of Genoa.

Consuls.—For the purposes of analysis, consuls may

in like manner be divided into two categories with respect to their particular functions, as follows:

1. Those who are in independent charge of a consulate as the principal officer.

2. Those who are assigned to other duty for the performance of special work, which may be in a subordinate capacity.

Whereas a consulate general has supervision over an entire country, reporting on developments from the national viewpoint, a consulate is restricted to a limited district, as for instance, several provinces.

The consul frequently has under him, not only the immediate staff of his consulate, but consular agents who act for him at distant points within his district where American interests are concerned.

Vice consuls.—Vice consuls may also be divided into two categories: career vice consuls, and non-career vice consuls. A career vice consul is a subordinate Foreign Service officer who has entered the service after examination and appointment by the President. He is subject to regular advancement to the highest grade of the service on the basis of demonstrated efficiency alone.

Non-career vice consuls, on the other hand, are clerks who have been employed for regular or routine office work. Such employees are frequently commissioned as vice consuls by the Secretary of State in order to enable them to administer oaths and sign documents of an official but unimportant character.

Interpreters. — Interpreters are American citizens who have advanced from the grade of student interpreter in the oriental languages. They are Foreign Service officers of the consular branch.

Student interpreters.—For a number of years it has been the practice to appoint student interpreters to the legation in China, the embassy in Japan, and the embassy in Turkey for the purpose of studying and perfecting themselves in the oriental languages. They are eligible to promotion to the grade of interpreter and also to the higher grades of the Foreign Service in the same manner as other Foreign Service officers. Student interpreters fall within the category of "Foreign Service officers, unclassified."

Consular agents.—A consular agent is usually a prominent American, or even a foreign business man located at a point within a consular district remote from the city in which the consulate is situated. His compensation is a moiety of the fees collected by him but not in excess of $1,000 per annum. He is bonded to the consul and acts for him.

Consular establishments.—The following tabulation shows the number of consular establishments and the total personnel as of September 30, 1924:

Offices:

Consulates General	50
Consulates	250
Vice Consulates	19
Consular Agencies	87
Combined Offices	2
Total number of offices	408

Personnel:

Career Officers	510
Consular Agents	41
Honorary Vice Consuls	33
Clerks and Other Employees	2,338
Total Personnel	2,922

Mode of appointment.—Consuls general and consuls are appointed by the President, by and with the advice and consent of the Senate. Congress, under its power to vest the appointment of inferior officers in the President alone, in the courts of law, or in the heads of departments, has vested in the President the power to provide for the appointment of vice consuls and consular agents under such rules and regulations as may be prescribed by him.[12] Accordingly, the consular regulations provide for the appointment of these officers by the Secretary of State, which has long been the common practice.[13]

Under the reorganization act, which is described in Chapter IX, it will be seen that consular officers have been recommissioned as "Foreign Service officers." Appointments hereafter will be made after examination and a period of probation in an unclassified grade to the position of Foreign Service officer, the consular commission being granted later in appropriate instances.

Duties of consuls general.—The exercise of supervisory authority by a consulate general gives to it the character of a clearing house for consular matters generally throughout its territory. All instructions from the State Department to consular officers and all replies thereto, as well as all reports of whatever nature, pass through the consulate general where they are examined.

The supervising consul general preserves consular precedents, enforces uniformity of practice under the regulations, interprets general instructions, counsels and advises consular officers in difficult matters, and reports upon their efficiency and personal qualifications as demonstrated in practice.

The duties of a consul general may be summarized as follows:

Under the direction of the Secretary of State, to maintain and promote all the rightful interests of American citizens, to protect them in all privileges acquired

---

[12]R. S. 1695.
[13]U. S. Consular Regulations (1896), par. 39.

by treaty or conceded by usage, and to facilitate trade relations between the United States and the country in which he is stationed.

To assume charge of an important consulate general, and give unity of direction to all consular establishments within the territory over which he exercises supervision.

To maintain personal contact with local officials, business men, and others of the country in which he is stationed, with a view to gathering information and reporting important commercial and political developments.

In certain non-Christian countries (China, Turkey, Siam, and Morocco), to exercise judicial functions through consular courts established under treaty for the trial of cases in which American citizens are involved.

To receive the papers of American vessels arriving at foreign ports and deliver them to the master after the obligations of the vessel towards the crew have been discharged. To issue bills of health to vessels clearing for the United States. To ship, discharge, and relieve American seamen; to settle disputes between the masters and the crews of American vessels; to investigate mutiny and other crimes on the high seas, and to return criminals to the United States for trial; to render assistance to American vessels in distress, and in the absence of the master, or other qualified officer, to take charge of wrecks and cargoes.

To certify invoices of all merchandise over $100 in value shipped to the United States from foreign countries, and to keep copies of each such invoice for the detection of customs frauds and the compilation of trade statistics; to enforce the customs regulations with respect to prohibited merchandise, and that which requires disinfection, or special documentation.

To execute notarial documents, take depositions, and perform all other acts which any notary public in the United States is authorized or required to perform. This includes all business or legal documents executed under the laws of all the States, territories, and insular possessions of the United States, including income tax returns, pension papers, copyrights, trade-marks, and the like, for the Federal Government.

To grant visas to alien immigrants, and restrict the numbers embarking for the United States under the quota law; to issue certificates to admissible Chinese.

To take charge of the estates of American citizens dying abroad without legal representatives, and to preserve such estates for delivery to the rightful heirs. To notify relatives of such deaths, and in many cases to arrange for burial, or shipment of the remains to the United States.

To make weekly reports to the Treasury Department on the health conditions prevailing within the consular jurisdiction, for the enforcement of quarantine, and the guidance of United States officials in matters of sanitary precautions. All bills of health and supplemental bills of health issued to vessels clearing for the United States contain such a statement of the health conditions prevailing at the port of departure.

To keep a register of all American citizens resident within the jurisdiction; to act as official witness to the marriage of American citizens, and to register the birth of children born of American parents.

To report disasters occurring within the foreign jurisdiction and extend all possible aid to American interests involved.

To assist in the enforcement of plant quarantine and regulations against the introduction of animal diseases.

To cooperate with the Department of Agriculture in the introduction of exotic plants into the United States, and report upon methods of combating insect pests and blights.

To cooperate with the Department of Labor in reporting upon matters relating to immigration and labor conditions abroad.

To cooperate with the Department of the Interior by reporting on mining, education, forestry, reclamation, and conservation.

To report on commercial matters; to reply to specific trade inquiries from American and foreign business men with a view to the extension of American trade; to make reports in accordance with questionnaires prepared in the Department of Commerce; to report valuable trade opportunities for the Department of Commerce; to gather information relating to the standing of foreign business firms for the World Trade Directory on which the Department of Commerce advises American exporters.

To cooperate with the Diplomatic Mission of the United States with relation to political or important economic developments.[14]

All consular officers do not perform all the duties ascribed to a consul general. At seaports, shipping matters are often predominant, while at inland posts these do not occur. At some posts the political factors are higher than the commercial, as for instance, during a foreign war or revolution. At other posts the immigration question is most acute, as for example, Naples, Italy, or Warsaw, Poland.

---

[14]The foregoing summary is necessarily incomplete, as the consular service assists every department and independent establishment of the United States Government, as well as all American interests having foreign relations. (See Chapter VII.)

Duties of consuls.— The duties of consuls are in every way similar to those of consuls general, exclusive of supervisory functions and those described as semi-diplomatic.

The scope of consular duties is so extensive that specialization is necessary. There are five consuls assigned to the consulate general at Paris and four consuls assigned to London, who are subordinate to the consul general and perform a specialized work. Commercial matters are handled largely in this way, as are also visa and immigration matters, shipping matters, and others of definite character. The Consular Service is capable of assigning to such specialized work a sufficient number of trained officers to meet all the demands that have from time to time been made upon it.

For example, the Federal Reserve Board required extensive detailed information regarding the fluctuation in the prices of commodities for the purpose of establishing its index numbers showing the cost of living abroad. With no additional overhead charge, American consular officers were able to absorb this work and to cable the required periodical reports to the United States.

Duties of vice consuls.—Vice consuls assume charge of the consulate in the absence of the consul. They are subordinate to the consul and act under his instructions. They conduct the routine work of the office, directing the other employees. They study conditions and make voluntary reports on trade and other matters.

Duties of interpreters and student interpreters.—Interpreters and student interpreters are consular officers and their duties partake of the nature of those of a consul or vice consul, their special qualifications in the difficult languages of the countries where they are stationed being merely an additional, though highly valuable, attribute.

Organization of a consulate general.—By way of bringing the various duties of consular offices to their concrete application, the following description of the organization of the consulate general of the United States at London is quoted from the testimony of Consul General Robert P. Skinner:

"I hold in my hand a register of our office, which I shall not read, but it may interest you if I select points from it to show the working organizations of an American consulate in one of the large commercial cities of the world.

"To start with, there is my own particular office. You can easily understand what that work is—general supervision, including supervisory jurisdiction over the other consulates in the United Kingdom."

The commercial department.—"Now, we come to a very interesting department, the commercial department. We have here 10 different employees. We have one employee who sits at the telephone from 9 o'clock in the morning until 5 in the evening answering inquiries about the rates of duty on particular commodities, customs administration laws, all sorts of commercial questions of that kind. In this department we carry on commercial correspondence and receive visitors. In the course of a year thousands of commercial travelers drop in who want addresses and specific and general information of every nature.

"During the year ended June 30, 1922, in this particular department there were 3,328 written replies to trade inquiries sent out. Our office made 396 trade reports of rather a comprehensive character, and we sent to the Federal Reserve Board reports by cable every month showing the fluctuations in prices of all the staple commodities. That is a very large work. We receive in our office every first-class trade journal in the United States dealing with important commodities, and we are in communication with the various trade exchanges which deal in the same commodities, and in these various ways we get the prices from day to day. These prices are at the command of our manufacturers."

The shipping department.—"The shipping department is one of the most interesting branches of our work at the present time, in view of the great interest taken in the mercantile marine. We have six employees in it, also a surgeon of the United States Public Health Service. In this department the clearance of vessels, shipment and discharge of seamen, execution of quarantine laws, checking of alien passports, correspondence relating to shipping matters, and consular reports on the same subject are handled. During the year ending June 30, 1922, we issued 640 bills of health in London. That means 640 different ships went to the United States; the quarantine officer looked after the health of 640 vessels, and all sorts of operations in connection with those ships.

"Mr. Cole. Those were American vessels?

"Mr. Skinner. No; vessels of all descriptions. In the same manner we cleared 232 American vessels, a very different matter. We received 228 marine notes of protest, which, of course, related to an infinite variety of casualties, minor and important. We shipped 364 seamen, discharged 210, looked after 4 who died, relieved 112, and viséed 582 crew lists relating to several thousand men.

"That is a very cold statement about a branch of our work that is really wonderfully interesting. We receive

Yankee skippers every day, and it is really inspiring to see them. Not very long ago a ship came in, owned by the captain and the watch officers. They had reverted to the old-fashioned way when the captain owned the ship.

"The most of our vessels that come into London are tramps. But we have also first-class American passenger ships that come into London, ships of over 10,000 tons, mostly one-cabin ships on which the fare is but $100 and they are sailing full."

The citizenship department.—"Then we come to the American citizenship department. Here we have five employees. Here we grant emergency passports, take applications for departmental passports and consular certificates, register births, and handle the manifold correspondence arising out of that. In connection with that we deal with the law of citizenship, and have a great many cases of expatriation, and all sorts of legal problems. As I was saying before some of the Members came in, it is in working out those problems that the future diplomat should get a better practical knowledge of what he is to do in the higher regions of the service than anywhere else. In this department, in the last fiscal year, we either extended or amended 4,371 passports; we granted 999 passports and we received 1,117 applications for new passports; reported 43 births and 160 registrations. This is a very dull statement but it represents a great deal of work."

Alien visé department.—"Then we come to the alien visé department. You hear a great deal about that in the United States at present. Here we see all aliens proceeding to this country. We have eight employees in this department. We pass upon the suitability of every immigrant proceeding to the United States, and that means a face-to-face inquiry into the various circumstances of his life."

The accounting department.—"Next is the accounting department of our organization, where we take in the money. Here we have eight employees. During the year ended June 30, 1922, we dealt with 37,554 consular invoices. That represented, you might say, about half of all the British goods that entered the United States. Of course, there is a great deal of work connected with that.

"Mr. Linthicum. How many employees are in your office?

"Mr. Skinner. We have 55."

The notarial department.—"Then we come to our notarial department. Here we have only two employees. We take depositions and perform notarial services of a varied kind and carry on the correspondence arising therefrom. During the year ended June 30, 1922, this department performed 8,270 separate services. That covered every activity that a man might conceivably think of."

The war claims department.—"Then we come to our war claims department. I suppose that in no other consulate in the world is there such a department as a war claims department. That is a product of the war. We have here three employees. From the beginning of the war, we have made up the record of every claim of commercial character for seized goods, seized ships, etc. We have followed the cases through, representing many of these claimants in the courts, and have collected hundreds of thousands of dollars for different people. We have collected, incidentally, the whole prize court history of the war, having classified every prize court judgment that has been handed down. I do not know whether that will serve anybody in the future, but we thought that something might arise when the concrete commercial history of the war as distinguished from the broader aspects of it might be of utility."

The statistical department.—"In our statistical department we follow the movement of exports from the United Kingdom to the United States. At any moment of the day we can tell you the value of wool or any other commodity that has been exported as represented in our invoices. In this department is also handled the outgoing correspondence. During the year ended June 30, 1922, we sent out 43,208 letters from our office. In the same time 903 instructions were received from the Department of State and we sent out 1,732 dispatches or formal reports.

"Mr. Cockran. Can you give us the amount of these 37,000 invoices? What do they aggregate in the year?

"Mr. Skinner. For the 11 months of 1922 the aggregate exports from London to the United States reached 29,663,287 pounds plus $8,924,681. Some of our invoices are expressed in pounds, some in dollars, and on account of the varying rates of exchange we are embarrassed because you can not reduce those pounds to dollars and get a fair statement of the facts, so we follow the practice of expressing our statistics in the currency in the invoices as stated.

"Mr. Cockran. So that your actual invoices for the 11 months of 1922 covered $160,000,000.

"Mr. Skinner. Yes; about that figure." [15]

Consular services.—The following tabulation shows the number of consular services of different categories performed during the fiscal year ended June 30, 1924: [16]

---

[15]Hearings before the Committee on Foreign Affairs on H. R 17 and H. R. 6357, pp. 197-202.

[16]Reports from six consulates missing.

Protection and welfare cases	44,104	Extradition cases		56
American deaths recorded..	1,315	Notarial services 170,083		
Estates handled	794	Marine protests		6,047
Registration of Americans.	5,740	American vessels entered ..	20,622	
American passport services	69,497	American vessels cleared ...	20,421	
Sanitary reports	15,230	Seamen shipped	24,120	
Trade reports (voluntary).	15,659	Seamen discharged	21,148	
Trade reports (requested).	12,684	Seamen deserted		2,603
Replies to trade inquiries..	53,850	Seamen deceased		145
Landing certificates	1,008	Seamen relieved		2,583
Alien passports viséed 405,406		Disinfection certificates ...		7,124
Chinese certificates	1,470	Bills of health		41,836
Depositions and commissions	678	Consular invoices..........816,361		
		Letters received 977,390		
		Letters sent 1,160,636		

The protective function.—The protection of American citizens in their rights and interests abroad, although primarily a diplomatic function, is at the same time one of the most important and, not infrequently, the most active of consular duties.

Cases of injury or of impaired rights assume a diplomatic character only when their aggravated nature or the degree of their importance renders necessary an approach to the central government.[17]

Treaties and international usage accord to consular officers important authority and a wide range of protective functions in dealing with the affairs of their compatriots. Thus in the consular convention between the United States and France it is provided that:

"The Consuls-General, Consuls, Vice-Consuls or Consular Agents, of both countries, shall have the right to complain to the authorities of the respective Govern-

---

[17]"Being often nearest to the scene of action, the protective function in first instance is frequently exercised by the consul rather than by the diplomatic representative. Only if prevented from fulfilling his duties of protection, in cases where communication with the central government is required, need he address the diplomatic representative accredited to the country, although, as a matter of fact, in every case of more than trifling importance the consular officer either directly informs the legation of the facts or forwards to the legation a copy of dispatches sent to the Department of State."—Borchard, "Diplomatic Protection of Citizens Abroad," p. 437.

ments, whether federal or local, judicial or executive, throughout the extent of their consular district, of any infraction of the treaties or conventions existing between the United States and France, or for the purpose of protecting informally the rights and interests of their countrymen, especially in cases of absence. Should there be no diplomatic agent of their nation, they shall be authorized, in case of need, to have recourse to the General or Federal Government of the country in which they exercise their functions." [18]

A very large proportion of the protection cases are of a minor order and are disposed of through consular action, the diplomatic mission being merely advised of the circumstances and kept informed of the progress made. The importance of the consular rôle in protecting the rights of Americans abroad may be judged by the fact that for the fiscal year ended June 30, 1924, the Consular Service dealt with 44,104 such instances. [19]

The protection of individuals.—Either in accordance with treaty agreements, or as an act of courtesy, the local officials in foreign countries generally inform the consul of any serious difficulties in which his compatriots

[18]Consular Convention of 1853. See Malloy, "Treaties, Conventions," etc., vol. 1, p. 530. Similar provisions are contained in treaties with a number of other countries.

[19]"In countries with which the United States have treaty stipulations providing for assistance from the local authorities, consular officers are instructed that it is undesirable to invoke such interposition unless it is necessary to do so. In cases of arrest and imprisonment, they will see, if possible, that both the place of confinement and the treatment of the prisoners are such as would be regarded in the United States as proper and humane. If a request for assistance is refused, the consular officer should claim all the rights conferred upon him by treaty or convention, and communicate at once with the diplomatic representative in the country, if there be one, and with the Department of State. When such requests are made in accordance with long-established usage, he should, when they are refused, make suitable representations to the proper local authority, and likewise advise the legation and the Department."—Printed Personal Instructions to Diplomatic Agents, 1885, quoted in Moore's Digest, vol. V, p. 101.

may be involved. The right of an injured person to communicate with his consul in such circumstances is rarely denied.

In case of death, where no legal representative is present, the consul takes possession of the estate for delivery to the legal heirs. He notifies the relatives or friends of the deceased, reports the circumstances to the Department of State, and in many instances arranges for the disposal of the remains either by burial or cremation abroad, or shipment to the United States for interment. During the fiscal year ended June 30, 1924, seven hundred and ninety-four estates of deceased Americans were taken into the custody of consular officers—an average of slightly more than two a day. In each consulate births, deaths, and marriages are recorded, and a register of American citizens residing abroad is kept. In case of civil commotion, the consul becomes the guardian of the interests of his fellow-citizens. On occasions consuls have sought and obtained the protection of United States warships or marines.

Distressed and destitute American seamen are afforded relief from funds provided for the purpose, and either given suitable employment on outgoing vessels, or returned to the United States. Cases of imprisonment for crime, or internment for insanity sometimes require very special solicitude and attention.

The protection of commerce.—From the national point of view it is perhaps with relation to commerce that the protective function assumes its chief importance. All manner of sharp practices are to be encountered in foreign trade, while even in the most legitimate commerce circumstances are constantly arising in which not only goods, but well-established rights are thrown into jeopardy. Foreign tariffs and commercial laws are a prolific source of troubles. Sudden changes in the rates of customs duties or in administrative requirements, secret agreements, discriminations, bounties, requisitions, embargoes, prohibitions against importations, customs decisions or rulings, all require a watchful eye, for at almost every moment somewhere in the world American trade is involved in these difficulties.

But it is not only export trade that is affected by a fortuitous, or an arbitrary turn of events in other lands. Importations play a vital part in our domestic life, and especially with respect to essential materials on which many of our important industries as well as our standards of comfort depend. Not infrequently obstacles of the most formidable character must be overcome in order to secure delivery on goods of foreign origin which are urgently required by American manufacturers or consumers.

Again, the infringement of trade-marks and patents, rejections of merchandise, bankruptcies, violations of contracts, frozen credits, and a score of other ills due to abuse or misfortune, beset the path of the foreign trader and become, in varying degrees of importance, cases for the consul. Practically no American commercial establishment or agency abroad escapes for any considerable period the necessity of invoking consular aid and protection, either in overcoming trivial annoyances or in obviating difficulties of a much graver character.

Shipping matters are peculiarly within the consular province. The rights of seamen, as well as those of the owners of vessels and cargoes, are all given their due measure of care and attention. Mutinies, disputes between masters and crews, the discharge and shipment of seamen, desertions, the removal of masters under certain circumstances, stipulations to secure the release of American vessels held for debts, surveys to determine the seaworthy character of vessels, wrecks, crimes committed at sea, and many additional practical problems are the every day work of seaport consulates.

Harbor dues, port facilities, hydrographic charts and other important data are reported as an aid to shippers.[20]

The commercial function.—A vast majority of consular duties are commercial, having to do directly with the extension of foreign trade or with its protection. These functions inhere in the nature of the office, being conceded by usage, conferred by treaty, and to an important extent, prescribed by statute.

The protection of commerce is described in the foregoing pages. The extension of commerce involves many important categories of activity, chief among which may be cited the gathering and reporting of trade information for dissemination by the Department of Commerce, direct answers to trade inquiries, reporting trade opportunities, supplying foreign merchants with information regarding American products, aiding the representatives of American firms in their dealings with foreigners, assisting in the settlement of trade disputes and in the collection of foreign debts, investigating and reporting the standing of foreign business firms for the World Trade Directory on which the Department of Commerce advises American exporters, keeping, compiling, and analyzing statistics of trade.

All consular officers are encouraged to make trade

---

[20]The Marine Journal of New York stated in its issue of April 19, 1924: "It is the grateful opinion of the steamship managers that American Consuls are quick to discern their opportunities to render a service to the merchant shipping of their country, and that the reports of trade and shipping conditions in countries beyond the seas are of steadily increasing practical character and importance."

reports on their own initiative from the moment they enter the service. In the daily routine of office work they are brought into personal contact with the foreign business community and first-hand information is always at their command. The material which they supply is given broad dissemination in the United States and has proved of the greatest value in keeping the American business public accurately informed of conditions and commercial opportunities abroad.[21]

At posts of recognized commercial importance, trained consular officers are frequently assigned for specialized work in trade matters, their entire attention being devoted to the subject. Intensive study of a particular territory, or of an industry, like cotton textiles, or of a world commodity, like oil, develops the expert type of foreign representative whose reports are not only interesting and instructive, but whose judgments are balanced and dependable.

The great emphasis that has been placed on trade-extension work since the war finds its reflection in the fact that within the past five years the volume of consular reports on commercial subjects has more than doubled. In like degree, the quality of these reports is steadily improving; they are becoming more specific in character, more analytical, more clearly presented, and despatched with greater timeliness. Almost one-half of the consular trade reports are made on the request of the Department of Commerce, and follow the frame-

---

[21] An interesting observation was made in the British House of Commons during the recent debate on the diplomatic and consular bill, by Sir Park Goff, who stated: "Spain is the jumping-off ground for South America, and immediately the United States came into the War all the sea ports of Spain and Portugal, and all the towns, were flooded with Consuls and Vice-Consuls, and so-called Naval Consuls from America, but if you scratched any one of these men you found a most astute and thoroughly capable commercial traveller."—Parliamentary Debates, Official Report, vol. 116, p. 296.

work of its *questionnaires*. All reports are graded and criticized in the Department of State, and the efficiency record of each officer in the service shows his relative rating in commercial work.

But the value of consular commercial work is not limited to aiding particular traders in the marketing of their wares. The reports of consular officers are used for national purposes; they are given concrete application in the Department of State to the solution of foreign problems and to the shaping of international policies.

Politico-economic functions.—The back-ground of diplomacy lies in the consular field. It is economic. It deals with minerals, agricultural production, manufactures, exports and imports, finance, the sources of wealth, the avenues of commerce, the balance of trade.

In this material age, the first duty of a nation is to provide for the economic welfare of its people. Where its own natural resources are deficient for this purpose, it must find other means; expansion, colonization, conquest, the control of keystone commodities, the export of capital, emigration, "peaceful penetration." Diplomatic policy follows the dictates of the national urge; it plays the hand of the nation as to what it possesses and what it needs; to-day it defends a treasure, to-morrow it seeks one; its stakes are food and shelter.[22]

---

[22]Witness the following recent observation in a foreign journal with respect to ourselves: "What will happen when the American people as a whole, and not merely a few American students of world affairs, begin to realize that the fallow fertility of their garden has been exhausted, and that, if their energies are to find employment and their needs satisfaction in the future, they must break new ground? Will they use their great but transient preponderance of material resources in order to conquer fresh reserves by some formidable adventure in imperialism? Evidently at this moment they are in a vacillating state of mind. A long national tradition of inward concentration and aloofness from external affairs cannot be reversed in a day; but while the Administration at Washington has been withdrawing its troops at the first opportunities from Coblenz and Vladivostock, and Congress has been rejecting treaty-commitments in Europe,

The consul functions in the economic domain. His duties and his habit of mind are analytical. He must watch commercial developments with respect to their political effect, and political changes in their economic repercussions. He must report on these, giving the figures, the facts, and the reasons.

Through a sudden burst of consciousness the broad utility of this domain of observation seems to have impressed itself upon the world. The foremost nations have made quick to reorganize their foreign services on an interchangeable basis with a view to providing consular training for diplomatic officers, or bringing consuls forward into the diplomatic field.[23] It is the principle of the Dawes plan in foreign affairs; the business or economic determination of political issues. Books on politico-economic subjects are appearing at a rapid rate in an attempt to discover to the world what every good consul should know already; namely, the hidden economic motives of international policy.

Diplomatic and consular coordination.—Secretary of State Robert Lansing, in his letter to Honorable John Jacob Rogers, January 21, 1920, stated:

"The fact that there are a number of consular officers stationed within the territorial jurisdiction of each mission, working in ignorance of the policies which it is endeavoring to promote, is further evidence of the lack of unity of purpose in our Foreign Service. Such a state of affairs leaves in the mind the impression of latent forces going to waste through want of cohesive organization.

American trade and finance have been extending their activities all over the world; and, where national wealth has been invested in certain quantities, it has hitherto been an almost automatic law of international relationships that political intervention should follow."—*The Nation & The Athenaeum*, London, October 4, 1924.

[23]Italy now expressly reserves forty diplomatic positions for consuls.

"We must gain the additional impetus that will be given to the forces of our diplomacy by harmonizing the efforts of these local consular units with those of the mission itself, thus enabling American policies and American conceptions to be reflected in their true light with the same vision and with united effort throughout the entire land to which these officers are accredited." [24]

The problem of diplomatic and consular co-ordination is thus succinctly posed. Formerly, through what is now recognized to have been an erroneous conception, the consular service of every nation was considered as functioning along detached commercial lines, far removed from the subjects of diplomacy. It is now seen that much of the basic data of diplomacy is in the hands of the consul; that his facts are important, that his sources are valuable, and that his economic training is urgently needed in coping with many of the present-day aspects of international problems.

Of course the ultimate aim is to develop a new type of diplomatist—one who possesses both political and economic qualities—but for the time being, as these qualities are separately possessed, they must be brought together by organization. To accomplish this, the activities of the Consular Service, with respect to its separate units in a given jurisdiction, must be brought to a focus in the supervising consulate general and there linked with the action of the diplomatic mission. In this synchronizing process, the consulate general becomes the point of juncture; the instrument of co-ordination. Here we find what may be considered the broadest phase of consular activity; that of plowing the international subsoil for the diplomatic mission; gath-

---

[24]Printed in the hearings before the Committee on Foreign Affairs on H. R. 17 and H. R. 6357, 68th Cong., 1st Sess., p. 32.

ering data and weighing facts — the advisory field.

The consular branch of the Foreign Service is entering new fields. The world is crying for commercial diplomats—for analysts who are able to determine what economic exigencies are dictating the motives of other nations, and what may be done about it, if anything.

A suitable instrumentality for such a purpose is not impossible or even difficult of achievement. It should be a definite goal in the scheme of Foreign Service reorganization as relating to the highest purpose for which it exists.

Bibliography.

Angell, James B.: "The Consular Service and the Spoils System"; *Century Mag.,* vol. 48, June, 1894.

. Adams, Robert: "Faults in Our Consular Service"; *North American Review,* vol. 156, April, 1893.

Borchard, Edwin M.: "The Diplomatic Protection of Citizens Abroad"; Banks Law Pub. Co., New York, 1915.

Bowman, S.: "The New World. Problems in Political Geography"; World Book Co., Yonkers on Hudson, 1921.

Carr, Wilbur J.: "The American Consular Service"; *American Journal of International Law;* 1:891 (1907).

Carr, Wilbur J.: "What Your Consuls Do"; *American Consular Bulletin,* January, 1922.

Caillaux, Joseph: "Whither France? Whither Europe?"; Knopf, New York, 1923.

Chicago Council on Foreign Relations, and Illinois League of Women Voters: "Conference on the Economic Aspects of International Affairs."

Clark, J. R.: "The Right to Protect Citizens in Foreign Countries by Landing Forces"; Washington, 1912.

Cooper, Clayton Sedgwick: "Foreign Trade Markets and Methods"; Appleton & Co., New York, 1922.

Hinckley, F. E.: "American Consular Jurisdiction in the Orient"; Washington, 1906.

Jones, C. L.: "The Consular Service of the U. S."; New York, 1906.

Loomis, Francis Butler: "The Foreign Service of the United States"; *North American Review,* vol. 169, September, 1899.

Moore, John Bassett: "Digest of International Law"; vol. 5, Gov. Printing Office, Washington, 1906.

Nelson, Henry Loomis: "The Need of Trained Diplomats and Consuls"; *Harper's Weekly,* vol. 45, July 15, 1901.

Parker, George F.: "The Consular Service of the United States"; *Atlantic Monthly,* vol. 85, April, 1900, and May, 1900.

Salles, Georges: *"L'Institution des Consulats, son Origine, son Developpement au Moyen-Age chez les Differents Peuples";* Ernest Leroux, Paris, 1898.

Stowell, E. C.: *"Le Consul: Fonctions, Immunites, Organization, Exequatur";* Paris, 1909.

Stowell, E. C.: "Consular Cases and Opinions"; Washington, 1909.

Spurr, J. E.: "Political and Commercial Geology and the World's Mineral Resources"; McGraw-Hill, New York, 1920.

Viallati, A.: "Economic Imperialism and International Relations during the Last Fifty Years"; Macmillan, New York, 1923.

Warden, D. B.: "The Origin, Nature, Progress and Influence of Consular Establishments"; Smith, Paris, 1813.

Wharton, William F.: "Reform in the Consular Service"; *North American Review,* vol. 158, April, 1894.

Wratislaw, A. G.: "A Consul in the East"; Blackwood, London, 1924.

CHAPTER VI

OTHER FOREIGN AGENCIES

Attachés.—The term *attaché* is applied to a numerous class of foreign agents attached to diplomatic missions for the purpose of conducting special investigations or performing duties within a restricted and specialized field of activity. As the title implies, they are not an integral part of the Diplomatic Service, and while they do not hold diplomatic rank in the sense of being in the line of representative succession, so as to act as chargé d'affaires ad interim, they are regarded as being attached to the mission. Their names appear in the diplomatic list and are certified to the authorities of the city as being members of the staff of the diplomatic mission.[1]

The diplomatic list at Washington dated April 1, 1924, contains the following designations of attachés connected with the foreign diplomatic establishments in the United States: Attaché; Military Attaché; Assistant Military Attaché; Assistant Military Attaché for Aeronautics; Naval Attaché; Assistant Naval Attaché; Naval Attaché for Aeronautics; Commercial Attaché; Assistant Commercial Attaché; Financial Attaché; Air Attaché; Agricultural Adviser.

Military attachés.—The official status and duties of military attachés were thus defined by Secretary of State Sherman:

---

[1]Moore, Acting Secretary of State, to Freiherr Speck von Sternburg, June 2, 1898, MS. Notes to German Legation XII, 139. Moore's Digest, vol. IV, p. 439.

"Each military attaché is, in a sense, an aide-de-camp to the ambassador or minister to whose embassy or legation he is appointed. The orders of the ambassador or minister will be obeyed, unless they manifestly conflict with orders or instructions given by the Secretary of War. In the latter case, the military attaché will respectfully notify the ambassador or minister of the circumstances which prevent a compliance with his orders, in which event the full particulars of the case must be at once forwarded to the Adjutant-General. It is the earnest wish of the War Department that the most harmonious relations should exist between the military attachés and their chiefs in the Diplomatic Service. Any military attaché whose relations with the chief of the embassy or legation to which he is assigned are not most cordial will request a recall. A dignified appreciation of his own position and courteous respect for his diplomatic chief will be expected of each attaché." [2]

Military attachés are foreign observers of matters relating to the national defense, and are constantly on the alert for new ideas which can be applied to their own armies. They study the technical aspects of such subjects as the organization of various arms and units; principles of training and instruction; comparison of requirements of technical material; equipment of the soldier and equipment of units of an army; military rations, clothing and shelter; the performance of aircraft, both heavier and lighter than air; care and training of animals; the service of supply; the cost of maintenance of troops; the organization and training of reserves; the mobilization of man power and industry.

"The Military Attachés are attached to our embassies and legations and, in addition to being the military ad-

---

[2] Cited in Moore's Digest, vol. IV, pp. 437-438.

visers of the Ambassador or Minister, they are specifically charged with the collection of information on the military situation in the countries to which they are accredited. These reports are forwarded to the Second Division of the General Staff of the War Department, where specially trained officers digest them and maintain an accurate study on each country with respect to the military situation. These are called Information Digests and are always kept up to date, as changes in the situations occur. * * *

"The Second Division of the General Staff maintains a section which is the central coordinating agency of the War Department for the administration of our military attaché offices abroad. This section is also the central coordinating agency of the War Department for the transmission of corresponding information concerning our military establishment to the Military Attachés of foreign embassies and legations in Washington." [3]

There are twenty-two United States military attachés with nine assistants from the line of the Army, five assistants from the Air Service and one assistant from the Ordnance Department. They are stationed in the capitals of twenty-two foreign countries, grouped so as to cover forty-seven in all.

Naval attachés.—Naval attachés act in the same general capacity with respect to the Navy as do military attachés with respect to the Army. The United States naval attaché system began with the establishment of the office of Naval Intelligence in 1882, and has since been maintained. The work of naval attachés is mostly of a technical character in the matter of procuring information on naval professional subjects, their relations

---

[3]Major H. W. T. Eglin, *Congressional Digest,* Jan., 1924.

with foreign governments in this regard being on a basis of reciprocal exchange.

They also act as representatives of the Navy Department in purchasing material abroad and conduct the required inspection of such material; the volume of this work in certain countries is such as to require the assignment of officers as assistant naval attachés. In the Orient, junior officers are on duty for the study of the Japanese and Chinese languages; they serve under the naval attachés.[4]

Secretary of State Root emphasized the importance of military and naval attachés as follows:

"The peculiar and delicate functions of military and naval attachés, combining membership of the official diplomatic representation of their own government with the added privilege of direct intercourse with other than the diplomatic branches of the foreign administration and even of official association, on some occasions, with the Head of the State and with the highest officers of its military establishment, make it desirable that American officers serving in those capacities shall enjoy no less privileges than their colleagues of other nationalities."[5]

Commercial attachés.—Commercial attachés are representatives of the Department of Commerce sent abroad for the purpose of gathering and reporting commercial and economic information and assisting in the promotion of the trade and commerce of the United States. They are appointed by the Secretary of Commerce and report directly to him. The commercial at-

---

[4]Commander W. W. Galbraith, in *The Congressional Digest*, January, 1924.

[5]Circular Instruction to American Diplomatic Officers, Feb. 14, 1906, quoted in Hyde, "International Law," vol. I, p. 414.

taché service dates from an appropriation carried in the act of July 16, 1914.

The duties of commercial attachés are described under the heading "Department of Commerce" and their relations with the Foreign Service are discussed in the next chapter.

The Department of Commerce.—The Department of Commerce is charged with the duty of fostering, promoting, and developing the foreign and domestic commerce, the mining, manufacturing, shipping industries, and the transportation facilities of the United States.[6]

Originally, the major portion of these activities were confided to the Bureau of Manufactures, the province of which was "to foster, promote, and develop the various manufacturing industries of the United States, and markets for the same at home and abroad, domestic and foreign, by gathering, compiling, publishing, and supplying all available and useful information concerning such industries and such markets, and by such other methods and means as may be prescribed by the Secretary or provided by law."[7]

Bureau of Foreign and Domestic Commerce.—In 1912 the Bureau of Manufactures and the Bureau of Statistics, both of the Department of Commerce, were consolidated into a single "Bureau of Foreign and Domestic Commerce"[8], which, since its establishment, has confined its activities almost entirely to the promotion of foreign trade. "With the exception of the studies of the cost of production from 1913 to 1917 and some minor activities during later years, the bureau has not

---

6Act of Feb. 14, 1903, Sec. 3, 32 Stat., 826.
7*Ibid.*, Sec. 5, p. 827.
8Act of Aug. 23, 1912, Sec. 1, 37 Stat., 408.

paid any particular attention to domestic trade problems." [9]

Cooperation of the Consular Service.—The same law by which the Department of Commerce (and Labor) was established likewise provided that "all consular officers of the United States, including consuls-general, consuls, and commercial agents, are hereby required, and it is made a part of their duty, under the direction of the Secretary of State, to gather and compile, from time to time, useful and material information and statistics in respect to the subjects enumerated in section three of this act in the countries and places to which such consular officers are accredited, and to send, under the direction of the Secretary of State, reports as often as required by the Secretary of Commerce of the information and statistics thus gathered and compiled, such reports to be transmitted through the State Department to the Secretary of the Department of Commerce." [10]

Honorable John Jacob Rogers of Massachusetts has explained the legislative intent of this provision as follows:

"Congress particularly recognized, it seems, that the attempt might be made by the Department of Commerce to extend its activities just in the way it has sought to extend them—by the commercial attachés. It regarded that as unnecessary. It recognized the fact that we had this large and expensive and efficient Consular Service spreading throughout the world. It therefore provided for a liaison between the Department of State on the one side and the Department of Commerce on the other side, and that is the purpose of the law

---

[9] "Bureau of Foreign and Domestic Commerce," *Service Monographs of the U. S. Government,* No. 29, Institute for Government Research, p. 1.

[10] Act of Feb. 14, 1903, Sec. 5, 32 Stat., 827.

which I have just read. That law specifically protects and cherishes the foreign service of the United States, and makes it clear that under the Department of Commerce, so far as the organic act was concerned, it was not the intent and the desire of Congress to have a new foreign service established and built up." [11]

In order to provide facilities for effective cooperation between the Department of State and the Department of Commerce, provision was made for an administrative unit as follows:

"A person, to be designated by the Secretary of State, shall be appointed to formulate, under his direction, for the instruction of consular officers, the requests of the Secretary of Commerce; and to prepare from the dispatches of consular officers, for transmission to the Secretary of Commerce, such information as pertains to the work of the Department of Commerce; and such person shall have the rank and salary of a chief of bureau, and be furnished with such clerical assistants as may from time to time be authorized by law." [12]

Until 1905 the Department of Commerce maintained no foreign representation of its own, being entirely dependent upon the reports of consular officers for its information, as seems to have been contemplated in the original act. For many years consular officers had been engaged in the preparation of commercial and general economic information, both for the use of the Department of State, in its bearing upon foreign relations, and for other departments. [13]

---

[11] Hon. John Jacob Rogers of Massachusetts, *Cong. Record,* 66th Cong., 2nd Sess., p. 3770.

[12] Act of Feb. 14, 1903, Sec. 11, 32 Stat., 830.

[13] The act of Aug. 18, 1856, provided: "Consuls of the United States in foreign countries shall procure and transmit to the Department of State authentic commercial information respecting such countries, of such

Trade commissioners.—In 1905 Congress granted an appropriation of thirty thousand dollars "for compensation at not more than ten dollars per day and actual necessary traveling expenses of special agents to investigate trade conditions abroad, with the object of promoting the foreign commerce of the United States." [14]

This was the beginning of the direct representation of the Department of Commerce abroad. Several years later (1911) their designation was changed to "Commercial Agent" and in 1914 they became known as "Trade Commissioners," which is their present designation.

At first these special agents were traveling representatives who gathered information and made reports on specific subjects but "the practice of sending out roving commissioners has been completely discontinued and has not been followed in the department for a number of years—for at least four or five years." [15] Trade commissioners are now assigned to the offices of the commercial attachés, or to particular posts. They have become resident agents.

Commercial attachés.—The act of July 16, 1914, carried an appropriation of one hundred thousand dollars "for commercial attachés, to be appointed by the Secretary of Commerce, after examination to be held under his direction to determine their competency, and to be accredited through the State Department, whose duties shall be to investigate and report upon such conditions in the manufacturing industries and trade of

---

character, and in such manner and form, and at such times as the Department may from time to time prescribe." (R. S. 1712.)

[14] Act of Feb. 3, 1905, 33 Stat., 681.

[15] Statement of Dr. Julius Klein before the Committee on Interstate and Foreign Commerce, Feb. 18, 1924; Hearings on H. R. 4517, p. 41.

foreign countries as may be of interest to the United States; and for one clerk to each of said commercial attachés to be paid a salary not to exceed $1,500 each; and for necessary traveling and subsistence expenses, rent, purchase of reports, travel to and from the United States, and all other necessary expenses not included in the foregoing; such commercial attachés shall serve directly under the Secretary of Commerce and shall report directly to him." [16]

Activities of the bureau.—The range of the activities of the Bureau of Foreign and Domestic Commerce is as follows:

Promotion of export trade; procuring and distributing data on markets for American goods; procuring and distributing names of merchants in foreign countries; procuring and distributing information regarding foreign tariffs and trade restrictions; procuring and distributing information regarding commercial laws in foreign countries; adjustment of trade disputes; stimulation of interest in export trade; assistance to foreign buyers; distribution of information regarding American industries; studies of technique of foreign trade; assistance in research work; collection and publication of statistics; annual and monthly statistics of the trade of the United States; special statistical compilations; statistical abstract of the United States; statistics of foreign countries; supplying information regarding investment opportunities in foreign countries; administration of the China Trade Act; studies of foreign industrial and commercial organization and methods; aid to industries purchasing raw materials; supplying

---

[16] Act of July 16, 1914, 38 Stat., 500.

information regarding domestic economic conditions and trade.[17]

The Department of Agriculture.—The Department of Agriculture maintains or sends abroad yearly some two hundred and thirty employees and collaborators from its various bureaus. Of this number about 150 are employed in Alaska and our insular possessions; while about 90 are in foreign countries outside the jurisdiction of the United States. These employees are experts along specialized lines. They deal with physical and biological problems relating to agriculture.

In each of our insular possessions—Alaska, Hawaii, Philippine Islands, Virgin Islands, Porto Rico—the Department of Agriculture maintains experiment stations, branches of the Weather Bureau and the Forest Service. These stations, conducted in a manner similar to that in which State agricultural experiment stations are operated, deal with problems affecting production, based upon soil, and climatic and other conditions.

Foreign agricultural agents.—The representatives of the Department of Agriculture in foreign countries may be classed in two distinct categories: (a) Those who are engaged in purely scientific research work; (b) Those who deal with the business operations of agriculture.

The first of these concern themselves with new varieties of plants, new methods of breeding and cultivation,

---

[17]"A great part of the information regarding foreign trade conditions is obtained from consular officers who are under the direction of the Secretary of State. * * *

"As the Bureau has representatives at only twenty-eight posts in twenty-seven countries, it is entirely dependent on the consular officers for data on many countries. It also relies on these officers for much detailed local information in countries where it has its own representatives, as consular officers are located at all important commercial centers."—Bureau of Foreign and Domestic Commerce, *Service Monographs of the U. S. Gov.* *No.* 29, Institute for Government Research, pp. 46 and 92.

methods of combating diseases and pests, and protective measures, or quarantine, against animals, plants, and seeds.

The Bureau of Plant Industry is now engaged in several important scientific investigations abroad, while the Bureau of Entomology, the Federal Horticultural Board, the Forestry Service, the Biological Survey, the Fixed Nitrogen Research Laboratory, and the Bureaus of Soils, Public Roads, and Animal Industry all have foreign agents in the field.

In addition to its own direct representatives the Department of Agriculture receives information from collaborators, who report on special agricultural problems, and interchanges material with the ministers of agriculture of other countries.

The business operations of agriculture relate primarily to foreign markets and competition, which of course include market reporting as well as various phases of farm management and agricultural economics. For this purpose a considerable organization is in operation at home, while in the foreign field a permanent, though comparatively small, staff of agents is maintained.

The Bureau of Agricultural Economics.—In 1914 there was established in the Department of Agriculture an Office of Markets, but the close relationship that was seen to exist between profitable production and successful marketing led to the consolidation, in 1921, of the Bureau of Farm Management and the Bureau of Markets and Crop Estimates into a single Bureau of Agricultural Economics.

The foreign agricultural economics work is carried out by experts from the various commodity divisions of the Bureau of Agricultural Economics, acting in cooperation with the commissioners of agriculture and other agents of the department resident abroad. In Europe these agencies are organized into a committee under the chairmanship of an Assistant Chief of the Bureau of Agricultural Economics. The field work is administered through the offices of the commissioners of agriculture located at London and Berlin. The office of the Permanent Delegate of the International Institute of Agriculture at Rome acts as a supplementary administrative center.

The department also maintains permanent offices at Vienna, observing the development of agriculture in the great competitive district of the Danube Basin and Southern Russia; at Marseilles, France, a research laboratory for combating insect pests; at Mexico City a commissioner of agriculture in charge of animal quarantine investigations; at Buenos Aires a commissioner of agriculture in charge of the investigations of South American competition in cereals, animal products and fruits. The Bureau of Agricultural Economics has experts in Europe studying the demand for agricultural products and factors of competition, with special reference to cotton, meats, meat products, fruits, and vegetables.

Treasury Department.—The Treasury Department maintains two field services abroad: (a) a corps of customs agents who deal with the enforcement of the customs laws of the United States; and (b) a corps of medical officers of the Public Health Service who enforce the laws and regulations relating to quarantine.

The work of the customs agents is described in its relation to the Foreign Service in Chapter VII.

The officers of the Public Health Service are detailed to consulates, and work in the closest collaboration with consular officers. There are forty-two such medical representatives abroad, stationed at various important points, principally ports which are in direct steamship communication with the United States.

Duties of public health officers.—The general duties of the foreign representatives of the Public Health Service are as follows:

To furnish to the consul and to the Surgeon General of the Public Health Service information concerning the prevalence of quarantinable and other communicable diseases; to countersign the bills of health issued to vessels leaving for ports in the United States, its possessions or dependencies; to withhold the bill of health until satisfied that the vessel, passengers, crew and cargo have complied with the quarantine laws and regulations of the United States; to inspect all vessels, passengers and crews sailing, or departing, for the United States from ports at which cholera, yellow fever or plague in men or rodents prevails, or at which smallpox or typhus fever prevails in epidemic form; to inspect all vessels carrying steerage passengers; to prevent the embarkation of persons infected with quarantinable diseases; to furnish advice on matters connected with their profession upon request of the consul; to examine claimants on the Veterans' Bureau when requested by the proper authorities.

Special regulations are in force with respect to ports at which quarantinable diseases are prevalent, requiring the exercise of careful vigilance and the enforcement of definite precautionary measures according to the nature of the case. This applies to ports where cholera prevails, or where yellow fever, plague, smallpox, typhus, or leprosy are to be found. The means of enforcement are applied to vessels, cargoes, crews, and passengers, and are controlled through the bill of health, which is an essential document for vessels entering the United States.

The United States Shipping Board.—The Shipping Board is not, strictly speaking, within the category of governmental agencies having to do with the conduct of foreign affairs. It is a commercial enterprise, engaged in transportation, for which purpose it maintains twenty-three foreign offices, all of which function either under the jurisdiction of the Vice President in charge of European affairs, at London, or of the Director for the Orient at Manila. However, the law imposes upon the Board two specific duties which border closely upon the investigational work of other governmental agencies.

The board is empowered to investigate the action of foreign governments with respect to privileges afforded and burdens imposed on vessels of the United States, and to make a report of the result of such investigations to the President, who is authorized to secure by diplomatic action equal privileges for United States vessels.

The board is also directed to investigate the relative cost of constructing vessels at home and abroad; to examine the rules under which vessels are constructed at home and abroad; to investigate matters relating to marine insurance, the classification and rating of vessels, and the navigation laws of the United States, and to make such recommendations to Congress as it may deem best for the improvement and revision of such laws.

It is understood that foreign investigational work is conducted through the established agencies abroad, or through the use of supercargoes.

Both in the solution of administrative problems and in the supplying of general shipping information the consular service is able to offer a substantial degree of cooperation.

United States Tariff Commission.— The Tariff Commission has power to investigate the tariff relations between the United States and foreign countries, commercial treaties, preferential provisions, economic alliances, the effect of export bounties and preferential transportation rates, the volume of importations compared with domestic production and consumption, and conditions, causes, and effects relating to competition of foreign industries with those of the United States, including dumping and cost of production.

The commission also makes investigations to assist the President in ascertaining the differences in cost of production in the United States and in foreign countries of articles covered by the dutiable schedules of the tariff act. These functions, although not requiring the maintenance of a permanent foreign establishment, not infrequently necessitate the sending of special investigators, who are experts in particular trades, to cover various regions as regards the prevailing economic conditions relating to tariffs.

The Federal Trade Commission.—Under the terms of the Webb-Pomerene law, associations solely and actually engaged in the export trade of the United States are, under some conditions, exempted from certain provisions of the Sherman Anti-trust Act of July 2, 1890, and the Clayton Act of October 15, 1914. Section 5 of the Webb-Pomerene Act provides that every export association shall file certain statements with the commission at specified times. Additional information as to its organization, business, conduct, practices, management, and relation to other associations, corporations, partnerships, and individuals, shall be furnished when so required by this commission.

In connection with the formation and operation of the export associations mentioned above, numerous economic and legal questions arise which necessitate examination and investigation by the commission. Price manipulations and unfair practices of competition, as well as foreign legislation relating to combinations, in so far as it may affect American trade, come within the scope of the commission's work under the law.

Pan American Union.—The Pan American Union was founded in 1890, under the name of the International Bureau of American Republics, in accordance with the action of the first Pan American Conference, held in Washington in 1889-90. At the fourth conference, held at Buenos Aires in 1910, its name was changed from the International Bureau of American Republics to the Pan American Union.

It is the official international organization of all the Republics of the Western Hemisphere, founded and maintained by them for the purpose of exchanging mutually useful information and fostering commerce, intercourse, friendship and peace. It is supported through their joint contributions, each nation annually paying that part of the budget of expenses which its population bears to the total population of all the Republics. Its general control is vested in a governing board made up of the diplomatic representatives in Washington of all the Latin-American governments and the Secretary of State of the United States. Its executive officers are a Director General and an Assistant Director, elected by the board. They in turn are assisted by a trained staff of editors, statisticians, compilers, trade experts, translators, librarians, and clerks.

It is strictly international in its scope, purpose, and control, and each nation has equal authority in its administration. Its activities and facilities include the following: publication in English, Spanish, Portuguese, with separate editions, of an illustrated monthly bulletin, which is a record of the progress of all the Republics; publication of handbooks, descriptive pamphlets, commercial statements, maps, and special reports relating to each country; correspondence covering all phases of Pan American activities; distribution of every variety of information helpful in the promotion of Pan American commerce, acquaintance, cooperation, and solidarity of interests. It also sets the date, selects the place of meeting, and prepares the programs for the International Conferences of the American States known as the Pan American Conferences, and is custodian of their archives.

The United States Section of the Inter-American High Commission.—The Inter-American High Commission was organized on the recommendation of the First Pan American Financial Conference, held in Washington May 24-29, 1915. It aims to bring about substantial uniformity in the commercial law and administrative regulations of the American Republics and more stable financial relations between Latin America and the United States, and, in general, to carry out the recommendations of the First and Second Pan American Financial Conferences, and cooperate in the formulation and effectuation of the program of the international conferences of American States in so far as this program bears directly on the purposes and work of the commission. The Second Pan American Financial Conference took place in Washington, January 19-24, 1920. The commission's work is directed by a central executive council, which is composed of the chairman, vice chairman, and secretary of the section which represents the country selected as headquarters of the commission for the interval between any two meetings.

The United States section was given statutory recognition by act of February 15, 1916. There are corresponding sections in the Republics of Central and South America and the West Indies.

The International Joint Commission.—The International Joint Commission was created by the treaty between the United States and Great Britain signed January 11, 1909, the object of which is "to prevent disputes regarding the use of boundary waters and to settle all questions which are now pending between the United States and the Dominion of Canada involving the rights, obligations, or interests of either in relation to the other or to the inhabitants of the other, along their common frontier, and to make provision for the adjustment and settlement of all such questions as may hereafter arise."

The commission consists of six members, three appointed by the United States and three appointed by Great Britain on recommendation of the Government of Canada. It was organized in 1911, adopted rules of procedure, and established permanent offices in Washington and Ottawa. It has jurisdiction over all cases involving the use or obstruction or diversion of boundary waters between the United States and Canada, of waters flowing from boundary waters, and of waters at a lower level than the boundary in rivers flowing across the boundary.

Under Article IX of the treaty, the International Joint Commission also is constituted an investigatory body, for the purpose of examining into and reporting upon any questions or matters of difference arising along the common frontier that shall be referred to it from time to time by either the Government of the United States or the Government of Canada.

Under Article X of the treaty, any questions or matters of difference arising between the high contracting parties involving the rights, obligations, or interests of the United States or of the Dominion of Canada, either in relation to each other or to their respective inhabitants, may be referred for decision to the International Joint Commission, it being understood that on the part of the United States such action will be by and with the advice and consent of the Senate and on the part of Great Britain with the consent of the Government of Canada.

Under Article VI of the treaty, the commission is charged with the measurement and apportionment from time to time of the waters of the St. Mary and Milk Rivers and their tributaries, these rivers lying partly in Montana and partly in Alberta and Saskatchewan, and being largely used for irrigation purposes in both countries.

International Boundary between Alaska and Canada and the United States and Canada.—A joint tribunal for the settlement of certain questions that had arisen between the United States and Great Britain in regard to the location of the boundary line between Alaska and Canada and the interpretation that should be given to certain portions of the earlier treaties defining that line, was provided for by the convention of January 24, 1903, between the United States and Great Britain. It was also provided that when a decision should be reached by the tribunal, each Government should appoint on its own behalf one or more scientific experts, who should with all convenient speed proceed together to lay down the boundary in conformity with the decision. The questions submitted to the tribunal were decided, excepting one in regard to 120 miles of the boundary of the "coast strip," and the award was signed October 20, 1903. By an exchange of notes between the Secretary of State and the British ambassador an agreement was reached in regard to the undecided portion of the "coast strip" boundary, thus concluding the diplomatic negotiations. Scientific experts were appointed to lay down the line in accordance with the award of the tribunal and existing treaties.

The convention of April 21, 1906, fixed the initial point of the boundary along the one hundred and forty-first meridian and made provision for the appointment of one commissioner from each Government to determine a telegraphic longitude on the one hundred and forty-first meridian and to trace and mark the meridian north and south so far as might be necessary to define the exact boundary and permanently to mark and chart that part of the boundary. The field work has been completed and the maps are now in course of preparation.

A controversy in regard to the location of mining claims in Whatcomb County, Washington, and uncertainty as to the location of the boundary line at other places along the forty-ninth parallel west of the summit of the Rocky Mountains led to an investigation and report on that portion of the boundary by both the United States and Canadian parties independently in 1901.

By concurrent action, the Governments of the United States and Great Britain in 1902 and 1903 made provision for the designation of commissioners of the two

Governments to act jointly for the purpose of renewing lost or damaged monuments and placing additional monuments where such were needed throughout the course of the boundary along the forty-ninth parallel of north latitude from the summit of the Rocky Mountains to the Gulf of Georgia.

By a treaty between the United States and Great Britain, signed in Washington, April 11, 1908, the marking of the boundary was divided into eight sections, and between the years of 1903 and 1915 the two international commissions marked the boundary between Alaska and Canada and the United States and Canada for approximately 3,700 miles out of a total of 4,150 miles, leaving only about 450 miles to be surveyed.

Arbitration of outstanding pecuniary claims between the United States and Great Britain.—The arbitration of a large number of outstanding claims between the United States and Great Britain, based upon the general arbitration treaty signed at The Hague, was provided by special agreement, signed on August 11, 1910, and ratified by the Senate on July 19, 1911.

The claims listed in the approved schedule cover: (1) alleged denial in whole or in part of real property rights; (2) acts of the authorities of either Government in regard to the vessels of the nationals of the other Government or for alleged wrongful collection or receipt of customs duties or other charges by the authorities of either Government; (3) damages to the property of either Government or its nationals or personal wrongs of such nationals alleged to be due to the operations of the military or naval forces of the other Government or to the acts of negligence of the civil authorities of the other Government; (4) contracts between the authorities of either Government and the nationals of the other Government.

The claims are prepared by the agents of each Government and submitted to a tribunal, constituted in accordance with Article 87 of The Hague Convention. The United States and Great Britain each appoints an arbitrator and the two arbitrators thus selected choose an umpire.

Each party to the agreement bears its own expenses. The expenses of the tribunal are defrayed by the two Governments, the amount so expended being deducted from the sums awarded by the tribunal.

International Fisheries Commission.—On March 2, 1923, the United States signed with Great Britain a convention for the preservation of the halibut fisheries of the northern Pacific Ocean, including the Bering Sea. Ratifications were exchanged October 21, 1924. By the convention, each Government agreed to appoint two members of an International Fisheries Commission, to pay the salaries and expenses of their representatives and to share equally all general expenses. The Commission is charged with making a thorough investigation of the Pacific halibut, reporting the results of its investigation to the two Governments, and making recommendations for the regulation of the halibut fisheries with a view to their preservation and development. Its duties are as follows:

To plan such scientific investigations relative to the life history and habits of the halibut as will reveal the present abundance of the species, the need for conservation measures and the kind of conservation measures which will best perpetuate the supply and at the same time admit of the fullest possible utilization of the existing supply. To conduct the carrying out of the details of such investigations, review existing literature on the subject, prepare reports for publication, and such kindred matters as come within the scope of such an investigation, including the proper interpretation and significance of the scientific data collected.

The North Pacific Halibut Act, approved June 7, 1924, giving effect to the convention, authorized an appropriation for 1925 of $15,000 for salaries and expenses of the commission. The Department of Commerce, under the terms of the convention, is obligated to carry out certain provisions, including cases of illegal operations, the arrest of persons, the seizure of vessels and the seizure and sale of fish. Similar work will be done by Canada.

International (Water) Boundary Commission, United States and Mexico.—This boundary was first established by the treaty of peace between the United States and Mexico of February 2, 1848, and subsequently modified by the treaty of December 30, 1853, generally known as the "Gadsden treaty." Under these treaties the boundary was defined and located "up the middle of the river" by the joint commission generally known as the Emory-Salazar Commission, during the years 1849 to 1856.

The present commission was created by the treaty with Mexico of February 18, 1889, for a term of five years, and was subsequently extended from year to year until the treaty of November 21, 1900, made its duration "indefinite." The duties of the commission, as declared in the treaties, are to locate and maintain the boundary between the United States and Mexico where it is affected by the Rio Grande and the Colorado Rivers and to avoid the difficulties occasioned by reason of the changes which take place in the beds of those rivers.

The commission has exclusive jurisdiction over all differences or questions that may arise on boundary between the United States and Mexico from the Gulf of Mexico to the Pacific Ocean, approximately 2,000 miles, consisting of some 1,300 miles along the Rio Grande and 25 miles along the Colorado River; also 680 miles overland boundary between El Paso, Texas, and the Pacific Ocean.

The question of the elimination of the "bancos" remained unsettled until the treaty of 1905. The word "banco" is used to describe a portion of land cut bodily from the mainland by the action of the river, bringing into question the nationality of such land. The duties of the commission are therefore to determine by survey and examination where, according to our treaties, the true boundary lies. According to our present arrangement, whenever an area cut off by the change in the channel exceeds 650 acres, or has as many as 200 persons residing on it, the jurisdiction remains in the country in which the land formerly was, and the old bed of the river remains the boundary, thus "eliminating" the "banco" from dispute as to nationality.

Mixed Claims Commission, United States and Germany. —The Mixed Claims Commission between the United States and Germany was established by executive agreement August 10, 1922, to determine the amount to be paid in satisfaction of Germany's financial obligations under the treaty concluded between the two Governments on August 25, 1921.

The United States agency began operations in the early part of October, 1922. The claims then on file numbered more than 12,000, representing an aggregate of $1,479,064,313.92, including the claim of the United States for the expenses of the Army of Occupation in the sum of $255,544,810.53. A great many of these claims have already been disposed of, and others have been prepared and submitted to the commission for its consideration.

Mixed Claims Commissions, United States and Mexico. —Under the conventions between the United States and Mexico, signed September 8, 1923, and September 10, 1923, respectively, two international commissions have been set up for considering claims of citizens of the two countries arising since 1868. One of these is a general commission, dealing with all usual claims, while the other is a special commission for the settlement of claims arising out of revolutions. The time stipulated for the presentation of claims to the general commission is one year, and to the special commission, two years, from the date of the first meetings of the commissions in August, 1924. The completion of the arbitration under the general convention is set for three years, and under the special convention, five years.

An element of difficulty lies in the restoration of destroyed evidence, the gathering of widely scattered testimony, and the finding of witnesses who have disappeared. Claims are presented through the Department of State, which has already received some twenty-five hundred. The total value of all claims, when filed, will amount to many millions of dollars.

International Bureau, Permanent Court of Arbitration. —The Permanent Court of Arbitration was created by the international treaty signed at The Hague, July 29, 1899, on the occasion of the First International Peace Conference.

The treaty provides for an international bureau establishment at The Hague, which shall serve as a record office for the court, and which shall be the channel of communication relative to the meetings of the court. It has custody of the archives and conducts all the administrative business. A permanent administrative council, composed of the diplomatic representatives of the signatory powers accredited to The Hague, and the Netherlands minister for Foreign Affairs, who acts as president, is charged with the establishment and organization of the International Bureau, and has entire control over the appointment, suspension, or dismissal of the officials and employees of the bureau, fixing payments and salaries, and controlling expenditures.

Some of the cases decided by the Permanent Court of Arbitration in which the United States has been directly interested are as follows: October 14, 1902, the Pius Fund of California between the United States and Mexico; in February, 1904, Venezuelan claims; September 7, 1910, North Atlantic fisheries case; October 25, 1910, Orinoco steamship case, United States and Venezuela.

Interparliamentary Union.—The Interparliamentary Union is composed of members of the various international parliaments, who favor the arbitration of international disputes. It deals with questions of public international law relating to the maintenance of peace.

In each parliament of the world, so-called "groups" have been organized for the purpose of bringing before the parliament questions concerning the amelioration of international relations. Conferences have been held annually, or biennially, since 1889.

The Bureau of the Interparliamentary Union, which is established at Brussels, Belgium, under the management of a general secretary nominated by the council, encourages the formation of international groups and keeps a list of members. It is the central organ of the groups in all that concerns their reciprocal relations.

International Institute of Agriculture.—This institute was created by the treaty of 1905, signed by 41 powers, for the purpose of collecting, studying, and publishing statistics and technical and economic information concerning farming, commerce in agricultural products, prevailing prices, and so forth.

Under the terms of the agreement, the leading nations of the world pledge themselves to exchange promptly and accurately information relating to livestock, seeded areas, agricultural production, imports and exports of agricultural products, prices of agricultural products, farm labor, land laws, and other pertinent facts pertaining to the economics of agriculture.

The cost of maintenance and operation is apportioned among the adhering nations. By way of facilitating the transmission of agricultural information, the United States Navy Department has placed its wireless service at the disposal of the institute and the Department of Agriculture free of cost. It is estimated that about thirty per cent of the foreign agricultural information received by the Department of Agriculture is supplied by the institute.

International Research Council.—Prior to the war the United States and many foreign governments were supporting a number of independent scientific associations and societies such as the International Geodetic Association, the Astronomical Association, the Seismological Association, and others of like character.

The organization of the International Research Council for the purpose of grouping these under a central control was proposed by the delegates of the National Academy of Sciences of the United States at an international conference held in London under the auspices of the Royal Society in October, 1918. This proposal was taken up at the second international conference held under the auspices of the Paris Academy of Sciences in November of the same year, and formally completed at Brussels in July, 1919. The purposes of the International Research Council are as follows:

To coordinate the different branches of science and its applications; to initiate the promotion of international associations or unions deemed to be useful to the progress of science in accordance with Article 1 of the resolutions adopted at the conference at London in October, 1918; to direct international scientific activity in subjects which do not fall within the purview of any existing international associations; to enter, through the proper channels, into relations with the governments of the countries adhering to the International Research Council in order to promote investigations falling within the competence of the council.

Under the auspices of the International Research Council the following bodies have been established:

The International Astronomical Union, The International Union of Pure and Applied Chemistry, The International Union of Geodesy and Geophysics, The International Union of Mathematics, and The International Union of Scientific Radiotelegraphy.

International Hydrographic Bureau.—The International Hydrographic Conference, held in London from June 24 to July 16, 1919, and at which delegates from 22 states were present, recommended the establishment of an international hydrographic bureau, with a view to effecting a permanent liaison among the national hydrographic officers of the world.

The International Hydrographic Bureau is the administrative office of an association of maritime states, having for its object the fostering of close and permanent relations between the hydrographic services of the associated states. It seeks to coordinate their efforts with a view to rendering navigation easier and safer in all the seas of the world; to secure the general adoption of the resolutions taken by the various international hydrographic conferences; to obtain uniformity in hydrographic documents; and to advance the theory and practice of the science of hydrography. It studies the hydrographic documents of the world and publishes lists of geographical positions, primary and secondary meridians, seamen's signals, and so forth. It also deals with the construction and use of hydrographic instruments and appliances, the principles of which have been approved by the national offices, the methods of hydrographic surveying and research, and all related subjects of scientific value and importance.

International Radiotelegraphic Convention.—On November 3, 1906, an international convention was signed at Berlin with a view to establishing uniform regulations in the use of wireless telegraphy. The convention was ratified by the United States in 1912. It provides that there shall be an international bureau, the duties of which are to collect, coordinate, and publish information of every kind relating to wireless telegraphy; examine the applications for changes in the convention or regulations; promulgate the amendments adopted; and generally perform all administrative work referred to it in the interest of international wireless telegraphy. It also provides for distress calls, and procedure to be followed.

The expenses of the international bureau are borne by all the contracting countries, its work being placed

in the charge of the International Bureau of Telegraphs
at Berne, Switzerland. As the convention provides that
conferences shall be held from time to time, the additional expenses incident thereto are borne by the signatory nations.

International Bureau of Weights and Measures.—By
the treaty of May 20, 1875, the United States became
a member of an international bureau created for the
purpose of establishing a uniform standard of weights
and measures. It is the function of this bureau to preserve the original standards of measurement and, upon
request, to furnish accurate copies to governments and
scientific institutions. From time to time there is held a
general conference, composed of delegates of the treaty
States, at which there is a discussion of scientific methods for perfecting the accurate reproduction of standards of measurement. The bureau has also become an
important scientific center for metrological observation. The instruments in the Bureau of Standards are
sent back from time to time to be compared in Paris
with the original standards in the international bureau.
The instruments used in the United States are copies of
the standards in the Bureau of Standards.

**International Commission on the Publication of Annual
Tables of Constants.**—This commission was appointed by
the Seventh International Congress of Applied Chemistry at its meeting in London in 1909, in which the
United States participated, and continued at the Eighth
International Congress in New York in 1912, of which
the United States had official charge.

The various members of the commission are responsible for the abstracting of the literature of their respective countries. With the help of suitable bodies of
abstracters, all periodicals and other publications con-

nected with chemistry, physics, and allied sciences are carefully examined as they are published, and numerical data likely to be of use, together with the bibliographic references, is entered on slips. These slips are sent to the members of the commission, who, after examination, forward them to the central office in Paris. The data are then classified and arranged in tables, which are published. All the data published in any one year appear in a volume for that year.

The demands for publications on the part of scientists and manufacturers in the United States have far surpassed those from any other country.

International Bureau of the Union for the Protection of Industrial Properties.—The United States is signatory to the convention for the Protection of Industrial Property concluded in Paris March 20, 1883, ratified and proclaimed June 11, 1887. An additional agreement was signed at Brussels December 14, 1900, and the original convention was revised at Washington, June 2, 1911, and proclaimed by the United States in 1913. The contracting countries constitute a Union for the Protection of Industrial Properties and for the mutual protection of their citizens or subjects in the matters of patents, trade-marks and commercial names. The International Bureau at Berne, Switzerland, is placed under the authority of the Government of the Swiss Confederation which regulates its organization and supervises its operation. It gathers information relative to the protection of industrial property and embodies it in a general statistical report which is distributed to all administrations. It considers questions of interest to the union and publishes a periodical on questions concerning the union.

Numbers of this periodical, like all the documents

published by the International Bureau, are distributed among the members.

The bureau holds itself at the disposition of the members of the union for supplying special information relating to the international service of industrial property. It makes an annual report. Expenses, within the total fixed by the convention, are regulated by the Swiss Confederation, which advances the amount and is reimbursed by the governments members of the union.

International Bureau for the Publication of Customs Tariffs.—The International Bureau for the Publication of Customs Tariffs was created by International Convention signed at Brussels July 5, 1890.

Its object is "to publish, at the common expense, and to make known, as speedily and accurately as possible, the customs tariffs of the various States of the globe and the modifications that may, in future, be made in those tariffs." Tariffs of the various countries are translated and copies transmitted to the signatory members.

Bulletins are issued containing information concerning legislative or executive provisions affecting tariffs.

International Statistical Institute at The Hague.—The International Statistical Institute was established June 24, 1885, at the Jubilee meeting of the Statistical Society of London (now the Royal Statistical Society). It is a voluntary association. Apart from contributions to the permanent office pledged by several governments, it has no official connection with any government. Its object is the promotion of statistics in both their scientific and practical aspects. The institute selects its members from among the citizens of various countries who have distinguished themselves in the field of statistics in the service of their governments or in private life. The number of regular members is limited to 200 and the number of honorary members to 20. No one state is to have more than one-fifth of the elected members, regular or honorary.

A permanent statistical office was established by a vote of the general meeting of the institute held at Vienna on September 10, 1913. It maintains a statistical library, prepares data for international comparisons, works for the unification of statistical methods, publishes an international year book and a periodical bulletin, and assists in preparing a working program for the biennial meetings.

International Trade-mark Registration Bureau.—The United States is a party to the convention for the protection of trade-marks signed at the fourth Pan American Conference of American States at Buenos Aires August 20, 1910, proclaimed September 16, 1916. The convention provides for the better protection of trademarks and commercial names through the creation of two trade-mark registration bureaus at Habana and at Rio de Janeiro. The bureau at Habana is now in operation. It deals with the registration of trade-marks coming from the United States, Mexico, Cuba, Haiti, Dominican Republic, San Salvador, Honduras, Nicaragua, Costa Rica, Guatemala, and Panama. The bureau at Rio de Janeiro has not been established, due to delay in ratification by the governments most directly concerned. Trade-marks in the United States may be registered at Habana, whereupon the bureau registers them in the other countries with the same effect as if the individual had made his application direct in each instance.

The International Railway Congress.—The participation of the United States in the International Railway Congress is not based upon treaty obligation. An appropriation to cover the cost of membership was first made in 1905.

The International Railway Congress is a permanent association established to promote the progress and development of railroads. The adherents of the congress are railway administrations and governments. Exclusive of the United States, there are about forty governments which contribute. The affairs of the Congress, its organization and programs, are regulated by an international commission, which it elects. The membership of the United States is of chief interest and benefit to the Interstate Commerce Commission.

International Office of Public Health at Paris.— International defensive action against epidemics was first urged by the French Government, which in 1851 called a sanitary convention to meet in Paris; this was followed by a second meeting in 1859. The epidemic of cholera of 1865 caused the holding of a third congress at Constantinople. Other conferences have followed at short intervals, that of Paris in 1903 being specially important as it was there decided to establish an international sanitary office to be situated at Paris.

The sixth sanitary conference, at Rome in 1907, drew up a formal convention for the new institution. The International Office of Public Hygiene at Paris is under the control of a commission composed of delegates from all the member States. Its main object is to "collect and bring to the knowledge of the participating States facts and documents of a general character concerning public health and especially regarding infectious diseases, notably cholera, the plague, and yellow fever, as well as the measures taken to check these diseases."

The United States ratified the convention, which went into effect in 1908.

The Pan-American Sanitary Bureau.—The Pan-American Sanitary Bureau was created pursuant to a resolution passed by the delegates of the American Republics at the Second International Conference of American States, in Mexico City, January 29, 1902. The bureau maintains permanent headquarters at Washington, D. C. Pan-American sanitary conferences of the American Republics are called by the chairman of the bureau, through the Pan American Union, under whose auspices its work is conducted.

The object of the bureau is to stimulate the carrying out of the ideas which are developed in the sanitary conventions and to prepare for the forthcoming conventions.

Conventions of the American States deal with means of checking the ravages of infectious and other diseases, establishing and enforcing sanitary regulations in those seaports hitherto shunned by the merchant marine because of the danger to life attending the landing of the crews or merchandise and the loading of vessels.

Expenses are apportioned among the various members on the basis of population. The Pan American Union has charge of the disbursement of the entire fund.

International Prison Commission.—Congresses for the discussion of penitentiary administration and reform have been held at irregular intervals since 1846. The International Prison Congress was organized on the initiative of the United States. Under authority of a joint resolution of Congress passed March 7, 1871, a commissioner was appointed to go to Europe and secure the cooperation of European Governments in the holding of an international congress for the discussion of all matters relating to the prevention and treatment of crime, the improvement of criminal law, and prison administration. The first meeting of the International Prison Congress was held at London in 1872. As a result of this meeting, the congress was organized on a permanent basis. Through an appropriation of June 11, 1896, the United States became an adhering member of the International Prison Commission, which is the permanent executive committee of the congress, and through which the different nations cooperate in securing information and in preparing reports on the subjects decided upon for investigation and discussion. This commission is composed of one representative officially appointed by each of the adhering governments and meets annually or biennially.

International Bureau for the Repression of the African Slave Trade.—Agreements for the suppression of the slave trade were made between Great Britain and France in 1833 and 1841. In the latter treaty some additional States joined. The congress of Berlin in 1885 took up the question again and determined in principle upon the more complete international organization of the preventive system. The Brussels conference of 1890 finally regulated the matter through a convention in which both slave trade and African slavery itself were made subject to strict international regulation. An office was established at Zanzibar for the purpose of superintending the enforcement of the general act. A second bureau was established at Brussels for the purpose of collecting information and publishing documents and statistics with respect to the slave trade. The Brussels general act also regulates the sale of liquor in the central belt of Africa. In regions where the natives have not yet become accustomed to the use of liquors, the traffic is entirely forbidden. For other parts a high minimum excise duty is fixed by the treaty. The bureau at Brussels acts as an intermediary between the treaty powers for the exchange of information concerning the liquor traffic in their respective African possessions.

The United States is a party to the general act signed at Brussels July 2, 1890, and to the convention signed at Brussels June 8, 1899. It is an adhering party to the convention signed at Brussels November 3, 1906, regulating the liquor traffic in certain parts of Africa.

The United States Court for China.—The United States Court for China was created by act of June 30, 1906, and given exclusive jurisdiction over all cases and judicial proceedings then within the jurisdiction of American ministers and consuls, except civil cases where the sum involved was not over $500 United States gold, and criminal cases where the punishment for the offense would not exceed $100 fine or sixty days' imprisonment or both. In the latter class of cases the court was given appellate jurisdiction and was charged with supervisory control over the exercise by consuls and vice consuls of the duties prescribed by law relating to estates of decedents in China.

By the diplomatic and consular act approved June 4, 1920, the judge of the United States Court for China was authorized to appoint a United States commissioner, who is, in addition, ex-officio judge of the consular court for the district of Shanghai, with all the authority and jurisdiction formerly exercised by the vice consul acting by virtue of the act of Congress of March 4, 1915.

The court holds sessions regularly at Shanghai and at stated periods at Canton, Tientsin, and Hankow, a session being required to be held in each city at least once annually.

Appeals from the final judgment and decrees lie to the United States Circuit Court of Appeals of the ninth judicial circuit, and thence to the United States Supreme Court.

The procedure is required to be in accordance with existing procedure in United States consular courts in China, as provided by law, except that the judge has power from time to time to modify and supplement said rules.

Bibliography.

Hughes, Charles Evans: "The Pathway of Peace"; An address delivered before the Canadian Bar Association at Montreal, September 4, 1923; Government Printing Office, 1923.

Reinsch, Paul S.: "Public International Unions"; Ginn and Co., Boston, 1911.

CHAPTER VII

THE PROBLEM OF INTERDEPART-
MENTAL RELATIONS

The nature of interdepartmental relations.—The Department of State, with its vast system of foreign representation, is intimately associated with all other departments of the government either in the enforcement of the laws of the United States or in the gathering and reporting of important material from foreign sources for their use.

The chief agency in this general scheme of cooperation is the Consular Service, the functions of which cover a wide range of such activities.

As relating to the first of these two categories, the following examples will serve to illustrate the manner in which consular officers are called upon to participate in the enforcement of the laws:

Administrative functions.—The tariff acts for many years have carried administrative provisions requiring the certification by consular officers of invoices covering all shipments of foreign merchandise to the United States over one hundred dollars in value and imposing many other highly important duties of kindred character.[1]

The selective immigration law makes the Consular Service an instrument for enforcing the quota system. Under this arrangement consular officers are entrusted

---

[1] See Act of October 3, 1913, 38 Stat., 185.

with important authority in the granting or the refusal of passport visas.[2]

The quarantine laws require the issuance by consular officers of bills of health to all vessels departing for the United States, and provide for the rendering of sanitary reports on health conditions in foreign countries.[3]

The merchant marine laws make the consul an important figure in dealing with the problems of ocean transportation, the relief and discharge of seamen, and the settlement of disputes between masters and crews.

The laws of all the States of the Union and of the Federal Government provide for the execution before consular officers of notarial documents of every description.[4]

Services for other departments.—In like manner the statutes provide for the gathering and reporting of various classes of information for the use of other departments of the Government, the following examples being illustrative:

"Consuls of the United States in foreign countries shall procure and transmit to the Department of State authentic commercial information respecting such countries, of such character and in such manner and form and at such times as the department may from time to time prescribe." [5]

Agricultural data.—"And they shall also procure and transmit to the Department of State, for the use of the Agricultural Department, monthly reports relative to the character, condition, and prospective yields of the agricultural and horticultural industries and other fruit-

---

[2] Act of May 26, 1924, 43 Stat., 153.
[3] Act of Feb. 15, 1893, 27 Stat., 450-1.
[4] R. S. 1750, amended April 5, 1906, 34 Stat., 101.
[5] R. S. 1712, amended June 18, 1888, 25 Stat., 186.

eries of the country in which they are respectively stationed;[6]

"And he (the consul) shall also report as to the character of agricultural implements in use, and whether they are imported to or manufactured in that country; as to the character and extent of agricultural and horticultural pursuits there.[7]

"And he (the consul) shall also furnish * * * at least once in twelve months, the prices current of all articles of merchandise, including those of the farm, the garden, and the orchard, that are imported through the port or place in which he is stationed."[8]

Imports and exports.—"It shall be the duty of consuls to make to the Secretary of State a quarterly statement of exports from, and imports to, the different places to which they are accredited, giving, as near as may be, the market price of the various articles of exports and imports, the duty and port charges, if any, on articles imported and exported, together with such general information as they may be able to obtain as to how, where, and through what channels a market may be opened for American products and manufacturers." [9]

Labor reports.—"In addition to the duties now imposed by law, it shall be the duty of consuls of the United States, annually, to procure and transmit to the Department of State, as far as practicable, information respecting the rate of wages paid for skilled and unskilled labor within their respective jurisdictions * * *" [10]

---

[10]*Ibid.*

[7]R. S. 1713, amended June 18, 1888, 25 Stat., 186.

[8]*Ibid.*

[9]Act of Jan. 27, 1879, 20 Stat., 273-274. *Note.* For a description of the services rendered for the Department of Commerce, see pages 200, 201.

[10]*Ibid.*

The Work of the Consul.

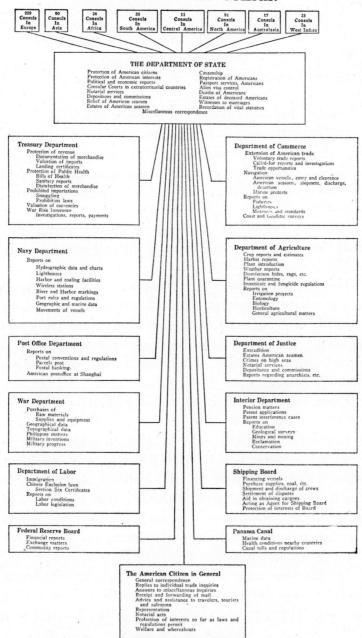

THE DEPARTMENT OF STATE

Protection of American citizens
Protection of American interests
Political and economic reports
Consular Courts in extraterritorial countries
Notarial services
Depositions and commissions
Relief of American seamen
Estates of American seamen

Citizenship
Registration of Americans
Passport services, Americans
Alien visa control
Deaths of Americans
Estates of deceased Americans
Witnesses to marriages
Recordation of vital statistics

Miscellaneous correspondence

Treasury Department

Protection of revenue
 Documentation of merchandise
 Valuation of imports
 Landing certificates
Protection of Public Health
 Bills of Health
 Sanitary reports
 Disinfection of merchandise
Prohibited importations
 Smuggling
 Prohibition laws
Valuation of currencies
War Risk Insurance
 Investigations, reports, payments

Department of Commerce

Extension of American trade
 Voluntary trade reports
 Called-for reports and investigations
 Trade opportunities
Navigation
 American vessels, entry and clearance
 American seamen, shipment, discharge, desertion
 Marine protests
Reports on
 Fisheries
 Lighthouses
 Measures and standards
Coast and Geodetic surveys

Navy Department

Reports on
 Hydrographic data and charts
 Lighthouses
 Harbor and coaling facilities
 Wireless stations
 River and Harbor markings
 Port rules and regulations
 Geographic and marine data
 Movements of vessels

Department of Agriculture

Crop reports and estimates
Market reports
Plant introduction
Weather reports
Disinfection hides, rags, etc.
Plant quarantine
Insecticide and fungicide regulations
Reports on
 Irrigation projects
 Entomology
 Biology
 Horticulture
 General agricultural matters

Post Office Department

Reports on
 Postal conventions and regulations
 Parcels post
 Postal banking.
American postoffice at Shanghai

Department of Justice

Extradition
Estates American seamen
Crimes on high seas
Notarial services
Depositions and commissions
Reports regarding anarchists, etc.

War Department

Purchases of
 Raw materials
 Supplies and equipment
Geographical data
Topographical data
Philippine matters
Military inventions
Military progress

Interior Department

Pension matters
Patent applications
Patent interference cases
Reports on
 Education
 Geological surveys
 Mines and mining
 Reclamation
 Conservation

Department of Labor

Immigration
Chinese Exclusion laws
 Section Six Certificates
Reports on
 Labor conditions
 Labor legislation

Shipping Board

Financing vessels
Purchase supplies, coal, etc.
Shipment and discharge of crews
Settlement of disputes
Aid in obtaining cargoes
Acting as Agent for Shipping Board
Protection of interests of Board

Federal Reserve Board

Financial reports
Exchange matters
Commodity reports

Panama Canal

Marine data
Health conditions nearby countries
Canal tolls and regulations

The American Citizen in General

General correspondence
Replies to individual trade inquiries
Answers to miscellaneous inquiries
Receipt and forwarding of mail
Advice and assistance to travelers, tourists and salesmen
Representation
Notarial acts
Protection of interests so far as laws and regulations permit
Welfare and whereabouts

American Consuls serve practically every branch of our Government, every business man and, either directly or indirectly, every private citizen.

This chart shows how information gathered by them is concentrated in the Department of State and then distributed to the various governmental agencies and to private concerns and individuals.

A Consul's more important duties are shown, but by no means all of them.

A chart of consular cooperation.—By way of illustrating the extent and the nature of consular cooperation with the various executive departments and independent establishments of the government, there is shown herewith a chart which condenses these functions into related groups under appropriate headings.[11]

In the gathering of information for the use of other departments, the consul frequently acts upon his own initiative, but quite as often he follows instructions from the Secretary of State which have emanated in substance from the interested department. Naturally this system has the effect of throwing the Department of State into intimate, daily contact with all other branches of the government.

The demand for foreign information.—Of recent years, as the foreign interests of the United States have expanded, the functions of the various executive departments have likewise broadened and the range of their observations is rapidly extending to the new international horizon.

Practically no subject of to-day especially in governmental administration can be understood broadly until it is examined in the light of foreign experiences; in other words, there is so much of value to be learned from other nations, or from an examination of the international aspects of our own problems, that every department of the government now feels the need of facilities for the gathering of data pertinent to the special subjects with which it deals.

In this way there has arisen a demand for information of almost every description from the leading foreign sources. Through what machinery is this demand to be

---

[11]See page 193.

met? Manifestly, either through the utilization of the established Foreign Service, or through a multiplicity of other agencies.

The absence of a definite policy.—In point of fact, there has been no clearly defined policy as to which of these courses should be followed, and as a consequence, both have been attempted by piecemeal. No sooner did the Consular Service become established on a suitable statutory basis to be of greatest value to the business interests of the country than a parallel service was developed in another department to which the lion's share of appropriations for the extension of commerce has been diverted.

But it is obvious that Congress will not permit these various departmental agencies to expand indefinitely; to establish and maintain agents in all parts of the world, paralleling at every point the work of our regularly accredited representatives. Apart from other considerations, the expense of it would be staggering. Whatever may be done in this regard, therefore, the cooperation of the Consular Service must remain the chief factor in the gathering of foreign information, and the Department of State the center of the interdepartmental system for its appropriate utilization.

Although the greatest attention has been drawn to this subject through the confusion of effort in the extension of foreign trade, the problem of interdepartmental relations is by no means limited to this single phase of activity. Practically every department of the government, within the sphere of its ever broadening functions, is in some manner reaching out to foreign fields.[12]

---

[12] At the conference on Training for Foreign Service held in Washington Dec. 31, 1915, Hon. P. P. Claxton, Commissioner of Education, stated: "One very important function that the American consular officer has performed is that of serving as agent in collecting information for the De-

This development has long been noted, and attempts, both legislative and administrative, have been made to find a workable solution.

A Senate resolution.—On October 3, 1919, the Senate passed a resolution calling upon the heads of the several departments and independent establishments of the Government to submit complete statements of their activities relating to the foreign commerce of the United States. These reports were compiled and printed [13] but no action has been taken thereon.

Views of Secretaries Lansing and Redfield.—Secretary of State Lansing in his letter to the Senate stated the case as follows:

"The Department of Commerce disseminates purely commercial information, whereas the Department of State rarely disseminates the political information which may have a direct bearing thereon. I hope that it may be possible to find means of treating these related subjects concurrently, by bringing them to a correct focus in the Department of State and charging that department with their appropriate utilization.

"By this suggestion I do not desire to leave the impression that the Department of State is in any wise

partment of the Interior and the Bureau of Education. I was recently telling some educational group at the Bureau of Education that few men can write such readable reports of education as these consular agents give us. Just how accurate they are I do not know; but they are straightforward and unusually readable. Some of you probably know that at the last meeting of the National Education Association a resolution was passed asking Congress to provide for educational attachés at the various legations, showing the growing desire which the educators of this country have for accurate information about education in foreign countries."

At present there is a bill pending (H. R. 5568, 68th Cong., 1st Sess.) for the creation of Agricultural Attachés; another (S. 3357) for the creation of Customs Attachés; and still another (H. R. 4517) for giving permanent character to the commercial attaché and trade commissioner service of the Department of Commerce.

[13]Sen. Doc. No. 190, 66th Cong., 2nd Sess.

grasping or that there is a tendency on its part to usurp the functions or absorb the work of other departments; it is seeking their aid rather than coveting their authority. The situation which I am attempting to reveal demands a substantial broadening and intensification of work and a coordination of the activities of those departments whose efforts are directed toward the extension of foreign trade; their work must be made contributory to the furtherance of general policy and shaped in deference thereto. In other words, as the Department of State must inevitably direct the foreign policy of the Government, it desires to utilize to the fullest extent the agencies of all other departments. By such means alone would it be possible to reach a maximum of effectiveness in the broad domain of our foreign relations. The old cumbersome methods, with their duplications, their lack of common authority, and their independent operations, ought to be abandoned.

"The Department of State is charged with the conduct of international relations, of which commercial intercourse is an essential part. Lack of cohesive effort in dealing with foreign trade disintegrates the force of general policy to a like degree." [14]

Secretary of Commerce Redfield stated in his reply to the Senate: "There can be no clear-cut commercial policy carried out by separate bodies that do not interfunction. Any industrial organization composed as is the commercial organization of the Government would fail, for the seeds of decay are planted in the very separateness of the component parts. It is not urged that these bodies should cease to be or that their functions should be altered. There are separate duties belonging

---

[14] Letter dated January 22, 1920; see Sen. Doc. No. 190, 66th Cong., 2nd Sess., p. 8.

to each, although many of those duties lie in a common field with the Department of Commerce." [15]

Report of the Bureau of Efficiency.—On January 26, 1920, the Bureau of Efficiency rendered an extensive report on the foreign trade promotion work of the various departments, which contained specific recommendations, but these were not given effect.[16]

At present a subcommittee of the Committee on Appropriations of the House of Representatives is understood to be studying this question in its bearing upon expenditures.

Administrative coordination attempted.—Honorable Wilbur J. Carr, writing in February, 1921, has thus described a practical administrative effort which had been lately undertaken with a view to coordinating the interdepartmental system in Washington:

"Early in 1919 the Secretary of State addressed a communication to the heads of all other executive departments, boards and commissions dealing directly or indirectly with questions of foreign trade, inviting each to designate a liaison officer to spend one or more days of each week in the office of the Foreign Trade Adviser of the Department of State. It was suggested that these

---

[15]Letter dated October 30, 1919; see Sen. Doc. No. 190, 66th Cong., 2nd Sess., p. 43.

[16]The recommendations of the bureau were:

"(1) That all resident foreign trade agents of the United States Government stationed abroad shall be assigned to the Department of State.

"(2) That all departments contemplating sending trade investigators or other trade agents abroad shall first confer with the Secretary of Commerce, who should be given full power to determine the lines of all trade investigations to be conducted in foreign countries.

"(3) That all Government agents abroad whose work regularly or incidentally results in the collection of foreign trade information of any description, be required to send the data thus collected to the Department of Commerce, through the Department of State, for publication and dissemination by the Department of Commerce or for transmission to other branches of the Government service for such use as they may deem proper."
—House Doc. No. 650, 66th Cong., 2nd Sess.

liaison officers would constitute a more or less informal interdepartmental board or weekly conference. This would eliminate duplication of effort, expedite the handling of matters calling for interdepartmental consultation, and harmonize the work of the various governmental agencies in Washington in economic matters. This suggestion was adopted." [17]

Mr. Carr continued: "The Economic Liaison Committee, as it has come to be called, has met every Wednesday morning since March 26, 1919. It has proved a success. To expedite the exchange of information, the members of the committee have been made the recipients for their respective departments of the consular and diplomatic economic reports referred to them by the Department of State. They interchange manuscript material in frequent informal conferences among themselves. They have eliminated much duplication of work through a system of monthly reports by which the developments and work in connection with foreign trade of each of the sixteen bodies represented on the committee are presented briefly before the regular weekly meetings. These reports are mimeographed and circulated among the responsible executive heads in each department. By means of subcommittees, the main committee investigates particular problems arising in our foreign relations on the economic side. The conclusions and recommendations appended to the reports of these subcommittees are always presented in alternative form, unless no differences of opinion have been discoverable. The findings of the committees are not binding on the executive heads, but plainly cannot be without a very considerable influence." [18]

[17]Hon. Wilbur J. Carr, in an article entitled "To Bring Our Foreign Service Up to Date," published in *The Independent*, Feb. 26, 1921.
[18]*Ibid.*

Since the disintegration of the office of Foreign Trade Adviser later in the year 1921, the activities of the Liaison Committee have diminished in importance and much of their original utility and significance has been lost.

As an important phase of the problem of interdepartmental cooperation is involved in the relations of the Department of State with the Department of Commerce, it seems appropriate to examine in some detail the outstanding issues that have developed in this connection.

A table of preliminary data.—The Consular Service is composed of 510 consular officers, and 2,412 clerks and other employees, making a total foreign personnel of 2,922. It maintains 408 consular offices in 87 countries (including outlying colonial possessions) which embrace all important regions of the world. The total amount expended for the Consular Service for the fiscal year 1924 was $4,995,426.38. The fees collected by the service during the same period amounted to $6,548,-001.30, or $1,552,574.92 in excess of the cost of the service.

The foreign representation of the Department of Commerce is composed of 14 commercial attachés, 42 trade commissioners, 34 assistant trade commissioners and 134 clerks and other employees, making a total foreign personnel of 225. There are 40 offices maintained in 35 countries (including outlying colonial possessions). The total cost of the foreign representation of the Department of Commerce for the fiscal year 1924 was approximately $1,000,000. No fees were collected.

Consular services for the Department of Commerce. —The Consular Service supplied the following material to the Department of Commerce for its use in 1923:

Voluntary trade reports.............................. 15,000
Trade reports requested by the Department of Commerce. 15,000
Copies of direct answers to trade inquiries............ 36,300
World Trade Directory Reports..................... 21,411
Trade opportunities................................. 3,453
Miscellaneous material............................. 2,200
    Total number of services in the form of material
      submitted.................................. 93,364

The Department of State and the Department of Commerce.—The relations between the Department of State and the Department of Commerce have encountered two spheres of conflict; one at home, involving the departments themselves, and the other abroad, involving the consular service and the corps of commercial attachés and trade commissioners.

Friction at home.—Formerly there existed in the State Department a Bureau of Trade Relations which was organized in accordance with the Act of February 14, 1903, as a connecting link with the Department of Commerce.[19] It dealt with the commercial activities of consular officers upon whose reports the Bureau of Manufactures [20] was almost wholly dependent for its information and for the material contained in its publication, "Daily Consular and Trade Reports." [21] The functions of the two bureaus, which were never clearly delimited, and which were still further blurred by the existence of a third bureau (Bureau of Statistics), often overlapped, giving rise to charges of administrative encroachment and non-cooperation.

In 1912, an investigation of this situation was made by the President's Commission on Economy and Efficiency, which recommended the consolidation of the three bureaus into a single Bureau of Foreign and Domestic Commerce. Accordingly, the Bureau of Sta-

[19]See page 158.
[20]Now the Bureau of Foreign and Domestic Commerce.
[21]Now issued weekly as *Commerce Reports.*

tistics and the Bureau of Manufactures, both in the Department of Commerce, were merged under the above designation, and appropriations for the maintenance of the Bureau of Trade Relations in the State Department were cut off, thus effectually terminating its existence.

As the study of commercial and economic conditions is essential to an understanding of foreign political questions, there soon arose in the Department of State an Office of Foreign Trade Adviser, under the direction of consular officers and economists, whose duty it was to follow important economic developments abroad in their relation to the conduct of the war. This work was carried over into post-war conditions, whereupon conflicts again arose with the Bureau of Foreign and Domestic Commerce, with the eventual result that the Office of Foreign Trade Adviser was, in June, 1921, disintegrated by action of the Secretary of State, and its economists assigned to the various geographical or political divisions, where their work continues as a part of the regular, analytical activities of the department.

Remnants of important duties relating to the commercial work of the consular service were then grouped into an administrative unit and assigned to the jurisdiction of the Director of the Consular Service under the designation, or departmental symbol, "DC-2." [22]

This unit is now the point of contact with the Bureau of Foreign and Domestic Commerce, its work being purely administrative.

Friction abroad.—In the meantime, first the commercial agents (later known as trade commissioners), and then the commercial attachés of the Department of

---

[22] With the abolition of the office of Director of the Consular Service and the elevation of Hon. Wilbur J. Carr to the position of Assistant Secretary of State, the designation is now changed to "A-C-C."

Commerce, were sent abroad with duties indistinguishable from those of consular officers with respect to trade matters. In every phase of the commercial work of the two services there appeared to be duplication of effort and of material, and an overlapping of functions; the one reporting directly to the Department of State, and the other reporting directly to the Department of Commerce.[23]

The commercial attachés set up separate offices and the trade commissioners traveled about. But as an independent agent of this government has no official status in any foreign country except as a part of the recognized establishment for the conduct of foreign relations, the facilities of the commercial attaché were found to be greatly restricted, whereupon his office was moved to the embassy or legation.[24]

In this position there naturally developed a form of direct contact between foreign governments and these agents of a domestic department which is not concerned in the conduct of foreign relations. This seemed to cross the wires of diplomacy; to bring into the diplomatic machinery an extraneous element in the form of a representative who bore no responsibility in matters of international policies, and yet was free to work through its official channels in direct relation with foreign governments.[25]

---

[23]"Nevertheless, it is believed that friction, inefficiency, and real danger to the harmony of international relations, may result if two independent departments of the Government are allowed to maintain diplomatic or consular representatives in the same foreign state. For, disguise it as you will, commercial attachés are now performing consular functions while they enjoy an anomalous diplomatic status."—National Civil Service Reform League, "Report on the Foreign Service" (1919), p. 95.

[24]As contact with the political work of the mission seems to have had a tendency to divert attention from purely commercial subjects, some have recently been moved back to independent offices.

[25]Senator Lodge: "There have been cases, I know—I do not care to go into them—where representatives of one of the other outstanding things,

Suggested remedies.—There have been many discussions and attempts to find a solution to this situation.[25a] It has been suggested that the commercial attachés should be transferred to the State Department; and again, that the Consular Service should be taken over by the Department of Commerce. Neither of these expedients seemed practicable, however, and both may now be considered as abandoned.[26]

The Consular Service is an essential arm of the State Department and all its vast range of activities, including its work along economic lines, belongs primarily to that department, as these are valued first in their relation to foreign affairs.[27]

I will not say what, have gotten in their heads the idea that they were representing the diplomatic side, and they have made representations to foreign countries which they ought not to have made. That is, they ought to be under the head of the mission, and first report to him, and get his authority. Otherwise, we may have all sorts of troubles. It is not good organization."—*Congressional Record,* 68th Cong., 1st Sess., p. 7859.

[25a]In 1920 the Committee on Appropriations of the House of Representatives failed to provide for the salaries of commercial attachés, but in the face of a vigorous protest from the business world, the item was restored to the bill. In defending the action of the committee, Hon. Wm. R. Wood of Indiana stated: "We believe the Foreign Affairs Committee or the Commerce Committee, or both, ought to get together and evolve some plan whereby we can get the worth of our money, where there would not be this continual duplication of authority and of money expended on the part of the United States and the attendant friction inherent with this mixed responsibility."—*Cong. Record,* 66th Cong., 2nd Sess., p. 3149.

[26]"Our ambassadors and ministers and consuls must necessarily work together harmoniously under the same direction and any considerable knowledge of the workings of such a system would leave no doubt in anyone's mind that it is impossible that the consular affairs shall be under the direction of any department of the Government except that which directs our foreign affairs."—Elihu Root, Secretary of State, in a memorandum to Mr. Carr, Dec. 19, 1908.

[27]"If Consuls possessed no other functions they would justify the expenditures made for their maintenance because of their usefulness in connection with the conduct of our foreign relations, in maintaining constant contact with local foreign officials, business men and individuals, and in enlightening the Department of State on matters relating to foreign policy, the protection of American rights and commercial and other opportunities in foreign lands. Indeed, they are the only officers of the United States abroad maintaining continuous contact with officials and citizens in the localities in which they are stationed in the manner in which diplomatic

The British experience.—In England where the same complex situation arose, a separate department was created to function in the twilight zone between the Foreign Office (State Department) and the Board of Trade (Department of Commerce). This experimental device, known as the "Department of Overseas Trade," cannot be said to have proved altogether successful. Within a period of five years following its establishment in 1917, it was investigated by six royal committees which made various and conflicting recommendations, apparently without finding a satisfactory solution.[28]

In discussing an important aspect of this subject, Sir S. Hoare, who presented the British foreign service reorganization bill in the House of Commons, stated:

"I believe that one of the lessons that we have learned during the War is that in a foreign country the nation can only be represented in face of the foreign Government by a single Department. The Germans tried a different principle, the principle of leaving their military Attachés, their naval Attachés, and their commercial Attachés practically independent of their Ambassadors, and the result was that you had the Ambassador with one policy and you had the Attachés with different policies, and very often diametrically opposite policies, in the same country. Let me give the House one example. There was a moment in the War when the German Minister in Christiania was carrying on some extremely delicate negotiations with the Norwegian Government. At that moment the German Naval Attaché, who had

---

officers maintain contact with foreign governments at the capital cities."— (Hon. Wilbur J. Carr, formerly Director of the Consular Service, now Assistant Secretary of State, "What Your Consuls Do," American Consular Bulletin, Jan., 1922.)

[28]The Faringdon Committee, 1917; the Tilley Committee, 1917; the Cave Committee, 1919; the Steel-Maitland Committee, 1919; the Holmes Committee, 1920; and the Geddes Committee, 1922.

an entirely different policy, was spending his time in smuggling dynamite bombs through the courier's bag. The House will see at once how hopeless is administration in a foreign country when you have the Ambassador with one policy and some other British official very likely with a totally opposite policy, and I believe that to put the Consular Service under the Board of Trade would mean that the Consular Service, with the Commercial Attaché possibly at the head, would have one policy and the Ambassador very likely would have a divergent policy. On this account I take the opposite view, that, so far from removing the Consular Service from the purview of the foreign service, I go the length of saying that the two services ought to be one single foreign service, that every diplomat ought to have an economic training, and that to many diplomats it would be a great advantage if at some time during their career they had served in one of the great and important Consulates of the world. Incidentally, that, of course, means that the Department of Overseas Trade must come directly under the Foreign Office." [29]

Views of Senator Lodge.—Senator Henry Cabot Lodge recently stated in the Senate: "I think the attachés who have been sent over by the Department of Commerce have done good work, but I think it is very prejudicial to any service to have it broken up into different compartments. This is the Foreign Service of the Government. It all belongs under the State Department. * * *

"I think having different services—some from the Agricultural Department, some from the Department of Commerce—is a bad form of administration. * * * this matter of building up little services in different

---

[29]*Parliamentary Debates, Official Report,* May 21, 1919, vol. 116, p. 285.

branches, just as we had at one time half a dozen little navies, is a bad form of administration."[30]

Unity in the foreign field.—It is of greatest importance in the conduct of our foreign relations that there should be no scattering of forces or confusion of effort either at the source of control in Washington, or at the point of execution abroad. Concentration is the one and absolute prerequisite to success, unity of command being as essential at all times in diplomacy as it was in the action of the allied armies in France. The Department of State, that is, the Secretary of State, as the spokesman of the President—is the only agency of the government authorized or competent to deal with foreign governments. Its functions are discharged through the diplomatic and consular branches of the Foreign Service which, in the nature of the case, must remain where they are, as instruments of the Department of State, quite irrespective of the activities of other departments.

Cooperation with such other agencies as have now penetrated the foreign field presents both human and technical difficulties. So far as the human side is concerned, already a commendable spirit has been developed with every prospect that it may be further strengthened and encouraged. In regard to the technical aspects, an understanding, a policy, and a definite formula of coordination and procedure must be adopted unless such confusion is to be created as will thwart even the best directed human efforts.

Views of Representative Rogers.—Honorable John Jacob Rogers, author of the foreign service reorganization bill, has declared in the House of Representatives: "The State Department is and must inevitably be the

---

[30]*Congressional Record*, 68th Cong., 1st Sess., p. 7858.

medium of communication, both political and commercial, between the United States and the other countries of the world. At one time political questions and commercial questions were largely in separate, water-tight compartments; or, at all events, they did not closely or vitally interrelate. But to-day, there is scarcely a political question arising in our foreign intercourse which is not also commercial, and there is scarcely a commercial question which is not also political. It therefore becomes far more important than in the past that one agency of the Government shall exercise direct supervision and control of the whole problem of foreign intercourse." [31]

Views of the Civil Service Reform League.—The report of the National Civil Service Reform League discusses the issue of divided control as follows: "The work of foreign trade expansion cannot be adequately handled unless each department recognizes and accepts the limitations imposed by the nature of its functions. There cannot be a divided authority in any foreign land. The sole responsibility for the conduct of our foreign relations must centre in the official representatives of the Department of State. If the present system of maintaining quasi-independent commercial attachés is continued, sooner or later some serious difference of opinion will arise and it is likewise possible that a foreign country might take advantage of the departmental difference or rivalry to injure us in our vital interests." [32]

Questionable aspects of trade extension work.—The issue is a complicated one, and has not been simplified by the fact that many prominent authorities have ques-

---

[31] *Cong. Record,* 66th Cong., 3rd Sess., p. 2192.
[32] "Report on the Foreign Service," National Civil Service Reform League (1919), pp. 100-101.

tioned whether, after all, a government can aid effectually in the extension of commerce otherwise than by protecting it diplomatically and maintaining an atmosphere favorable to its development through the removal of obstructions and the cultivation of friendly international relations.[33]

On this point Lord Bryce has expressed serious misgivings, both as to the value and as to the desirability of governmental activities in the commercial domain. He says:

"An experience of many years leads one to believe, first, that Governments accomplish less in the long run for the trading interests of their respective nations than is believed, and, secondly, that they often do harm by inducing their traders to relax their own energy and lose the keenness of their initiative. The dangers to a state and a people, which seem almost inseparable from the mixing of general national policy with the pecuniary interests of business firms or classes, are more serious than is commonly realized. Money can exercise as much illegitimate influence in democracies as elsewhere." [34]

The essential sphere of governmental activity does not lie in the direct extension of trade; it consists rather in the furtherance and protection of commercial rights

---

[33]The last British committee to investigate the Department of Overseas Trade, which was composed of prominent business men, recommended in part as follows: "It appears to us that this sort of canvassing is absolutely outside the scope of ordinary Government business, and ought not to be paid for by the taxpayer. * * * Indeed, so far as large firms are concerned, we are satisfied that through their own agents they are quite able to handle their own business affairs, and so far as small firms are concerned, we understand it is done to a large extent through Associations to which they subscribe or by their own individual efforts. We are convinced that a Government Department in this country which has no financial responsibility in suggesting or recommending operations to the mercantile community will do no practical good."—Second Report of Committee on National Expenditure (Cmd. 1582), London, 1922.

[34]Bryce, "International Relations," p. 109.

and the building of a basis of profitable intercourse, which are diplomatic and consular functions. In this sense the work of our foreign representatives is analogous in character to that performed by the governmental engineers in the development of navigation. They do not create commerce, which is quite capable of finding its own way; their duty is to open a channel and maintain it free of sand-bars and snags, thus providing an economic situation favorable to trade. So with the agents of the Government abroad. The treaty structure and the whole fabric of international commercial agreements are of diplomatic origin, while their application, their interpretation, and all interventions or representations invoking them, or urging the recognition of rights acquired through them, are exclusively the functions of diplomacy. One constructive foreign policy, or diplomatic action, can do more to broaden the opportunities for international commerce than could be accomplished through the efforts of any known number of commercial representatives, or any measurable volume of published trade intelligence.[35] Dependable commerce is not possible where a favorable diplomatic atmosphere does not exist. The work of the State Department and of the Foreign Service is, therefore, a prerequisite and a continuing necessity in the development of profitable trade relations.

---

[35]"The relation between world trade and world politics is now so close that it is hardly possible to draw a line between political activities which are purely political and those which have an ultimate effect upon commercial relations. The duties of diplomatic officers at the present time are so closely related to the commercial and economic interests of their countries that it can certainly be said that their work has a direct relation to the foreign commerce of the United States and is an essential instrumentality in its promotion. * * * In the extension of foreign trade it should not be overlooked that the role of diplomacy is almost a preponderant one."— Robert Lansing, Secretary of State, Letter to the Senate, Jan. 22, 1920, in response to Senate Res. 203, 66th Cong., 2nd Sess., Sen. Doc. No. 190, p. 5.

An economic basis versus paternalistic aid.—The services performed by the Government in the extension of trade may be grouped broadly into three categories, namely: the publication of general information; the circularizing of firms known to be interested in particular matters; and direct aid to individual business concerns. Thus far these services have all been performed gratuitously.

There being no tangible method of appraising the results of such activities, little is known of their true value, and therefore no dependable estimate can be made as to the proportion of waste involved. Under these circumstances it is exceedingly difficult for Congress to act with enlightened discretion in the matter of providing appropriations.

As business interests which are of sufficient importance to engage in export trade are amply able, and would doubtless be quite willing, to pay reasonably for such services as are profitable to themselves, there appears to be no good reason why the system should not be made to yield sufficient revenue to cover its own expense, as in the case of the consular service. Indeed, the very test of its value would seem to lie in whether or not it can be placed on an economic basis instead of on a basis of subsidy. The only theory on which these services may not be sold for their cost is that they are not worth their cost, and are therefore a waste of public money.

Furthermore, a system of fees would tend to stimulate the initiative of exporters in their own behalf and as rapidly as they could render themselves independent of the Government in the conduct of their own business affairs they would do so.

The present method is paternalistic, tending to decrease their self-reliance and to place upon the Government responsibility for their failures. If the Government, by the expenditure of several million dollars per annum, can develop export trade by maintaining agents abroad for the gathering of foreign commercial intelligence, surely we should expect from a national business organization no less success in the same field. But so long as the Government is willing to act gratuitously and to assume the blame, every encouragement will doubtless be given for it to monopolize the work of foreign trade extension, thus throwing this vital phase of our commerce more and more out of business channels and more and more into governmental hands. Such a maladjustment could not cope with the organized business methods of our chief competitors. On what theory is paternalism in foreign trade defensible when the same principle is so jealously excluded from the domestic field as stifling to normal business?

As rapidly as possible the Government should shift the responsibility for the direct extension of trade to business hands, concentrating its powers and its influence on the legitimate functions of supplying general information, protecting and safeguarding established commerce, and opening up new opportunities through diplomatic action.

There are, of course, certain classes of material which the Foreign Service is in a peculiarly favorable position to supply, and which can be obtained through no other established agency or medium. Even greater emphasis than heretofore should be placed on this work.

The basis for a system of fees.—A statistical check-up on the present system would either prove its value or reveal its shortcomings; it would disturb nothing that is worthy of perpetuation, but would eliminate the waste involved.

There are eight classes of services susceptible of being placed upon a basis of fees which, in proportion to their value, should yield supporting revenue. They are as follows:

1. *World trade directory reports.*—These are in the nature of specific information relating to the character and standing of foreign firms. While they do not purport to vouch for the credit rating of such firms, important facts are given as a guide to American exporters, the data being gathered and the reports compiled almost exclusively by consular officers. Each such report entails considerable investigation abroad and should be assimilated with other consular services on a basis of fees.

2. *Foreign trade opportunities.*—The representatives of both the Department of State and the Department of Commerce report foreign trade opportunities which may be of interest to a single firm, or to several competing firms. Notice of these is either published or transmitted to interested exporters confidentially. The trade opportunity service could be placed on an annual subscription basis, and in the case of non-subscribers, a separate fee could be exacted for the information supplied in each case.

3. *Foreign tariffs.*—Information regarding foreign tariffs is gathered from three main sources: (a) from consular officers, (b) from the representatives of the Department of Commerce, (c) from the International Bureau for the Publication of Customs Tariffs at Brussels, Belgium, to which the United States Government is an adhering member.

The Department of Commerce issues a quarterly

publication entitled "Foreign Tariff Notes" which consists mainly of compiled material reprinted from "Commerce Reports," regarding changes in foreign tariffs. It also issues a "Foreign Tariff Series," consisting of monographs relating to the tariff or customs regulations of a single country, or dealing with the tariff on related classes of commodities in several countries.

It would seem fitting that all specific and compiled foreign tariff information should command an appropriate fee. A subscription service of foreign tariff information could be administered with ease.

4. *Foreign commercial laws.*—Information is gathered by the Consular Service and by the representatives of the Department of Commerce relative to foreign commercial laws. This service, like that of foreign tariffs, could easily be placed on a subscription basis with a schedule of specific fees for material supplied to non-subscribers.

5. *Commodity questionnaires.*—Many requests are received from individual sources or from groups of manufacturers and exporters for investigations into the foreign trade status of commodities in which they are interested. Some of these relate to a single country, some to several countries, and some to the entire world. The circular *questionnaires* sent out for this purpose vary in length from half a dozen simple questions to more than a hundred complex and technical items. Both the consular service and the representatives of the Department of Commerce gather the information, which is submitted in report form and coordinated in the Department of Commerce.

A schedule of fees for these surveys could be adjusted to the importance of the work involved, taking into consideration both the length of the *questionnaire,* and the extent of the territory to be covered.

6. *"Commerce Reports."*—This publication, which is compiled from consular reports and the reports of the representatives of the Department of Commerce, is issued weekly, and copies are circulated at an annual subscription charge of $3.00 in the United States and $5.00 abroad. This subscription charge does not cover the entire cost of printing. It would seem that a publication of this character, which gives current commercial information gathered from all parts of the world at a cost of hundreds of thousands of dollars to the Government, might be placed on a subscription basis several times as high as that now required without unduly burdening those who profit of its contents.

7. *Special publications.*—Various circulars and bulletins, handbooks and monographs are issued by the Department of Commerce, based upon the material supplied by its own representatives and by consular officers. The circulars and bulletins are usually distributed widely without charge, while the handbooks and monographs are sold at prices ranging from five cents to twenty-five cents, but mostly at ten cents per copy. These figures could easily be adjusted to cover the cost of publication in each case.

8. *Trade letters.*—Replies to individual trade inquiries by consular officers and the representatives of the Department of Commerce cover a wide range of material gathered from foreign sources. Some of these are general in character, while others are correspondingly specific and detailed. In all cases where the information thus transmitted is seen to be of definite value, and to have been gathered at some expenditure of effort, a fee should be charged. As copies of all an-

swers to trade inquiries written by consular officers are transmitted to the Department of Commerce, it would not be a difficult matter to assess an appropriate fee within a given range.

It is pertinent here to observe that according to the established tariff of consular fees, a consul is required to make an additional charge of $1.00 per hour or fraction thereof for services rendered outside the consulate. Answering a specific trade inquiry often requires many hours of outside work and yet no fee of any description is charged for either the material gathered or the time, no matter how valuable the former may have been to the interested person.

The Department of State and the Department of Agriculture.—The relation between the Department of State and the Department of Agriculture, while of ever increasing importance, are far less complicated and involved than are those which have been described in connection with the Department of Commerce.

Here we find a wide field of cooperation, but one in which there is no overlapping of functions, and very little duplication of effort or material.

The Department of Agriculture depends upon four main sources for its data regarding agricultural developments in foreign countries: (a) its own agents; (b) the International Institute of Agriculture at Rome, Italy; (c) the Consular Service; and (d) the agents of the Department of Commerce.

Agricultural agencies.—The foreign representatives of the Department of Agriculture are invariably specialists in particular phases of agricultural work and are sent abroad for the accomplishment of definite tasks of a scientific or technical character. Some two hundred and thirty of these, including collaborators and employees, are assigned to such duty annually, about one hundred and fifty being stationed in Alaska and the insular possessions of the United States and ninety in foreign countries.

As the Consular Service maintains no offices within our own territorial, or insular possessions, its field of operation in foreign countries is not intensively covered by agricultural agents and therefore the duties devolving upon it are correspondingly important and exacting. The International Institute of Agriculture assembles statistics and makes reports on the principal crop producing and consuming areas of the world with regard to the major agricultural products. Some twenty-five such areas are covered in the telegraphic communications of the institute. This material is said to be of the greatest value to the Department of Agriculture in judging general conditions, but apart from the keystone crops and the principal centers of consumption with which it deals, there remain many subjects of interest and importance on which the institute does not report.

Consular cooperation.—The reports of consular officers, therefore, are used both as a check against the data supplied by the Institute of Agriculture, and as complementary thereto with respect to other phases and areas of agricultural activities on which regular and systematized data are required. Consular reports on agricultural subjects are transmitted at the rate of about 400 a month,[36] and form in the aggregate some twenty per cent of all agricultural information received from foreign sources.

---

[36]Statement of Dr. Louis G. Michael, Foreign Agricultural Economist, before the Committee on Interstate and Foreign Commerce.—Hearings on H. R. 4517, 68th Cong., 1st Sess., p. 87.

But in addition to issuing agricultural reports, consular officers perform several important administrative functions for the Department of Agriculture, such as assisting in the enforcement of plant quarantine and insecticide and fungicide regulations. To their efforts are also due, in large measure, many of the successful and profitable results achieved by the Office of Foreign Seed and Plant Introduction of the Bureau of Plant Industry, in the matter of introducing into the United States exotic fruits, flowers, grains and vegetables.[37]

Method of cooperation.—In procuring agricultural information of a specific character through the Consular Service, the present practice is for the Department of Agriculture to supply printed or typewritten forms or *questionnaires* which are mailed out with appropriate instructions from the Department of State. The Foreign Service Section of the Bureau of Agricultural Economics acts as a contact agency with the Department of State in transactions of this character. There is, as yet, no separate contact office in the Department of State for the development of this work, all reports on agricultural subjects being handled by "A-C-C," which

---

[37]Dr. David Fairchild, Chief Plant Explorer of the Department of Agriculture has stated, in describing the work of the Office of Foreign Seed Introduction: "This organization in the Department of Agriculture is peculiarly a result of the helpful and friendly assistance of our diplomatic and consular officials abroad and the chiefs of the Consular Bureau of the State Department in Washington, who have in every possible way facilitated the foreign work. The pages of the sixty-five printed 'Inventories of Plants Imported' are filled with references to the work done by our consuls, either on their own initiative, in answer to requests from Washington, or to aid our Agricultural Explorers when abroad, to whom they have been of the greatest assistance and encouragement, going out of their way to assist them with advice and support whenever they got into difficulties. They have made expeditions into the remote corners of their districts to get plants which we were anxious to secure, and they have interviewed in our interest hundreds of foreign plant experts and furnished their opinions for publication regarding valuable plants and their uses."—*American Consular Bulletin,* August, 1921.

is the same administrative unit as in the case of the Department of Commerce.

"In our plan of coordination we aim at eliminating useless duplication by furnishing the Consular Service with *questionnaires* pertaining to specialized agricultural products or specialized phases relative to production, consumption, etc., of these products that are not covered by the work of the International Institute." [38]

The Department of State and the Treasury Department. —The relations with the Treasury Department present still another character of cooperation. Here the Consular Service is engaged in performing administrative duties having to do with the documentation of foreign merchandise, and the detection of customs frauds, evasions, and undervaluations which deprive the Government of legitimate revenue.

Experience is said to show that approximately ninety per cent of the undervaluation of foreign merchandise is of a technical character as distinguished from deliberate misrepresentation with fraudulent intent.

Customs representatives.—The customs representatives sent abroad by the Treasury Department are experts in tariff matters and their work is directed towards the correction of all forms of irregularity under the law. As the documentation of all merchandise intended for export to the United States is performed in the consulates, the Treasury agents act in direct and continuous relation with consular officers, through whom they are afforded facilities for carrying on their investigations. The technical nature of such work necessarily requires all consular officers to devote considerable attention to

---

[38]Statement of L. G. Michael, Hearings before the Committee on Interstate and Foreign Commerce on H. R. 4517, 68th Cong., 1st Sess., p. 87.

the details of customs procedure which forms a part of their regular duties.

A plan of cooperation.—By way of developing these functions and affording to the Treasury Department a now under way which contemplates the application of maximum of effective cooperation, an arrangement is several important principles of collaboration.

According to the present understanding, all consular instructions relating to customs matters are to be codified and consolidated into a single general instruction for easy reference. In the Department of State a contact office is to be established under the direction of a consular officer of field experience who will specialize in this phase of consular administration. Correspondingly, a contact office is to be designated in the Treasury Department, thus providing a channel for the informal transaction of current business.

Instruction facilities afforded.—The Treasury Department has provided facilities in the Customhouse in New York for the reception of consular officers on visit to the United States, and the State Department is to detail such officers to the Customhouse for several days during their periods of leave in order that they may receive first-hand instruction in the problems of customs administration. The Department of State will also afford to the officials of the Treasury Department facilities for appearing before the Foreign Service School and instructing new appointees in all essential phases of the customs work. Furthermore, it affords to the customs representatives abroad facilities for laying before the appropriate supervising consuls general, or Foreign Service inspectors, any deficiencies in consular practice relating to customs matters which may have been noted within their jurisdictions. In this manner the supervisory control may be exercised for the correction of defective practices and for giving effect to the wishes of the Treasury Department.

The valuation of work.—On the other hand, the Treasury representatives are required to report all cases of effective assistance rendered by consular officers, and the Treasury Department undertakes to valuate such assistance; for example, to report to the Department of State that information revealed by a consular officer has led to the detection of undervaluations, or frauds, the correction of which has netted the United States Treasury a given sum of money in added duties.

The technique of this arrangement lies in the connection here established between the efficiency record of the officer and his duties for another Department. A stimulus is thus afforded for winning distinction and promotion in the performance of such duties.

A system of cooperation abroad.—Following a recent understanding arrived at in conference between representatives of the Department of State and the Department of Commerce, with other departments agreeing, the President has prescribed rules and regulations in the form of an important Executive order which seems destined to reduce appreciably the chances of interdepartmental controversy arising from conflicts of authority and duplication of effort in the foreign field.[39] It provides for a fortnightly conference under the direction of the diplomatic chief of mission, of all foreign representatives of the United States stationed in the same city, for the purpose of securing a free interchange of information bearing upon the promotion and protection of American interests. Complete inventories of all

[39]Executive order of April 4, 1924.

economic and trade reports in preparation or in contemplation are to be exchanged at these conferences. There is also provided a definite system for the regular exchange of material and for collaboration in the preparation of reports.

In all cases of collaboration, or where material supplied by one officer is utilized by another, full credit therefor is to be given.[40]

Following the promulgation of the Executive order, the Departments of State and Commerce issued to their respective foreign representatives an identic instruction, precising the manner in which such credit is to be given.[41]

Coincidental with the promulgation of the Executive order, the following explanatory statement was issued by the White House:

"It is the purpose of the Executive order herewith promulgated to establish in the foreign service of the United States the basis for a coordination of effort in advancing American economic and commercial interests which will eliminate unnecessary duplication of work and encourage representatives of this Government in foreign countries to cooperate more fully in the accomplishment of their respective missions. The order does not modify the existing functions of the several executive departments, nor will it affect any changes hereafter made in these functions by subsequent act of Congress. As originally proposed it applied only to relations between foreign officers of the Department of Commerce and the Consular Service. In its perfected form it is reciprocal in nature and all inclusive in scope, placing alike upon all representatives of this Government abroad the responsibility to assist their colleagues of the

---

[40]See Appendix I.
[41]*General Instruction Consular*, May 24, 1924.

foreign service in the performance of all regularly assigned duties.

"It may be appropriately stated that the regulation of interdepartmental relations in the foreign field as herewith ordered is in harmony with the effort now proceeding through the Bureau of the Budget and the Joint Congressional Committee on Reorganization to realize a balance in administrative relations which will conserve the public funds. It is confidently expected that in effect this regulation will give purposeful unity to the activities of this Government in foreign countries, and in so doing will give additional impetus here at home to the endeavor being made to practice intelligent economy in public expenditures through coordination of the work of the several executive departments.

"In this matter the Executive has had the friendly and most helpful counsel of Members of the Congress acquainted with the practical phases of administrative problems in the foreign service." [42]

The urgent need for interdepartmental reform.—"One of the most pressing needs of our Government is an adequate reorganization and coordination of the various departments, boards, and commissions concerned in the supervision and control of our foreign affairs. Some fifteen authorities practically independent in action issue orders and regulations affecting our international relations. Each one of these intends to maintain a close cooperation with the State Department and with the other branches of the government, but in practice the results are far from satisfactory." [43]

It has been urged that Congress should clarify the

---

[42]Cong. Rec., 68th Cong., 1st Sess., p. 7779.
[43]Report of the National Civil Service Reform League on "The Foreign Service" (1919), p. 91.

interdepartmental situation by legislative enactment, but until a workable solution is found, such a course does not appear feasible as it could be accomplished only by the application of an arbitrary formula. Again, it has been argued that the solution rests with the executive departments in arriving at a basis of cooperation among themselves. These divergent views merely confirm the fact that no acceptable formula has been found, for neither Congress nor the departments would hesitate to act were a suitable course of action to be discovered.

Composite nature of the problem.—The chief difficulty seems to lie in the fact that so far the problem has been dealt with in fragmentary form as occasion arose, the broad issue of foreign representation not having been visualized as a composite whole. It is obvious that a number of departments must send abroad, from time to time, technical and scientific experts for specialized investigations, but it is equally obvious that such specialists cannot be planted about over the entire world.[44] The established Foreign Service, therefore, must continue to supply the bulk of material required by other departments, and the Department of State must remain the natural and inevitable center of the interdepartmental system. No formula can succeed which fails to take into account this elementary fact. Any other adjustment would shift the control of foreign relations to the eccentric and upset its equilibrium altogether.

---

[44] "While I am not in the least prepared to dispute the value of highly technical training of that description, and while we are the first to recognize the necessity for experts from the Department of Agriculture, if you will, in foreign countries—stressing the knowledge of technical phases of production, such as this problem that you indicated—but I am inclined to question the necessity for peppering the world with hundreds and hundreds of experts on all forms of commodities."—Dr. Julius Klein, Chief of the Bureau of Foreign and Domestic Commerce, in a statement before the Committee on Interstate and Foreign Commerce, Hearings on H. R. 4517, p. 120.

When other departments desire material from foreign sources, they must either request the Department of State to procure it through the established Foreign Service, or they must send their own representatives abroad.[45] As this necessity is inescapable, why should not the peculiar position of the Department of State be turned to constructive account by utilizing it as the center, or rallying point in a system of coordination?

Coordination or duplication.—Logic would seem to dictate that the established Foreign Service should be utilized to the highest practicable degree and only supplemented by other agencies in so far as its own officers may not be qualified or equipped to perform a given task. But this elementary principle does not seem to be of universal acceptation. Indeed, the recent tendency has been to duplicate or parallel the Foreign Service machinery with an ever increasing number of other agents, not for specialized work, but for the same work that consuls are regularly performing. The growing demand for coordination is due not only to the proportions which this practice has already assumed, but to the evident possibilities of its further and almost unlimited extension. Instead of strengthening and equipping the Foreign Service for its important duties, appropriations which might be applied to that end are diverted to the development of other and competing agencies within the same jurisdiction. A workable plan of coordination is rapidly becoming imperative. Furthermore, such a plan should not be difficult of achievement if conceived with due regard to the necessities of the case. The Department of State must not only cooperate

---

45 Even in the case of the Department of Commerce, which maintains a considerable number of foreign representatives, some 15,000 consular reports on commercial subjects were submitted in 1923 on the specific request of that department.

with other departments; it must interact with them, and its Foreign Service must be directed and administered with special relation to their needs. This means that an interlocking system is a prime necessity; not an artificial and arbitrary device, involving a transference of authority or of jurisdiction, but a common-sense arrangement of economy, efficiency, and mutual assistance.

The interlocking system.—The interlocking of other departments with the Department of State is not a new idea. It was attempted to a limited degree in the operations of the "liaison committee";[46] it is partially expressed in the present adjustment with the Department of Commerce; it functions to a like degree with the Department of Labor in the administration of the passport visa system; it is in operation with the Shipping Board; and it is assuming most encouraging form with the Treasury Department and the Department of Agriculture.

What seems to be required to make it an effective instrument of coordination is that these existing fragments should be gathered together and fitted into a composite whole. The conduct of interdepartmental relations should form a definite functional domain for one of the Assistant Secretaries of State, who should be charged with the duty of coordinating the work of the Foreign Service—especially the consular branch—with that of all other departments of the Government.

Under the Assistant Secretary there should be a separate contact office for each department, the interests of which are of sufficient importance to merit specialized attention. In like manner, in each of the corresponding

---

[46] See page 198.

departments there should be a similar bureau of contact for the transaction of current business with the Department of State on an intimate and informal basis. This group of contact officers, together with their supervisory chiefs, should form an interdepartmental council for the solution of administrative problems.

It should be the duty of each link of contact officers to develop the scope and improve the methods of co-operation, and to draft regulations and instructions to that end for the guidance of officers in the foreign field.

Practical application of the system.—With this general framework of organization, the requirements of each department could be readily ascertained and such administrative action taken as would meet its various needs.

Consular posts in particular areas could be strengthened by the assignment of qualified officers for special duty, as is now the practice in certain instances; special investigations could be undertaken by the detail of such officers as might be necessary, and when occasion required, Foreign Service officers might even be transferred temporarily into the service of other departments.

By way of developing the technical qualifications of Foreign Service officers for such duties, new appointees in the Foreign Service school should be intensively instructed in interdepartmental requirements. To this end a certain number of students in each class might be given topical assignments and specifically designated to familiarize themselves thoroughly with the needs of the interested departments. In this way each specialized subject thus assigned would take the character of a major theme for the young officer eager to distinguish himself by a display of special ability. The law now authorizes the Secretary of State to order Foreign Service officers home on leave and to utilize a portion of their time in the Department of State. By a further application of the foregoing principles, these officers might be assigned the task of studying the needs of a particular department and of applying the results at their posts abroad. Other officers on voluntary leave could be encouraged to give a portion of their time to similar preparation.

By compounding the needs of all departments in this manner, and linking the performance of such duties with the efficiency records of Foreign Service officers as an integral part of their careers, the service would soon demonstrate a surprising degree of specialized ability and an efficient system of interservice functioning would be realized. The established Foreign Service is capable of absorbing in this manner and of performing with ever increasing effectiveness the totality of all usual and regular duties of the Government abroad.

Bibliography.

American Academy of Political and Social Science, 1899: "The Foreign Policy of the United States, Political and Commercial."

Bureau of Efficiency Report, House Doc. No. 650, 66th Cong., 2nd Sess.

Carr, Wilbur J.: "To Bring our Foreign Service Up to Date"; *The Independent*, February 26, 1921.

"Foreign Commerce of the United States, Letters from the Heads of Executive Departments"; Sen. Doc. No. 190, 66th Cong., 2nd Sess.

Institute for Government Research: "Bureau of Foreign and Domestic Commerce, Service Monograph of the United States Government No. 29"; Johns Hopkins Press, Baltimore, 1924.

National Civil Service Reform League: "Report on the Foreign Service"; New York, 1919.

Schuyler, Eugene: "American Diplomacy and the Furtherance of Commerce"; Scribner's Sons, New York, 1886.

CHAPTER VIII

DEFECTS IN THE OLD FOREIGN SERVICE ORGANIZATION

Nature of foreign service deficiencies.—It is not difficult to find the fundamental errors in the old, or rather, the recent organization of the Foreign Service. Honorable Walter Hines Page wrote from his post in London:

"But the realness and the bigness of the job here in London is simply oppressive. We don't even know what it is in the United States, and, of course, we don't go about doing it right. If we did, we shouldn't pick up a green fellow from the plains of Long Island and send him here. We'd train the most capable male babies we have from the cradle." [1]

Lamentations of this character from a great and revered ambassador in the midst of his foreign experiences should arouse us. We know the reproach is merited, and have known it for years. We know that while the attention of our country has been absorbed in domestic affairs—in the application of democratic principles at home—our Foreign Service has remained the prey of spoilsmen, a close corporation for millionaires, and a fundamental contradiction of our most cherished institutions.

President Taft's criticism.—It was not without some feeling on this score that President Taft, in 1910, was moved to declare:

---

[1] Hendrick, "Life and Letters of Walter Hines Page," Letter to Frank Doubleday, Dec. 28, 1913, vol. 1, p. 166.

"We boast ourselves a democratic country. We say that there is no place within the gift of the people to which we may not select the most humble inhabitant, providing he be fit to discharge its duty, and yet we have an arrangement which makes it absolutely impossible for anybody but a millionaire to occupy the highest diplomatic post. Now I ask you whether that is consistency; whether it is not the purest kind of demagogy. By demagogy I mean the advancement of an argument which seems to be in favor of democracy but which, when it actually works out, is in favor of plutocracy." [2]

The first and most important defect in the foreign service, therefore, was the fact that only men of wealth could afford to accept the important posts. This was the result of a system, or practice, which it is easy to illustrate: The American Ambassador at London received an annual salary of $17,500 a year, with no additional allowances of any sort; not even a house to live in. [3]

The British Ambassador at Washington receives an annual salary of $12,500 and an additional lump sum allowance for representation purposes sufficient to bring his total compensation up to approximately $97,350. [4] Besides this, a home completely furnished and staffed, is placed at his disposal.

The difference between these two totals of compen-

[2]Extract from address of President William Howard Taft before the National Board of Trade, Jan. 26, 1910.

[3]An embassy building in London was donated to the U. S. Gov. by J. P. Morgan, and its acceptance authorized by Congress by act of March 2, 1921. Due to delays in altering, repairing and furnishing the building, it is not yet occupied.

[4]Hearings before the Committee on Foreign Affairs, 68th Cong., 1st Sess., on H. R. 17 and H. R. 6357, Statement of Hon. Wilbur J. Carr, pp. 154-155.

sation is what the American Ambassador is expected to pay out of his own pocket for the privilege of representing the United States.

In other words, an American Ambassador is expected to carry the burden of all expenses except those of the office, or chancery.[5]

The testimony of Honorable John W. Davis.—By way of bringing the situation close home, it is enlightening to examine the testimony of Honorable John W. Davis regarding his recent experiences while Ambassador to Great Britain as the successor of Honorable Walter Hines Page under the Wilson administration. He says:

"I am quite sure that my establishment in London was more modest than that of any other ambassador there. My house was not large; my whole establishment was the most modest. I did not do a great deal of entertaining. I only did the entertaining which was indispensable to return the courtesies which I officially received. Of course, you can not always take and never give. You must entertain the officials of the Government who entertain you to be recognized as on a friendly footing with them.

"I paid as rent for my own house $8,000 in round figures—that is, I paid 1,500 pounds sterling, plus rates

---

[5]"The present system is very much as if we were to say to one of our admirals, 'We are appointing you commander in chief of the Atlantic Fleet. You will have a salary appropriated by Congress of $10,000. You will now make a trip around the world, calling at the ports specified by the Secretary of the Navy, doing such entertaining as may be necessary for the good of the service; you will make necessary purchases of provisions, coal, and other supplies, and fight any battles that may be necessary, but you need not render an accounting from any of this, as you will pay it out of your salary.' Nobody would be surprised if the admiral said he was unable to work on these terms—but that is exactly what the Government expects from diplomatic officers to-day."—*Ibid.*, Statement of Hon. Hugh Gibson, U. S. Minister to Poland, p. 19.

and taxes, which are the real estate rents on it; which it cost me every year I was there, roughly. There was also a very low rate of exchange which I had in my favor the whole time, the low rate of exchange on the pound sterling, which went once as low as $3.30 and ran from that to $4.10, and up and down. Living as I was, without any ostentation—it was not a time for ostentation, and had I been a multimillionaire I would not at that particular time, under the circumstances, have indulged in the slightest ostentation whatever; the British people were just coming out of the war, were all distressed, still had the wounds on their persons and were bowed down with financial difficulty, and any man who would have made a display at that time would have made himself unpopular; it was eminently a time for conservatism and quietude—but with all that, living as I was, counting the expenses of myself and family, which is small, it cost me, roughly, three times my salary every year I was there, between fifty thousand and sixty thousand dollars. I do not believe that anybody could possibly have done it, done it decently, with any less expenditure than that. Now, of course, that is not fair." [6]

These same general conditions applied in varying degrees to all the important diplomatic posts of the service, with this exception: that the same salary ($17,500), was paid to all ambassadors; those to Peru, Chile, Cuba, and other countries, where the demands for representation are not so great as in London.

Abuses of the system.—In selecting men to fill these high positions, the President was not actually free, under his constitutional powers, to appoint men of experience and ability, or even those who reflected his own

---

[6] *Ibid.*, Statement of Hon. John W. Davis, p. 208.

political views. His range of choice was restricted, first
of all, to a few men of wealth who were willing to serve,
and spend, and who might, or might not, possess ability
or fitness for the positions; and secondly, he labored
under great political duress.[7]

This state of affairs has at times led to obvious abuse
through the practice of awarding diplomatic appointments to those who have contributed generously towards
the campaign funds of the successful party.[8]

Americans who wonder at the open practice of selling
titles of nobility in England should remember that these
are mere social ornaments, conferring no public authority upon their recipients, or purchasers; whereas, the
barter of important diplomatic positions is a serious
abuse of power, susceptible of jeopardizing the very
security of the nation, to say nothing of humiliating it
before the world.

If ability, experience, or talent were to be gained by

---

[7]Secretary of State John Hay wrote to Prof. G. P. Fisher, July 2, 1902:
"I have made no appointments in the foreign service since I entered the
State Department and the President himself, with all possible good-will, is
hardly ever able to make an appointment upon his own judgment and discretion. All other branches of the Civil Service are so rigidly provided for
that the foreign service is like the topmost rock which you sometimes see
in old pictures of the Deluge. The pressure for a place in it is almost
indescribable."—Thayer, "Life of John Hay," vol. II, p. 193.

"In truth, the President is often forced to send abroad men who are not
in harmony with his own ideals, * * *

"And the very prospect of a possible political appointment leads to
political blackmail. The necessary support for measures of recognized
value can at times be secured only at the price of political barter and
humiliating compromises."—National Civil Service Reform League, "Report
on the Foreign Service" (1919), pp. 52-53.

[8]"Resolved: That the National Civil Service Reform League through its
Executive Committee expresses its earnest remonstrance against the bestowal by the President of high offices of State in return for the contribution of large campaign funds. It must regard any appointment made on
account of such contribution as implying a forgetfulness of the trust conferred upon the Chief Executive, as a violation of the professions upon
which the present Administration came into power and as an example
which, if followed, must lead to the destruction of free institutions."—
Adopted 1893. *Ibid.*, Appendix A, p. 108.

such means, a point of practical justification might be pleaded in defense, but far from producing results so desirable, the political bestowal of diplomatic appointments serves to block the promotion of trained diplomatists, to discourage those who have made diplomacy a life career, and to produce in our Foreign Service such anomalous situations as would be ludicrous were they less shocking. Instances are not wanting where high diplomatic positions have been sought because of the personal sentiments of the applicant for the foreign country in question. In such conditions it might come to pass, especially in moments of international stress, that the American representatives in different countries would very easily take on the color of their environment, producing an inharmony of *pros* and *antis* respecting the affairs of foreign nations, which would render their cooperation with each other impossible and their judgment extremely faulty and undependable.

The result of the system of appointments for so long prevalent in the United States is strikingly shown in the table on page 235, which is taken from the report of the National Civil Service Reform League on the Foreign Service:

"The Diplomatic Corps on August 4, 1914.

(Comparative table showing the diplomatic experience of the representatives of France, Great Britain, and the United States at the important European posts when the European War broke. The table indicates the experience of the respective Ambassadors and Ministers at their posts and the previous training fitting them for the discharge of their duties.)

	Diplomatic Representative	Length of Service at Post Prior to Aug. 4, 1914	Previous Diplomatic Experience
BERLIN			
France	J. Cambon	7 years	10 years
Gt. Britain	Edw. Goschen	6 years	39 years
United States	J. W. Gerard	1 yr. 16 days	0
BERNE			
France	J. B. Beau	3 yrs. 2 mos.	27 years
Gt. Britain	E. M. G. Duff	1 yr. 1 mo.	25 years
United States	P. A. Stovall	1 yr. 2 mos.	0
BRUSSELS			
France	A. Klobukowski	3 yrs. 2 mos.	22 years
Gt. Britain	F. W. Villiers	8 yrs. 6 mos.	21 years
United States	Brand Whitlock	8 mos.	0
CONSTANTINOPLE			
France	L. M. Bompard	5 years	27 years
Gt. Britain	Louis Mallet	10 mos.	20 years
United States	H. Morgenthau	11 mos.	0
LONDON			
France	P. Cambon	16 years	16 years
Gt. Britain	————	————	
United States	W. H. Page	1 yr. 4 mos.	0
PARIS			
France	————		————
Gt. Britain	F. L. Bertie	9 years	22 years
United States	Wm. G. Sharp	2 mos.	0
PETROGRAD			
France	G. M. Paleologue	7 mos.	31 years
Gt. Britain	Geo. W. Buchanon	3 yrs. 8 mos.	35 years
United States	Geo. T. Mayre	1 month	0
ROME			
France	P. E. Barrere	16 years	17 years
Gt. Britain	J. R. Rodd	5 years	25 years
United States	Thos. N. Page	1 yr. 2 mos.	0
TOKYO			
France	A. Gerard	8 years	26 years
Gt. Britain	W. C. Greene	1 yr. 8 mos.	35 years
United States	G. W. Guthrie	1 yr. 3 mos.	0
VIENNA			
France	A. I. Dumaine	2 yrs. 3 mos.	35 years
Gt. Britain	M. W. Bunsen	9 mos.	26 years
United States	F. C. Penfield	1 yr. 1 mo.	12 years
WASHINGTON			
France	J. Jusserand	12 years	26 years
Gt. Britain	C. A. Spring-Rice	1 yr. 4 mos.	31 years
United States	————	————	————

The importance of a trained service.—Every other great nation trains its diplomats to a non-partisan respect for the government and the policies of their own country, and to an objective attitude towards the affairs of other nations.

The National Civil Service Reform League has taken a determined stand in advocacy of a trained diplomatic service in all grades from ambassador down.[9]

However, there is some question as to the extent to which this is immediately possible, because of constitutional barriers. The greatest hope for a true remedy lies in the newly created Foreign Service, where every facility seems to be provided for the development of diplomatic representatives of broad training and experience, and for their advancement to the grades of minister and ambassador on a basis of merit as against the claims of purely political contenders. If the impetus now given to this principle succeeds in enlisting a sympathetic public opinion, a great and constructive step forward will have been achieved.[10]

The inadequacy of diplomatic salaries.—The Diplomatic Service, below the grade of minister, was placed on a civil service basis in 1909, but the stability of its

[9]"At the meeting of the Council of the National Civil Service Reform League, July 26, 1918, President Richard H. Dana, reading a summary of the report of the special War Committee, said:

" 'It seems imperative that the League should take a fearless, uncompromising stand on the application of the merit principle to foreign service all along the line, especially in view of the shameless barter of these positions.'

"The governing body of the League, its Council, accepting the report of the War Committee, voted unanimously:

" 'That the League advocates the extension of the merit principle to all grades of the consular and diplomatic services.' "—*Ibid.*, pp. 45-46.

[10]Secretary of State Hughes, in an address before the American Foreign Service Association on Oct. 1, 1924, declared:

"I feel that our highest posts, those of Ambassadors, will in time be largely filled by men coming up through the legations, through the missions. That is the end to be achieved, to have a career which goes through to the top, and it can be done if we have the feeling through the country that this service is not merely worthy because of its objects or because of the capacity of certain of its members, but because the whole Service is instinct with energy and strength and is fortified by sound preparation and thorough training."—*The American Foreign Service Journal*, Nov., 1924.

merit system rested solely upon the insecure basis of a presidential Executive order.[11]

It had no statutory status, and at any moment might have been swept away or thrown open to political appointments by the stroke of a pen.[12]

The highest paid salary was that of diplomatic secretary, class one, who received $4,000 per annum. Officers of this class were usually designated as counselors of embassy or legation. There was no assurance of promotion to the grade of minister, even after a life-time of training and experience, or by way of recognition either for demonstrated ability or distinguished service. Thus the most to which a diplomatic secretary might reasonably aspire was a salary of $4,000 in a position of subordination to a chief of mission, who, in many cases, possessed no previous diplomatic experience and very little knowledge of the practical workings of foreign relations. The salary range of $2,500 to $4,000 was so inadequate, as measured by the financial requirements of these positions, that appointments were necessarily restricted to young men of wealthy families who were able and willing largely to pay their own way. Thus the applied principle of "plutocracy," to which President Taft referred, extended throughout the entire service.

The income qualification.—Under the British system there was until 1919, a "property qualification" of £400 ($1,946) income per annum required of all candidates for the Diplomatic Service. This was a relic of aristocratic practices, and has now been swept away

---

[11]Executive order of Nov. 26, 1909.

[12]"The executive orders are subject to executive repeal. The only hope for real reform is by removing the appointments from political influence. Not until the executive orders shall be put into the form of legislation by Congress, in response to a strong popular demand, will real and permanent reform in the consular service of the United States be attained."—Foster, "Practice of Diplomacy," pp. 241-242.

by democratic reform. While there was no such acknowledged income requirement in the United States, the administrative result was the same. Secretary of State Hughes has expressed himself with characteristic vigor in condemnation of the anomalous situation thus created:

"It is a most serious thing to be compelled to say that a young man without means, who desires to marry and bring up a family after the American tradition, cannot be encouraged to enter one of the most important careers that the country has to offer. I say bluntly that no American can face the facts without a sense of humiliation, and he is compelled to qualify his boasting of our intelligence and civilization so long as this condition continues." [13]

The same anomalous situation was discussed by Honorable John W. Davis as follows:

"Over and over again, while I was in London, young men and good men in the diplomatic service would come to me in great personal concern and ask me frankly whether I thought they ought to stay in the service. I always asked them what their financial condition was.

"If I found that they had no or at best meager resources beyond their official salary, I told them with great regret that I thought they were doing an injustice to themselves, and that at the earliest opportunity they ought to leave the service and get into something that was not a blind alley." [14]

Limited field of selection.—Very naturally the number of young men who were able to finance a career of

---

[13]Address before the Chamber of Commerce of the United States, May 18, 1922.

[14]Hearings before the Committee on Foreign Affairs on H. R. 17 and H. R. 6357, 68th Cong., 1st Sess., pp. 205-206.

this character was very limited, and the proportion of those who were likely to possess the qualifications of a diplomatist was smaller still. This had the effect of limiting the field of selection to a few willing candidates, and of forcing the acceptance of a goodly number of these in order to fill vacancies. In such circumstances it became exceedingly difficult to enforce a service standard other than to require a reasonable degree of academic education, which is altogether an insufficient test.

In this connection it is interesting to note the results of diplomatic examinations as regards the number applying and the number accepted during the representative years 1919 to 1922. It should be explained that the examination held in Paris in 1919 was a concession to the men of the A. E. F.

Date of Examination	Number Designated	Number Actually Taking	Number Passed	Number Appointed
May 19-21, 1919	17	12	9	9
May 26-31, 1919, at Paris, France.	181	181	24	13
Jan. 26-28, 1920	19	11	7	7
Oct. 18-21, 1920	26	17	13	13
July 11-15, 1921	48	42	17	17
July 10-13, 1922	41	34	12	10
Aug. 16-18, 1922	5	2	1	1
Total	337	299	83	70

Motives and types of candidates.—But aside from practical considerations, the attractions of the service were obvious, as it offered varied experiences of an agreeable and broadening character under the most favorable of auspices; namely, as the distinguished representative of a great nation, to which status, by law and tradition, there attaches a multitude of special privileges and immunities quite beyond the reach of the same individual in his personal capacity.

Thus the desire to enter the service was altogether natural, while the motive in so doing was more likely to be of a frivolous, than of a serious character. To particularize, social affairs rather than foreign affairs were apt to be the source of ambition in this case. This fact is evidenced by the amusing allusion of Honorable Hugh Gibson, United States Minister to Poland (now Minister to Switzerland) in the following extract from his testimony before the Committee on Foreign Affairs:

"We have a small number of men who ought not to be in office and who would not be there if we could offer attractions to better men. They constitute a dead weight on the back of the Diplomatic Service and nobody resents their presence any more than we do, or as much as we do. They are one of our principal problems and until they are removed we are going to labor under a very heavy handicap. You hear very frequently about the boys with the white spats, the tea drinkers, the cookie pushers, and while they are a very small minority, but they make a noise entirely disproportionate to their numbers. * * * Our great problem now is to attract enough men so that we will have a real choice of material and crowd out those incompetents and defectives. If we can do that we can build up the service, but until we can do that we can not hope to do it.

"The Chairman. Until such time as that, two or three men of the type you mention will discredit a whole nation.

"Mr. Gibson. There is no doubt of it.

"The Chairman. As a rule they do not do much work.

"Mr. Gibson. We have some of the type who do not do any work.

"The Chairman. As a rule they are men of inde-

pendent influence, and therefore feel that they are more
or less free from governmental control.

"Mr. Gibson. And they are so long as we can not
get men from whom to choose." [15]

Administrative difficulties.—The hearings at this
point turned to the practical difficulties of administering the service under such conditions:

"Mr. Rogers of Massachusetts. I have heard a story
which will typify the situation which now prevails where
a secretary asked for a year's leave of absence to go
big-game shooting in central Africa. He could not be
spared. He was a pretty good official and there were
no reserves and the leave was denied him. He said, 'All
right, I will go on leave or retire from the service.' They
did not have anybody that they could call in his place,
and therefore they said to him, 'You can have your
year's leave of absence.' I do not know whether you
are familiar with that particular incident, but is not
that the sort of thing that results from the inability to
have first-rate reserves pushing for the opportunity for
appointment as vacancies arise?

"Mr. Gibson. It makes it hard to have a very effective discipline if you can not replace a man when he
should be put out of the service. I have talked at some
length about the undesirables in the service because I
feel that they constitute a serious problem. However,
I hope I have not conveyed the idea that they are numerous. They are not. They constitute a small minority—a very small minority. I can not say a negligible
minority, because they do us too much harm to be ignored. The unfortunate thing is that they discredit the
majority in the eyes of the general public. Having said
so much about them I should like to add a few words

_____

[15]Hearings on H. R. 17 and H. R. 6357, 68th Cong., 1st Sess., pp. 40-41.

about the rest of the service. The large majority of our men make up a group of which we can be very proud indeed. No other branch of the service can show their superiors in ability, industry, devotion, loyalty, and sound Americanism. I don't believe any country has a finer group of men in the classified ranks of the foreign service. If we can offer these men enough to justify them in remaining in the service of the Government and can reinforce them with new men chosen by competition it will not take long to give us by far the best service in the world, and if we are to take proper care of our interests the best will be none too good." [16]

Progress nevertheless.—It is indeed encouraging that under a faulty system, and in the face of so many grave handicaps, the Diplomatic Career Service should have justified itself so amply. John Hay was a diplomatic secretary, to which fact, more than to any other, we owe the great world policy of the Open Door. He was a distinguished ambassador and an able Secretary of State.

Others have won, and are winning, distinction to a degree which augurs well for the future diplomacy of the United States under the vastly enlarged opportunities afforded by the reorganized Foreign Service.

Let us examine the situation as it now stands with respect to erstwhile diplomatic secretaries who have been called to fill the higher grades of ambassador or minister, or the commanding positions in the Department of State.

Ambassadors.—Of the thirteen ambassadorial posts, four are now held by service men:

Honorable Edwin V. Morgan, Ambassador Extraordinary and Plenipotentiary to Brazil.

---

[16] *Ibid.*

Honorable Henry Prather Fletcher, Ambassador Extraordinary and Plenipotentiary to Italy.

Honorable John W. Riddle, Ambassador Extraordinary and Plenipotentiary to Argentina.

Honorable William Phillips, Ambassador Extraordinary and Plenipotentiary to Belgium, which embraces also the position of Envoy Extraordinary and Minister Plenipotentiary to Luxemburg.

Ministers.—Of the thirty-eight posts of minister, thirteen are now filled by men who acquired their training as diplomatic secretaries as follows:

Honorable Hugh S. Gibson, Envoy Extraordinary and Minister Plenipotentiary to Switzerland.

Honorable H. Percival Dodge, Envoy Extraordinary and Minister Plenipotentiary to the Kingdom of Serbs, Croats and Slovenes.

Honorable Hoffman Phillip, Envoy Extraordinary and Minister Plenipotentiary to Uruguay.

Honorable William W. Russell, Envoy Extraordinary and Minister Plenipotentiary to Dominican Republic.

Honorable Arthur Bailly-Blanchard, Envoy Extraordinary and Minister Plenipotentiary to Haiti.

Honorable Peter Augustus Jay, Envoy Extraordinary and Minister Plenipotentiary to Rumania.

Honorable Ulysses Grant-Smith, Envoy Extraordinary and Minister Plenipotentiary to Albania.

Honorable Charles S. Wilson, Envoy Extraordinary and Minister Plenipotentiary to Bulgaria.

Honorable Lewis Einstein, Envoy Extraordinary and Minister Plenipotentiary to Czechoslovakia.

Honorable Fred Morris Dearing, Envoy Extraordinary and Minister Plenipotentiary to Portugal.

Honorable Montgomery Schuyler, Envoy Extraordinary and Minister Plenipotentiary to Salvador.

Honorable Robert Woods Bliss, Envoy Extraordinary and Minister Plenipotentiary to Sweden.

Honorable Irwin B. Laughlin, Envoy Extraordinary and Minister Plenipotentiary to Greece.

Undersecretaries of State.—During the Harding-Coolidge administration, Secretary of State Hughes has selected his chief assistant from the trained diplomatic officers of the service without exception:

Honorable Henry Prather Fletcher, Undersecretary of State, March 7, 1921, to March 6, 1922.

Honorable William Phillips, Undersecretary of State, March 31, 1922, to April 12, 1924.

Honorable Joseph Grew, Undersecretary of State, April 16, 1924 (still in office).

Assistant Secretaries of State.—The same practice has been followed in selecting assistant secretaries of state. It should be noted in this connection that the position of Second Assistant Secretary, which has come to be considered a permanent position, was filled with great distinction by Honorable Alvey A. Adee for forty-two years until his death in July, 1924.[17] Also, that the newly created assistant secretaryship has been filled by the advancement of Honorable Wilbur J. Carr, former Director of the Consular Service, who has served in the Department of State for thirty-two years. The promotion of Mr. Carr constitutes a conspicuous recognition of merit and service experience.

The assistant secretaries who have been selected from the diplomatic service during the Harding-Coolidge administration are as follows:[18]

---

[17]Now filled by Honorable John Van A. MacMurray.

[18]The numerical distinction formerly made between Assistant Secretaries of State was abolished by the Act of May 24, 1924, Sec. 22.

Honorable Fred Morris Dearing, March 11, 1921, to February 10, 1922.

Honorable Leland Harrison, March 31, 1922 (still in office).

Honorable Robert Woods Bliss, March 15, 1921, to January 30, 1923.

Honorable J. Butler Wright, June 11, 1923 (still in office).

Honorable John Van A. MacMurray, November 19, 1924.

But it is not enough that these men have been promoted and that others will follow. As the report of the Civil Service Reform League very justly points out:

"Even more important than the principle of appointing Ministers by promotion from the grade of secretary is the recognition of the need to retain those men who have once received such promotion. At present some of the best men almost prefer to decline promotion for fear they may be beheaded with a change of administration. * * *

"Some objection has been made to the promotion of consuls to Ministers. It has been suggested that consuls would generally prefer to remain as they are; in any event, until the diplomatic service pays a living wage. Without doubt the latter reform is a prerequisite of any real improvement in our diplomatic service." [19]

Deficiencies in the Consular Service.—Turning to the Consular Service, we find a situation which, if less exaggerated with respect to some of the deficiencies noted in the diplomatic branch, was none the less hopelessly limited from the standpoint of opportunities and rewards. The scale of compensation was much higher than that paid in the corresponding grades of the diplomatic

[19] Report on the Foreign Service (1919), p. 58.

service, while the burden of expenditure arising from the nature of the work was generally lighter. So far, these were favorable factors. There were two positions of consul general, class one, which paid $12,000 per annum, and the range in the other classes was from $8,000 downward to $2,000 for principal officers. There was also a corps of vice consuls of career on salaries of $3,000, $2,750, and $2,500, and a corps of consular assistants whose salaries were from $2,000 to $1,500.

The grade of consul general, class one, corresponded in rank to that of counselor of embassy in the diplomatic service, whereas the salaries attaching to these two positions were $12,000 and $4,000, respectively.

Service interchange impossible.—No further evidence is required to demonstrate the impracticability of an interchange of personnel. It would scarcely be feasible to transfer a consul general of high rank to a diplomatic position of like rank on one-third his consular salary. But this was not the only barrier to such transfers. There was an administrative regulation against it.[20]

Again, a young man could enter the Consular Service without a private income, as many did, and live modestly on his earnings, although he could not hope to save from that source. The consular personnel, therefore, was generally unavailable for transfer, as the question of independent means had not entered into their selection

---

[20]Transfers from one branch of the foreign service to another shall not occur except upon designation by the President for examination and the successful passing of the examination prescribed for the service to which such transfer is made. Unless the exigencies of the service imperatively demand it, such person to be transferred shall not have preference in designation for the taking of the examination or in appointment from the eligible list, but shall follow the course of procedure prescribed for all applicants for appointment to the service which he desires to enter. To persons employed in the Department of State at salaries of eighteen hundred dollars or more, the preceding rule shall not apply and they may be appointed, on the basis of ability and efficiency, to any grade of the diplomatic service."
—Executive order, Nov. 26, 1909.

and appointment. In this regard a vast majority of them were not financially qualified for the Diplomatic Service. But it not infrequently happened that an officer in one branch of the service would show marked aptitude and ability for the other. A consular officer might be eminently fitted, and might have demonstrated unusual talent for work of a purely diplomatic character, whereas his aptitude for consular work might have been less distinctive. Conversely, a diplomatic officer might have displayed unusual ability in matters relating to consular practice. While the assignment to duty of both these officers might have been fully recognized as a waste of their best talents, and their careers limited accordingly, they could not be interchanged.

The system of separate administration.—Thus were the two services administered separately and apart—in water-tight compartments, so to speak—while in point of fact they were two branches of the same service, functioning under the same department, in the same foreign field, often in the same city, and along lines as closely related as distinction would permit.[21]

But the Diplomatic Service was effectually closed to consular officers, and being the superior of the two services, there developed a sort of rivalry between them which not infrequently took the form of petty prejudices, producing an atmosphere devoid of the essential spirit of cooperation. Sir S. Hoare, who advanced the British foreign service reform bill, commented upon this

---

[21]"There has long been too great a distinction between the political interests of the Diplomatic Service and the commercial interests of the Consular Service. Both are engaged in political work, and both are engaged in commercial work. You cannot at this time take economics out of diplomacy."—Sec. of State Charles Evans Hughes, Address before the Chamber of Commerce of the United States, Washington, May 18, 1922, Senate Doc. No. 206, 67th Cong., 2nd Sess., p. 9.

point in the House of Commons in urging the principle of interchangeability as follows:

"Take another reason for discontent. * * * Take the fact that, for some purpose or other that I do not understand, the Consular Service is held to be inferior to the Diplomatic Service. The fact that Consuls, many of whom have a unique knowledge of the countries in which they are serving and of the languages of those countries, many of whom are doing work of first importance—the fact that these men see themselves inferior in status to the Diplomatic Service, seems to me to be not only a justifiable cause for discontent within the Service, but an absolutely indefensible position." [22]

The principle of interchangeability. — Honorable John Jacob Rogers, in discussing the purposes of interchangeability, stated the case as follows:

"Usually the young secretary in the past has gone from the law school or the college right into the foreign service. He has had no opportunity to know business or to learn business methods. He has had no advantage in age or experience which gives him a sufficiently level head to withstand the temptations of society abroad. I have seen very young men go into the foreign service. They were incessantly invited out to dinner, feted and treated with distinction by people of fashion and position. They lost their heads and their Americanism at the same time. They lost their sense of perspective and values.

"Do not think that I am speaking of all of them. I fear that I am speaking of a considerable portion of them. Now, if we start in a young man at the consulate he is not going to have a fuss made about him socially—

---

[22] Lieut. Col. Sir S. Hoare: Debate in the House of Commons, May 21, 1919.

he may be in Singapore or on the West Coast of Africa, or in Central America, where there is no society. He will learn business methods. He will acquire poise and sense and discrimination. He will learn to keep his head when later he is on duty at a European capital. He is going to be a more useful man to himself always, and that means that he is going to be a more valuable public servant to the United States. He will have a grasp of business and trade and politics. We shall get rid of the caste system, of a system where the diplomatic side of the service sometimes looks down on the consular side. We shall create a spirit of loyalty to a single unified foreign service and not primarily loyalty to the side of the Service to which the individual member belongs." [23]

Limitations of the consular career.—While promotions from the Diplomatic Service to the grade of minister were sometimes made, as we have seen, no appointments of this character were made from the Consular Service. It is clear, therefore, that the consular service led only to an *impasse,* there being no hope of reward beyond the grade of consul general.

London and Paris were the only two posts of the first class, and when these were filled, more than five hundred aspiring consular officers below that grade found their prospects of a life-time limited to vacancies arising in the $8,000 class, in which there were fourteen officers, or in the $6,000 class, in which there were only ten. As the service, since 1906, has operated on a civil service basis, many of the higher positions had come to be filled by men of long experience but who were advanced in years, many of them beyond the age of active service.[24]

---

[23]*Cong. Record,* Feb. 6, 1923, p. 3203.

[24]"The conditions just described are further aggravated by the fact that as both the diplomatic and consular service have operated on a civil service

There being no provision for retirement, these faithful and valuable representatives could not be dropped, nor could they be relegated to inferior positions, unbefitting the dignified rank which they had won through merit and achievement.

As the hope and prospects of many younger officers were dependent upon room for advancement, the foreclosure of these positions proved destructive of morale and discouraging to the service spirit. In these circumstances, seeing little prospect of rewards, either in distinction and honor or in the matter of money compensation, many of the best officers of the service reached a point where they felt themselves forced to consider other means of providing for themselves and their families. This was a comparatively easy matter for some of them, as the consular career is conspicuously a training ground for men who can succeed in important business enterprises.

The loss of good men.—There are many instances of consular officers being tempted away from the service, in which they were drawing salaries of five or six thousand dollars, by business offers of twenty-five or thirty thousand dollars a year. While some have accepted such positions, others have declined. In the absence of independent means, from the moment a consul entered the service he had a sense of operating under the law of diminishing returns, realizing that he could never hope to save, that he could barely live respectably and fittingly on his salary, and that eventually he would be

basis for a number of years, many positions in the higher grades are now occupied by men of advanced age who can not be removed to make way for younger and more efficient officers. There is no provision for their retirement and yet as their numbers increase from year to year these superannuated officers clog the service, cutting off promotion for all below them."— Secretary of State Charles E. Hughes, *The Congressional Digest*, January, 1924.

confronted with the problem of facing old age without the assurance of continued support. Due to the tropical risk and other hazards incidental to the service exigencies, it was difficult and often impossible to obtain life insurance.

Such meager savings as might be effected through thrift were all expended in returning occasionally to the United States for the purpose of refreshing the viewpoint and regaining the inspiration of the American atmosphere. As the Government bore none of the expense of such visits, a substantial fraction of the consular salary was obligated in advance by the necessity of accumulating a margin from petty savings sufficient to meet the burdens of the next trip home.

In the light of these organic deficiencies, it is easy to appreciate the appeal of Secretary of State Hughes when he inquired:

"Where is the Government to look for its candidates, offering as it does on the one hand an underpaid diplomatic career to which young men of talent and ability cannot aspire in the absence of private incomes, and on the other hand a consular career which is too restricted in its promise of reward to satisfy their legitimate aspirations?" [25]

Bibliography.

Carr, Wilbur J.: "To Bring Our Foreign Service Up to Date"; *The Independent,* February 26, 1921.

Congressional Digest: "Foreign Service Reorganization"; Washington, January, 1924.

Dennis, Alfred P.: "The Foreign Service of the United States"; *North American Review,* February, 1924.

---

[25]*Congressional Digest,* p. 122, Jan., 1924.

Hill, David Jayne: "Shall We Standardize Our Diplomatic Service"; *Harper's Magazine,* April, 1914.

Hughes, Charles Evans: "An Interview" (by Wm. H. Crawford); *World's Work,* June, 1921, p. 129.

MacClintock, Samuel: "A Unified Foreign Service"; *American Political Science Review,* November, 1922.

Osborne, J. B.: "Trade Protection Work of the Dept. of State"; *Pan-American Union Bulletin,* XXXIII, 1134-36, December, 1911.

CHAPTER IX

THE REORGANIZED FOREIGN SERVICE

Legislative objectives.—Taking cognizance of the nature and the extent of Foreign Service deficiencies under the old system, we find that they cover a wide range of maladjustments and fundamental limitations sufficient to stifle the interest both of the public and of those who were inclined to aspire to either branch of the service as a career. In approaching the question of reorganization, therefore, Congress found itself confronted with the following unsatisfactory state of affairs.

The foremost foreign nations had already reshaped their Foreign Service establishments to accord with post-war conditions.

Whereas the United States, for numerous and obvious reasons, requires a Foreign Service as strong as that of any other country, it was recognized that the existing organization had reached the limits of possible development and that it could be improved only by fundamental changes in its legislative status.

The entire adjustment was "plutocratic" and ill-designed to reflect, towards the foreign world, either the realities of American life or the principles for which the country stands.

It was conducive to political abuse and therefore could not command the full public confidence.

It confuted the principle of specialized training, and negatived the value of ability and experience.

It placed the unbiased judgment of the trained an-

253

alyst in a position of inferiority to that of the prejudiced partisan, thus coloring our outlook on international affairs with the tinge of internal differences.

To the popular mind it not infrequently gave to the great art and science of diplomacy the aspect of a social struggle.

There were no rewards commensurate with the efforts required and the qualities demanded.

There was little appeal to strong men, and less incentive to take full advantage of the opportunities of their career than to live in the enjoyment of its petty privileges.

The foundation of the Foreign Service structure was insecure, resting solely upon the basis of an executive order which a partisan wave might have swept away.

Artificial distinctions and awkward barriers were raised on every hand: against the acceptance of men without private incomes; against the transfer of a consular officer to the Diplomatic Service; against the transfer of a diplomatic secretary to the Consular Service; against the elevation of either of these to the higher grades; in other words, against the most elemental attractions for the type of personnel which must constitute the essence of an effective organization

The reorganization act of May 24, 1924.—Addressing itself to the substantial task of meeting these shortcomings the act of May 24, 1924, visualizes four principles of reform:

1. The adoption of a new and uniform salary scale with a view to broadening the field of selection by eliminating the necessity for private incomes and permitting the relative merits of candidates to be judged upon the basis of ability alone.

2. The amalgamation of the diplomatic and consular

branches into a single Foreign Service on an interchangeable basis. This is designed to relieve the limitations of the present consular career and effectually
coordinate the political and the economic branches of
the service.

3. The granting of representation allowances with a
view to lessening the demands on the private fortunes
of ambassadors and ministers and rendering it practicable to promote a greater number of trained officers to
those positions.

4. The adoption of a suitable system of retirement
as the means of maintaining a high standard of efficiency under the merit system.

Amalgamation and interchangeability.—Section 1 of
the act consolidates the Diplomatic and the Consular
Services into a single Foreign Service by providing
"That hereafter the Diplomatic and Consular Service of
the United States shall be known as the Foreign Service
of the United States."

There is then created the new, official designation, or
title, of "Foreign Service officer," which is defined as
denoting permanent officers in the Foreign Service below the grade of minister, all of whom are subject to
promotion on merit, and who may be assigned to duty
in either the diplomatic or the consular branch of the
Foreign Service at the discretion of the President.

Heretofore officers in the Foreign Service have drawn
their salaries by virtue of the fact that they were diplomatic secretaries or consular officers, but under the new
law, salary attaches to the title of Foreign Service officer. In other words, the office of secretary in the Diplomatic Service and that of consul carry no salary. All
diplomatic secretaries and consular officers have been
recommissioned as Foreign Service officers and all fu-

ture appointments to the service will be under that title, which has become the exclusive source of remuneration.

It is stated in Section 4 of the act "that Foreign Service officers may be appointed as secretaries in the Diplomatic Service or as consular officers or both," but as such appointments are made by the President under his constitutional powers, this provision is not mandatory. An officer in the Foreign Service may, and some will, hold three commissions: one as a Foreign Service officer, which controls his salary status; another as consul general, consul, or vice consul, which authorizes and empowers him to act in a consular capacity; and the other as diplomatic secretary, which authorizes and empowers him to perform diplomatic duties. Foreign Service officers assigned to the consular branch will act under their consular commissions; whereas, those assigned to the diplomatic branch will act under their commissions as diplomatic secretaries.[1]

The new title of Foreign Service officer does not, therefore, abolish or supersede the title of diplomatic secretary or consul. It is merely the common source of salary and the hinge of interchangeability.

Interchangeability defined.—Honorable John Jacob Rogers, author of the reorganization bill, has clearly defined the operation of interchangeability as follows:

"I desire if possible to make visual exactly the mechanics involved in this transferability feature. Let us imagine that the diplomatic service is a tall perpendicular pole. Near it and of equal height, but in no way connected with it, let us imagine a consular pole.

"The diplomatic pole has four notches equally spaced

---

[1]"Provided further, That all official acts of such officers while on duty in either the diplomatic or the consular branch of the Foreign Service shall be performed under their respective commissions as secretaries or as consular officers."—Sec. 4, Act of May 24, 1924.

from the bottom to the top. These represent the four promotion and salary classes. The consular pole, strangely enough, has about twenty-five notches more or less equally spaced from the bottom to the top. When a man starts climbing either the diplomatic or the consular pole he necessarily sticks to the one task. No matter how much better he could climb the other pole if given the chance, he is, in practice, never allowed to prove this. Once he starts upon his life climb he is never permitted to transfer across to the other pole. What we are proposing in the reorganization bill is very simple. We are making the two poles into a ladder by putting in 9 rungs, equally spaced from the bottom to the top. Every man now in either branch of the service and found worthy of retention will be placed opposite one of these 9 class and salary rungs. A Consul General of high class or a counsellor of embassy will be placed at the first rung, and so on down, in accordance with considerations of ability and seniority. Those newly taken into the Foreign Service of the United States—which is the name of the ladder we are now creating—will start in on the bottom rung. The rungs serve not only as a convenient basis for classification and for salary scale, but they serve also as a medium by which a man who has been doing diplomatic work can be transferred across for the consular work, or vice versa. The ranks of the consular service and of the diplomatic service having been assimilated there can be no confusion. Every man will be an officer in the Foreign Service of the United States of a particular class and instantly available for work either on the consular side or on the diplomatic side." [2]

---

[2] Address before the International Institute of Politics, Williamstown, Massachusetts, August 21, 1923.

Foreign service officer a statutory title.—There are nine classes of Foreign Service officers, ranging in salary from $9,000 in class one to $3,000 in class nine.

Below class nine there is an unclassified grade into which have been grouped the vice consuls of career, consular assistants, interpreters and student interpreters, who are subordinate officials, and whose salaries range from $3,000 to $1,500.

Appointments to the position of Foreign Service officer are made by the President, by and with the advice and consent of the Senate. The office, however, is of statutory creation, in which regard it differs from that of diplomatic secretary (public minister), or consul, which are both constitutional. The distinction is of noteworthy importance in that it marks the final evolution of the service to a basis of stability and permanence. Heretofore the examination tests required of candidates have been in the nature of self-imposed restraints upon the President, which he might at any time waive or modify by a special or general Executive order. The power was his alone to decide whom he should appoint as diplomatic secretary or consul, subject only to confirmation by the Senate. But the same is not true of Foreign Service officers. The Constitution makes no mention of such positions, nor are there any powers or duties attaching to the office which would confuse it with the office of public minister or consul. In fact, it has no duties at all, and there is not a single act that can be performed under the title of Foreign Service officer except that of receipting and accounting for official salary. Therefore, the position being a statutory office, Congress was free to prescribe qualification requirements, and to stipulate under what conditions appointments should be made. This it has done as follows:

Conditions of appointment.—"That hereafter appointments to the position of Foreign Service officer shall be made after examination and a suitable period of probation in an unclassified grade or, after five years of continuous service in the Department of State, by transfer therefrom under such rules and regulations as the President may prescribe: Provided, That no candidate shall be eligible for examination for Foreign Service officer who is not an American citizen: Provided further, That reinstatement of Foreign Service officers separated from the classified service by reason of appointment to some other position in the Government service may be made by Executive order of the President under such rules and regulations as he may prescribe.

"All appointments of Foreign Service officers shall be by commission to a class and not by commission to any particular post, and such officers shall be assigned to posts and may be transferred from one post to another by order of the President as the interests of the service may require: Provided, That the classification of secretaries in the Diplomatic Service and of consular officers is hereby abolished, without, however, in any wise impairing the validity of the present commissions of secretaries and consular officers." [3]

While the President is still free, under his constitutional powers, to appoint a diplomatic secretary or a consular officer, quite independently, as heretofore, there is no salary attaching to those positions, and a special appropriation would in each case be required.

Furthermore, the old Executive orders relating to the appointment of such officers have not been repealed, and

---

[3]Sec. 5, Act of May 24, 1924.

they carry qualification requirements similar to those now applicable to Foreign Service officers. The new enactment is in no sense to be construed as an encroachment upon the presidential powers of appointment. The service has for many years, and under five successive administrations, operated on a civil service basis by the voluntary action of the President, with congressional acquiescence or concurrence.

Stability by common consent.—Secretary of State Elihu Root, in 1906, when the first step towards establishing the merit system in the Consular Service was being undertaken, stated in the hearings:

Secretary Root: "I think there can gradually be built up a rule of action by the concurrence of the President and Congress, which it would be very difficult for any administration to break away from. * * * To make the change without an understanding means a row. It means a fight. It means hard feeling. And any improvement in such a system ought to come by general consent, and this classification is going a little way on the part of Congress toward indicating the acceptance of a little different system——

Representative Garner: "To helping the President to get away from the Senate? (Laughter.)

Secretary Root: "To help him to get away from a bad practice in which both Houses have concurred." [4]

That is precisely what has now been accomplished.

Again, in 1912, when the second step towards stabilization was under consideration, Acting Secretary of State Wilson stated that the great virtue of the new provision was in "upholding the hands of the President and relieving him from a horrible amount of pressure,

[4]Hearings before Committee on Foreign Affairs, Feb. 16, 1906.

giving him a fair chance to make good appointments in the foreign service." [5]

In the case of the act of May 24, 1924, President Harding heartily endorsed the plan of reorganization,[6] as did also President Coolidge,[7] who gave prominence to the need of Foreign Service reorganization in his first message to Congress.

The new classification.—Section 3 of the act provides:

"That the officers in the Foreign Service shall hereafter be graded and classified as follows, with the salaries of each class herein affixed thereto, but not exceeding in number for each class a proportion to the total number of officers in the service represented in the following percentage limitations: Ambassadors and ministers as now or hereafter provided; Foreign Service officers as follows: Class 1, 6 percentum, $9,000; class 2, 7 per centum, $8,000; class 3, 8 per centum, $7,000; class 4, 9 percentum, $6,000; class 5, 10 percentum, $5,000; class 6, 14 percentum, $4,500; class 7, $4,000; class 8, $3,500; class 9, $3,000; unclassified, $3,000 to $1,500."

The effect of the percentage limitations imposed upon the various classes, although in the nature of an administrative restriction, is not so exacting in this regard as to interfere with the working of the merit system. There will always be a sufficient number of vacancies to provide for merited promotions. The number allowed in each class with relation to the total personnel of the service is so graduated as to give pyramidal form to the

---

[5]Hearings before the Committee on Foreign Affairs, March 17, 1912, p. 73.

[6]See letters to Senator Lodge, dated Aug. 24, 1922, and to Hon. John Jacob Rogers, dated Sept. 1, 1922, printed in hearings on H. R. 17 and H. R. 6357, 68th Cong., 1st Sess., p. 25.

[7]Letters to Hon. Stephen G. Porter and to Hon. John Jacob Rogers, ibid., pp. 34-35.

classification scale, while the retirement system affords an outlet for the upper classes, thus providing a natural channel of advancement.

Reclassification and recommissioning.—By way of recommissioning the men in the service to their respective classes of Foreign Service officers, it was provided that the Secretary of State should on the date on which the act became effective, certify to the President the records of efficiency of all officers and—except in the case of those found to merit reduction in rank, or dismissal from the service—recommend their recommissioning as follows:[8]

"Secretaries of class one designated as counselors of embassy, and consuls general of classes one and two as Foreign Service officers of class one.

"Secretaries of class one designated as counselors of legation and consuls general of class three as Foreign Service officers of class two.

"Secretaries of class one not designated as counselors, consuls general of class four, and consuls general at large as Foreign Service officers of class three.

"Secretaries of class two, consuls general of class five, consuls of classes one, two, and three, and Chinese, Japanese, and Turkish secretaries as Foreign Service officers of class four.

"Consuls of class four as Foreign Service officers of class five.

"Secretaries of class three, consuls of class five, and Chinese, Japanese, and Turkish assistant secretaries as Foreign Service officers of class six.

"Consuls of class six as Foreign Service officers of class seven.

[8] See pages 293, 294.

"Secretaries of class four and consuls of class seven as Foreign Service officers of class eight.

"Consuls of classes eight and nine as Foreign Service officers of class nine.

"Vice consuls of career, consular assistants, interpreters, and student interpreters as Foreign Service officers, unclassified." [9]

By a special provision, consuls general of class one were not required to suffer a reduction in salary because of their recommissioning, but this applied only to one officer, as the other consul general of that class was retired on account of age.

The following table shows the result of the reclassification, effective under the reorganization plan, together with the permissible number in each class:[10]

CAREER PERSONNEL OF THE FOREIGN SERVICE
(As of September 30, 1924)

Class	Consular	Diplomatic	Total	Permissible Number
1	16	12	28	38
2	16	3	19	44
3	39	12	51	51
4	21	27	48	57
5	55	8	63	63
6	50	28	78	88
7	92	9	101	—
8	84	19	103	—
9	7	—	7	—
Unclassified—$3,000	40	—	40	
Unclassified—$2,750	30	—	30	
Unclassified—$2,500	55	4	59	
Unclassified—$1,500	5	—	5	
Totals	510	122	632	

[9] Sec. 7, Act of May 24, 1924.
[10] It will be noted that the number in the last three classes and in the unclassified grade are not restricted; therefore, the total number for the entire service at any given time is likewise unrestricted. This will be governed by appropriations.

Foreign service inspectors.—It is provided in section 3 of the act "that as many Foreign Service officers above class 6 as may be required for the purpose of inspection may be detailed by the Secretary of State for that purpose;" and in section 10 it is stated: "That the provisions of section 4 of the act of April 5, 1906, relative to the powers, duties, and prerogatives of consuls general at large are hereby made applicable to Foreign Service officers detailed for the purpose of inspection, who shall, under the direction of the Secretary of State, inspect the work of officers in the Foreign Service, both in the diplomatic and the consular branches."

It has been seen that the duties prescribed for inspectors by section 10 of the act of April 5, 1906, relate solely to the Consular Service,[11] whereas there will now be inspections in both branches. Owing to the nature of diplomatic work, and the delicacy of examining into the affairs of an important mission, the instructions under which an inspector will act with relation to an embassy or legation are very appropriately left to the determination of the Secretary of State in each case. The inspectors for this work will doubtless be drawn from the diplomatic branch, while those detailed for consular inspections will of necessity be consular officers.

Salary and expenses of inspectors.—Formerly the salary of a consular inspector was $5,000, in addition to which he was allowed actual and necessary travel expenses, and not exceeding an average of $8.00 per day for subsistence.

Foreign Service inspectors may be selected from any of the first five classes and will continue to draw their

---

[11]See page 21.

regular salaries as Foreign Service officers. Honorable Wilbur J. Carr has explained the desirability of this change as follows:

"An inspecting officer requires a very special kind of personality and experience, and it is my observation that there ought to be a very wide range of selection in the service. The officers, of course, are all taken from the service, but you can not always find enough men in one class who are especially qualified for that particular duty, which after all is a very difficult duty and requires a certain special kind of personality and a certain kind of experience. So it would be in the interest of better administration, I am sure, if you should broaden the range of selection in that respect." [12]

In addition to salary, a Foreign Service inspector is allowed travel and subsistence expenses, but here again there is an important change. The old system of accounting in minute detail for every item of expenditure, keeping vouchers therefor, translating these from various foreign languages into English and converting foreign moneys into their dollar equivalent under fluctuating exchange conditions, imposed an enormous burden of routine work upon these important officials who were without stenographic assistance, and therefore forced to do their own calculations and typing. It is now provided: "That the Secretary of State is authorized to prescribe a per diem allowance not exceeding $6, in lieu of subsistence for Foreign Service officers on special duty or Foreign Service inspectors." [13] This dispenses with the necessity for detailed accounting.

---

[12] Hearings before Committee on Foreign Affairs on H. R. 17 and H. R. 6357, 68th Cong., 1st Sess., p. 183.
[13] Sec. 14, Act of May 24, 1924.

Representation allowances.—An outstanding feature of the act is contained in section 12, which provides:

"That the President is hereby authorized to grant to diplomatic missions and to consular offices at capitals of countries where there is no diplomatic mission of the United States representation allowances out of any money which may be appropriated for such purpose from time to time by Congress, the expenditure of such representation allowance to be accounted for in detail to the Department of State quarterly under such rules and regulations as the President may prescribe." [14]

In seeking the presidential approval of this provision, Secretary Hughes explained it as follows:

"The principle of providing representation allowances is one which is well established in the practice of other nations and among the important business interests of this country. In relation to the Foreign Service it is a corollary to the Government ownership of embassy and legation buildings abroad as a means of lightening the burden of personal expense on our ambassadors and ministers. While it is not deemed advisable to request appropriations for this purpose at the present time, I believe it important that statutory provision should be made therefor in order that suitable funds may be provided at a later date and in such proportion as the special exigencies may require." [15]

The inadequacy of the salaries paid to the diplomatic representatives of the United States is so traditional and the consequences since the beginning of the Government have been so humiliating, so undemocratic, and

---

[14] Act of May 24, 1924.

[15] Letter to the President dated August 22, 1922. See Hearings before the Committee on Foreign Affairs on H. R.17 and H. R. 6357, 68th Congress, 2nd Sess., p. 24.

so disabling to our envoys that it seems appropriate to let the pages of history speak for themselves in describing the need and the importance of some change in the adjustment.

John Adams to John Jay.—From his post in London on December 15, 1785, John Adams addressed a letter to "His Excellency John Jay, Secretary of State," on the inadequacy of the salaries of our ministers abroad, which read in part as follows:

"In this state of things, I must be cautious. I am not able to pay the scribes, like an exchequer; nor to promise them pay or promotion, like an opposition. And, indeed, paragraphs in our favor seem only to provoke ten inventions against us. Something might be done in time, however, by mixing in conversation, and explaining or contradicting the grossest and worst abuses. But this can be done, in these countries, only by the civilities of the table, and by a liberal hospitality, in which we are much straitened. House rent, furniture, carriage, and a certain number of servants, with the daily expenses of living, which cannot be avoided, without becoming the scorn of the world, and without being insulted by every footman and porter, consume all, and more than all, our allowance.

"I feel for the circumstances of my country as much as any man in it, but I am sure those circumstances will not be mended by extreme parsimony in the support of her servants and negotiators in Europe. When your ministers are seen to take rank of nobles and bishops at St. James', who spend many thousands a year, and are observed to live at home and appear abroad, with what is called '*la plus infame économie*,' which is the expression every day in vogue, you will find that neither you nor they will be considered as of any consequence. Your ministers abroad must keep a table for the entertainment of strangers who are presented at court, and consequently to them, to return the civilities that are shown them by foreign ministers, and by people of high rank in the country. They ought to keep a table, at times, for the entertainment of men of letters and eminence in arts and sciences, by which they might remove the prejudices of the world against their country and themselves, and attract some attention and good will to both." [16]

Another letter from John Adams.—In a subsequent communication to the Secretary of State Mr. John Adams points out:

"There is a certain appearance, in proportion to rank, which all the courts of Europe make a serious point of exacting from every body who is presented to them.

"I need not say to you, sir, because you know it perfectly, that American ministers have never yet been able to make this appearance at court; they are now less able to do it than ever. I lament this necessity of consuming the labor of my fellow-citizens upon such objects, as much as any man living; but I am sure that the debasing your ministers, so much below their rank, will, one day, have consequences of much more importance to the husbandman, artisan, and even laborer." [17]

James Monroe to the Auditor.—In a letter dated December 17, 1810, addressed to the Auditor, James Monroe observed:

"The reason in favor of an increase of the salaries of our ministers abroad, are as strong as for an increase of that of those at home, if not much stronger; and there is one reason, of great force, which is peculiarly

[16]"Foreign Relations," vol. 5, House Doc. No. 94, 22nd Cong., 2nd Sess.
[17]*Ibid.*

applicable to the former. The spirit of our Government, and the manners of our people, not only authorize, but inculcate economy at home in the expenditure of our public functionaries; but that indulgence cannot be enjoyed by those abroad, however consonant it may be to their habits and inclinations, or necessary to their circumstances." [18]

John Quincy Adams to the Secretary of State.—In a letter from his post in London to the Secretary of State, dated July 31, 1815, John Quincy Adams stated:

"It is needless to say to you, or to any person having been in the same capacity here, that the annual salary of an American minister is insufficient to support a man with a family—I say not, in the style of high official rank, but in the decency becoming a private gentleman." [19]

A second letter from John Quincy Adams.—In a subsequent letter dated September 30, 1816, relating to his experiences while again on mission to London Mr. John Quincy Adams stated to the Secretary of State:

"An experience of the expense of living here, for upwards of four months, even under all the privation to which I have submitted, has confirmed me in the desire to be recalled as early in the spring as the President may find it convenient to replace me, if, upon the construction of the law, the Legislature should refuse an appropriation for the outfit." [20]

Report of Louis McLane, Secretary of the Treasury, 1831.—In his report dated December 7, 1831, Louis McLane, formerly Minister to Great Britain, then Secretary of the Treasury, made the following statement:

---

[18]*Ibid.*
[19]*Ibid.*
[20]*Ibid.*

"The salaries of the public ministers abroad must be acknowledged to be utterly inadequate, either for the dignity of the office, or the necessary comfort of their families. At some foreign courts, and those whose relations towards the United States are the most important, the expenses incident to the station are found so burdensome, as only to be met by the private resources of the minister. The tendency of this is to throw those high trusts altogether into the hands of the rich, which is certainly not according to the genius of our system. Such a provision for public ministers as would obviate these evils, and enable the minister to perform the common duties of hospitality to his countrymen, and promote social intercourse between the citizens of both nations, would not only elevate the character of his country, but essentially improve its public relations." [21]

Edward Livingston to President Jackson.—On January 31, 1833, Secretary of State Edward Livingston addressed a letter to President Jackson in which he stated:

"A minister to a foreign power, whatever may be his grade, is the accredited agent of his country. If he is forced, from the inadequate compensation that is allowed him, to live in a manner that will not allow him to associate, on an equal footing, with others of the same grade, he is deprived of many of the advantages which social intercourse affords, to perform essential duties, and to gain important information, which can only be obtained by mixing in the first circles. It is not expected, nor should I recommend, that his allowance should be such as to enable him to vie, in expense of living, with the ministers of monarchs, who allow extrava-

---

[21] *Ibid.*, Report of the Secretary of the Treasury of 7th Dec., 1831.

gant salaries, and who, themselves, have large fortunes, which they expend in addition to their official allowance: but he ought to have the means of returning civilities which he receives—of giving to his countrymen a plain hospitable reception when they visit the place of his residence; and, above all, he ought to have an allowance that will enable him to meet the expenses absolutely necessary for the due performance of his official duties, without trenching on his salary so much as to render it entirely incompetent to his necessary and decent support. * * *

"But, to represent the dignity of the country, and, on a scanty salary, to transact its most important concerns abroad, we send a man whom we provide with none of these necessaries for the transaction of his business; we force him to do all the drudgery of the office with his own hands, and either to live in some obscure place, where his countrymen blush to find him fixed, when, after some difficulty, they have discovered his tavern residence; or, at the expense of his own fortune, to provide what is necessary for the interest and dignity of the Government. The usual answer to these representations is that, notwithstanding all these inconveniences, candidates are always found eagerly seeking these appointments. But it must be remarked that these candidates are of two kinds. First, men of wealth, who are willing to purchase the honor of the station at the expense of their private fortunes. But, although these are not always the fittest, in other respects, for the place, they are sometimes selected, and their appointment is popular, because there seems to be no objection to a minister's keeping up a decent appearance provided he does it at his own expense. Secondly, there are others who seek these appointments, because they make false calculations on the consequences. They resolve to be very economical, to live within their income, and to be drawn into no extravagance. But, on arriving at their place of destination, they find that expenses which might, with prudence, have been avoided here, are inevitable abroad. Civilities are received which must be returned; strangers are introduced who must be entertained; their countrymen call on them, and must be treated hospitably. In short, they find themselves obliged to live as others do; or, to forego all the advantages which social intercourse would give them in the business of their mission. The consequence is, that all our ministers return with impaired fortunes, however firm their resolutions have been to avoid unnecessary expense. It is possible there may be exceptions; but they are certainly very rare. If, then, none of the ministers we have sent abroad, however prudent, have been able to live for the salaries that are allowed them, the conclusion is inevitable, that the salaries ought to be increased, or the ministers should be recalled. If the mission is useful it ought to be supported.at the public, not at private expense; and the representatives of a great nation ought not to be obliged to employ, in devising parsimonious expedients for their support, that time and those talents which ought to be occupied in the service of their country." [22]

Walter Hines Page to Edward M. House.—Although the pages of our foreign relations are replete with testimonials of this character, there is none which strikes more deeply home than the lament of Walter Hines Page, Ambassador to Great Britain, in his letter

---

[22]Letter from Secretary of State Edward Livingston, to President Jackson, Jan. 31, 1833, vol. 5, "Foreign Relations." House Doc. 94, 22nd Cong., 2nd Sess.

to Colonel Edward M. House, dated February 13, 1914, which reads in part as follows:

"Of course I am open to the criticism of having taken the place at all. But I was both uninformed and misinformed about the cost as well as about the frightful handicap of having no Embassy. It's a kind of scandal in London and it has its serious effect. Everybody talks about it all the time: 'Will you explain to me why it is that your great Government has no Embassy: it's very odd!' 'What a frugal Government you have!' 'It's a damned mean outfit, your American Government.' Mrs. Page collapses many an evening when she gets to her room. 'If they'd only quit talking about it!' The other Ambassadors, now that we're coming to know them fairly well, commiserate us. It's a constant humiliation. Of course this aspect of it doesn't worry me much—I've got hardened to it. But it is a good deal of a real handicap, and it adds that much dead weight that a man must overcome; and it greatly lessens the respect in which our Government and its Ambassador are held. If I had known this fully in advance, I should not have had the courage to come here. Now, of course, I've got used to it, have discounted it, and can 'bull' it through— could 'bull' it through if I could afford to pay the bill. But I shouldn't advise any friend of mine to come here and face this humiliation without realizing precisely what it means—wholly apart, of course, from the cost of it." [23]

Testimony of Honorable John W. Davis.—The successor to Walter Hines Page as Ambassador to Great Britain was Honorable John W. Davis, who came at his own expense to Washington to testify before the

[23]Hendrick, "Life and Letters of Walter H. Page," Letter to Colonel House, Feb. 13, 1914, vol. I, p. 233.

Committee on Foreign Affairs in favor of the reorganization bill. In regard to the need and the desirability of representation allowances Mr. Davis stated:

"There is one other thing in the bill on which I have a pretty deep personal feeling, and that is the provision for representation allowances to the diplomatic officers of the Government. Of course, that is an old subject. To those who have had any experience with it, it is rather a sore subject. It is notorious that we never have paid to our ministers, and especially to our ambassadors in the larger capitals, a salary on which it was possible for them to live, let alone to carry on the ceremonial activities that are indispensable in those positions. Those ceremonial activities, if we choose to call them that, are not mere matters of display or pride or ostentation. A certain amount of that sort of thing, as all of us here as reasonable men know, is indispensable in an exalted position of that sort. To a certain extent the country itself is judged by the style in which its representatives live abroad. Human nature being what it is, men, people, officers, and nations are judged to a large extent by appearances. It may be sometimes a false standard, yet none the less it is a standard which men employ, and the country itself must inevitably be judged to a certain extent by the appearance that its representatives present.

"There is another side of it that is not so often realized by the man in the street which is even more important than that. My belief is that what the diplomatic officer under present-day conditions furnishes to his Government, the most valuable thing he furnishes, is a personal knowledge of the men who are controlling the activities of the nations with which his Government deals. * * *

"The bearing of that on this question of expense is that you can not get an acquaintance with human beings unless you associate with them. You have got to get acquainted in that particular circle. You have got to get upon terms of social intimacy, as far as opportunity permits, with men who are responsible for the governmental policy, and that, of course, necessarily involves the interchange of those courtesies that go to make up human intercourse. That means expense. It is the same sort of expense account that the manufacturer has for his salesmen when he sends them out and gives them a salary, plus expense account, to be spent in cultivating the good will of their customers.

"If I had my way about it, a perfectly free hand, I say to you frankly I would not raise the salary of an ambassador, possibly not of a minister, in the Government service; not because I do not think they earn their salaries. A man in any of these positions who is of any account at all earns his salary many times over in his service to the Government. They are not sinecures; they are really very hard-working posts. But you can not raise those salaries, as it seems to me, without getting them out of proportion to the other salaries that are paid in the governmental establishment. While you pay your Chief Justice $16,500 and Cabinet officers $12,000, and so on down the line, I do not think that in due proportion you can raise the salaries of your ambassadors and ministers, but you can do what every other Government does, and give them what the French call *frais de réprésentation,* expense of representation, which will cover these necessary expenses, which they must undertake, which they must assume, if they are to become really useful to the Government in their positions. I think there ought to be—and I am glad this bill takes it up in that form—that there ought to be a lump appropriation given to the Secretary of State to be disposed of by him in his discretion, and, of course, with accountability to Congress and to the Treasury, in allotting to the different diplomatic posts such expenses of representation as would fairly enable them to meet these indispensable expenditures, which are not in their nature private, but which are really incurred for the benefit primarily of the Government they represent." [24]

Honorable Theodore E. Burton, Temporary Chairman of the Republican National Convention.—As a fitting climax to the age-long effort to adjust in suitable measure the compensation of our diplomatic representatives, Honorable Theodore E. Burton, Temporary Chairman of the Republican National Convention, in his keynote speech of June 10, 1924, claimed the following merits for this feature of the reorganization act:

"We have passed and the President has approved the so-called Rogers Bill, placing our diplomatic and consular service, with its rapidly increasing importance, on a higher plane and giving opportunities to others than millionaires to occupy the more important positions." [25]

Home leave and re-Americanization.—Section 15 of the reorganization act provides:

"That the Secretary of State is authorized, whenever he deems it to be in the public interest, to order to the United States on his statutory leave of absence any Foreign Service officer who has performed three years or more of continuous service abroad: Provided, That the expenses of transportation and subsistence of such

---

[24]Hearings on H. R. 17 and H. R. 6357, 68th Cong., 1st Sess., pp. 207-208.

[25]*New York Times*, June 11, 1924.

officers and their immediate families, in traveling from their posts to their homes in the United States and return, shall be paid under the same rules and regulations applicable in the case of officers going to and returning from their posts under orders of the Secretary of State when not on leave: Provided further, That while in the United States the services of such officers shall be available for trade conference work or for such duties in the Department of State as the Secretary of State may prescribe."

The purpose of this enactment is three-fold:

(a) It serves to bring officers back for the refreshment of their views on affairs in their own country.

(b) It provides facilities which many could not afford from their meager savings.

(c) It permits the Department of State to take advantage of their presence for work within the Department or for trade conference work among Chambers of Commerce and important business organizations.

The first of these objects is of fundamental importance.

Views of Thomas Jefferson.—Thomas Jefferson, when Secretary of State under President Washington and later when President himself, adopted a very definite policy with respect to representatives remaining abroad so long as to lose touch with affairs in their own country. On this subject he wrote in 1801:

"Very soon, therefore, after entering on the office of Secretary of State, I recommended to General Washington to establish, as a rule of practice, that no person should be continued on foreign mission beyond an absence of six, seven, or eight years. He approved it. On the only subsequent missions which took place in my time, the persons appointed were notified that they could not be continued beyond that period. All returned within it except Humphreys. His term was not quite out when General Washington went out of office. The succeeding administration had no rule for anything so he continued. Immediately on my coming to the administration, I wrote to him myself, reminded him of the rule I had communicated to him on his departure; that he had then been absent about eleven years, and consequently must return. On this ground solely he was superseded. Under these circumstances, your appointment was impossible after an absence of seventeen years. Under any others, I should never fail to give to yourself and the world proofs of my friendship for you, and of my confidence in you. Whenever you shall return, you will be sensible in a greater, of what I was in a smaller, degree, of the change in this nation from what it was when we both left it in 1784. We return like foreigners, and, like them, require a considerable residence here to become Americanized." [26]

Although conditions to-day are vastly changed, owing to the development of rapid communication, which renders the position of a foreign representative less isolated, the need has been felt constantly for some provision which would lend itself to the re-Americanization of the officers in the Foreign Service. There are some, especially in remote posts, who are unable to defray the expenses of themselves and their families to the United States for periods of years, to the disadvantage both of themselves and of the Government. [27]

---

[26] President Jefferson to Mr. Short, Oct. 3, 1801, 2 Randall's Life of Jefferson, 672. Quoted in "Moore's Digest," vol. IV, p. 460.

[27] "It is a disadvantage to the public service that diplomats, living perpetually abroad, not only lose touch with the public opinion of their own country but also, if they remain long at the same post, unconsciously assimilate the outlook of the country where they reside. In both cases, too,

Evidences of legislative policy.—That the policy has definitely changed in this regard is evidenced not only by the enactment of appropriate legislation, but by the tenor of the discussions in Committee when this provision was under consideration. The following excerpt from the hearings affords convincing evidence of this fact:

"The Chairman. What do you think of the idea of a rule that would require our foreign representatives to spend one-third or one-fourth of their time in the United States, a rule somewhat like that which the Navy has?

"Mr. Gibson. That would be an excellent thing, not only for the Government but for the individual.

"The Chairman. Do you approve of that?

"Mr. Gibson. I do. I do not know that you could make it rigid without allowing for emergencies which might make it undesirable for a man to absent himself from his post—

"The Chairman. I do not mean a hard and fast rule, but a general policy.

"Mr. Gibson. There is no doubt that a man does get out of touch with conditions in America if he stays away more than two years at a time, and one can not be a thoroughly efficient representative unless he keeps in close touch with what goes on at home.

"Mr. Browne. In that case would you have to have some substitute to send back to those positions?

"Mr. Gibson. It would mean having a rotation.

"The Chairman. You mentioned the fact that one of our secretaries at London was granted leave as he planned a lion hunt in Africa. Do many of them fol-

the views they chiefly imbibe are those of officials and not those of the general public." Kennedy, "Old Diplomacy and New," p. 190.

low that practice when they secure leave instead of returning to the United States or go somewhere on the
Continent?

"Mr. Gibson. Most of the people that I know
when they get leave do try to come home. There are
times when a man is not able to come home to take his
leave. The expense is very large, and that is a major
consideration, but I find that most of our people come
home when they do have the opportunity, or else they
get out of touch.

"The Chairman. How do you feel about bringing
them home and putting them to work at the State Department as the Navy does?

"Mr. Gibson. The Department of State does that
now, and it ought to be, of course, of benefit to the department and the service. When a man comes back to
the field from the department he is of greater value to
a mission than if he comes from another mission abroad.

"Mr. Rogers of Massachusetts. If the committee
would refer to H. R. 551 it will serve to indicate my
views on what ought to be done here: * * *

"In other words, Mr. Gibson, does it not seem appropriate, if it is such a good thing from the United States
standpoint to have these men come back, that they ought
to be assisted in coming back?

"Mr. Gibson. For a concrete example I will cite one
of our consuls-general who has not been home for several
years. He wants to come home, but he has a family to
look after and can not scrape the money together to do
it. Unless the Government makes it possible for him
it will be a year or two before he can come back home.
That is not sound from the Government's point of view
in that it prevents the officer from developing his
greatest usefulness—but he would be justified in resent-

ing the implication that he does not want to come home, but would like to spend that leave on the Continent." [28]

The retirement system.—It would be futile to attempt to construct a permanent service without an outlet. All positions in the upper classes would soon fill up with men subject to removal only for cause or death. This condition would very soon clog the service and block all prospect of promotion on merit. The act makes provision in Section 18 for a system of retirement and disability, which is separate and distinct from that of the civil service retirement and disability system, established by the law of May 22, 1920. However, in many of its provisions there are points of basic similarity, and obvious adaptations of the general principles of the civil service retirement and disability law to the special requirements of the Foreign Service. A full discussion of the retirement feature is given in Chapter XI.

Assignment to the Department of State.—Following out the practice established by the Act of February 5, 1915, which authorized the assignment of diplomatic and consular officers to the Department of State, there is a provision in the new law authorizing the assignment of any Foreign Service officer for such duty without the loss of class or salary for a period of not more than three years unless the public interests demand further service, when such assignment may be extended for a period not to exceed one year. [29]

Commissioner, chargé d'affaires, minister resident, diplomatic agent and counselor.—Section 17 provides:

"That within the discretion of the President, any Foreign Service officer may be appointed to act as com-

---

[28]Hearings before the Committee on Foreign Affairs on H. R. 17 and H. R. 6357, 68th Cong., 1st Sess., pp. 47 and 48.

[29]Sec. 14, Act of May 24, 1924. See also page 31.

missioner, chargé d'affaires, minister resident, or diplomatic agent for such period as the public interests may require without loss of grade, class, or salary: Provided, however, That no such officer shall receive more than one salary."

By the act of July 1, 1916, creating the position of counselor of embassy or legation, the President was authorized to designate and assign any diplomatic secretary of class one to that position. Under Section 16 of the reorganization act the President may, when he considers it advisable so to do, designate and assign any Foreign Service officer as counselor of embassy or legation.

Bonds of Foreign Service officers.—For many years all consular officers, upon assuming office, were required to give a bond for the true and faithful accounting for all fees, moneys, and properties of the Government.[30] No requirement of this character having been made with respect to diplomatic secretaries, the reorganization act amends the previous law by extending its provisions to all Foreign Service officers, who are now required to give a bond in a penal sum of not less than their annual compensation. The bond covers by its stipulations all official acts of such officers whether as Foreign Service officers, or as secretaries in the diplomatic service, or as consular officers.

Official fees.—In like manner, those provisions of the act of April 5, 1906, relating to official fees and the method of accounting therefor, as applied heretofore in consular practice, are now extended to the diplomatic branch of the service, where the collection of certain fees is in some instances authorized.

---

[30] R. S. 1697, 1698.

Private secretaries to ambassadors. — It having been thought by Congress that an ambassador should be provided with facilities for selecting his own confidential clerk or private secretary, authorization for appropriations for that purpose is included in the act, where it is stated that they "shall be appointed by the ambassador and hold office at his pleasure."[31]

Recall to active duty.—Section 19 provides:

"In the event of public emergency any retired Foreign Service officer may be recalled temporarily to active service by the President and while so serving he shall be entitled in lieu of his retirement allowance to the full pay of the class in which he is temporarily serving."

Bibliography.

American Consular Bulletin: (Containing articles descriptive of the Rogers Act), Washington, D. C., July, 1924.

Grew, Joseph: "Danish Foreign Service Reorganized"; *American Consular Bulletin,* Washington, October, 1921.

Lay, Tracy: "Foreign Service Reorganization"; *American Political Science Review,* November, 1924.

Van Dyne, F.: "Our Foreign Service"; Rochester, 1909.

Williams, H. O.: "Foreign Service Changes World Wide"; *American Consular Bulletin,* Washington, May, 1921.

---

[31] Sec. 13, Act of May 24, 1924.

CHAPTER X

THE CONTROL OF FOREIGN SERVICE PERSONNEL

The importance of personnel administration.—The Foreign Service is not only interchangeable, but is directly competitive in every class and grade with respect to the men of both branches. The fidelity and earnestness of its officers, their discipline, their spirit of cooperation—in short, the success of the entire system—turns upon the important question of personnel control.

Many provisions of the reorganization act relate specifically to matters of personnel, prescribing the mode of reclassification, of appointment, assignment, transfer and promotion.

These are sketched only in general outline, however, the details of administration being left largely to such rules and regulations as the President may prescribe. As presidential Executive orders issued under these conditions have the force of law, it is obvious that from the viewpoint of service administration the rules and regulations which govern the system are of equal importance with the act itself. The administration of personnel at the time the new regulations were promulgated had already reached a high stage of development in the Consular Service but was less scientifically treated in the Diplomatic Service.

The duties of consular inspectors.—Coincidentally with the establishment of the merit system in 1906, there was created a corps of five consular inspectors appointed

284

and commissioned by the President as consuls general at large, and invested with broad authority and responsibility, as follows:

"They shall make such inspections of consular offices as the Secretary of State shall direct, and shall report to him. Each consular office shall be inspected at least once in every two years. Whenever the President has reason to believe that the business of a consulate or a consulate general is not being properly conducted and that it is necessary for the public interest, he may authorize any consul general at large to suspend the consul or consul general, and administer the office in his stead for a period not exceeding ninety days. In such case the consul general at large so authorized shall have power to suspend any vice consular officer or clerk in said office during the period aforesaid. The provisions of law relating to the official bonds of consuls general, and the provisions of sections seventeen hundred and thirty-four, seventeen hundred and thirty-five, and seventeen hundred and thirty-six, Revised Statutes of the United States, shall apply to consuls general at large."[1]

The system of inspection.—Mainly through the work of the inspectors the process of determining the relative standing of officers in the field, as regards their efficiency, ability, and general fitness, was reduced to a tangible method of valuation from which a definite standard for the service was evolved. With only five inspectors it proved impracticable to cover the entire service every two years, as required by law, and consequently their number was increased to seven in 1919.

For the purposes of inspection, the service was divided into seven inspection districts or zones, as follows: Eastern Europe; Western Europe; Mexico and the

[1] Act of April 5, 1906.

West Indies; Central and South America; Central Asia and Africa; The Far East; and British North America. The officer assigned to British North America has his headquarters in the Department of State.

The work of consular inspectors was not confined to a mere appraisal of men. It embraced every detail of consular work with particular emphasis upon uniformity in consular practice, the standardization of forms, methods, and equipment, the furtherance of administrative policy and the encouragement of service cohesion and *ésprit de corps*. Perhaps no more careful audit has ever been attempted in any department of the Government than that with which the consuls general at large were charged. From the accumulated experience obtained through their searching investigations, precise formulae for estimating and reporting upon the qualifications of officers have been deduced and established in practice.

The inspector's report.—The rating of an officer in the inspector's report takes five main divisions, each being further reduced to five related subdivisions which form the basis of percentage estimates. The following table shows the relative weight given in these reckonings to various qualifications, although it is necessary to explain that the descriptive word in each case is interpreted in its broadest, rather than in its narrow sense. For instance, "Honesty" includes purity of thought, candor and conscientiousness; "Morality" embraces decorum, general behavior, moral courage, rightmindedness, and conduct in accordance with the usual proprieties of social life; "Sobriety" includes temperament, self-control, moderation in conduct, speech and act. The résumé here given is merely the final reckoning page or summary of the inspector's report, resulting from thirteen lengthy sheets of discussion based upon a questionnaire of pertinent data of which the following may be cited as an example:

"*Standing.* Does the officer command the respect of the community; extent and character of acquaintance; (a) among Americans; (b) among other foreigners; (c) among nationals? Do the members of his family contribute favorably to his standing?"

RATING OF AN OFFICER

Character:	POSSIBLE		ACTUAL
1. Honesty	100		......
2. Morality	100		......
3. Sobriety	100		......
4. Decision	100		......
5. Tact	100		......
Average	100	5)	......

Intellectual and Social Qualifications:	POSSIBLE		ACTUAL
6. Education	100		......
7. Languages	100		......
8. Judgment and discretion	100		......
9. Personality	100		......
10. Standing	100		......
Average	100	5)	......

Administration:	POSSIBLE		ACTUAL
11. Knowledge of regulations	100		......
12. Ability in consular practice	100		......
13. Promptness	100		......
14. Force	100		......
15. System	100		......
Average	100	5)	......

Commercial functions:	POSSIBLE		ACTUAL
16. Knowledge of local conditions	100		......
17. Accuracy and reliability	100		......
18. Initiative	100		......
19. Assistance to American commerce	100		......
20. Quality and volume of reports	100		......
Average	100	5)	......

RATING OF AN OFFICER (*Continued*)

Service Spirit:	POSSIBLE	ACTUAL
21. Interest in the service	100	......
22. Loyalty	100	......
23. Subordination	100	......
24. Cooperation	100	......
25. Readiness to serve at any post	100	...,...
Average	100 5)	......
	5)	...,..
Rating		

STANDARDS FOR GRADING

96 to 100..........Excellent.	81 to 90..........Average.
91 to 95..........Very good.	76 to 80..........Fair.
	75 and below.:.....Poor.

The office of consular personnel.—On September 1, 1921, the handling of consular personnel matters in the department was concentrated in an Office of Consular Personnel, which was in the nature of a fact-finding agency, confining its activities to the accumulation, preservation and analysis of personnel data, as contrasted with administration and direction. The work of the Office of Consular Personnel was strictly confidential, its duties being:

(a) To keep the efficiency records of all officers and employees of the Consular Service.

(b) To collect, collate, and record pertinent data relating to consular personnel.

(c) To maintain contact with consular officers and employees while on visit to the United States.

(d) To bring to the attention of educational and other institutions and individuals the advantages of the consular career.

(e) To interview applicants and prospective applicants for the Consular Service.

(f) To keep as a part of the efficiency records of consular officers and employees all portions of the reports of consuls general at large, consuls general, consuls, and others, which relate to consular personnel.

Reports by supervising officers.—Immediately following the establishment of the personnel office, an instruction was sent to the field requiring supervising consuls general to render annual efficiency reports upon the principal consular officers stationed within their supervisory jurisdictions.[2]

Substantially the same form was employed for this purpose as that used by the inspectors. In this way the facilities for procuring accurate information relative to the activities of consular officers abroad were considerably enlarged.

Since 1917 it had already been required that all principal officers should submit annual efficiency reports on the subordinates within each consulate, including consuls detailed for duty as vice consuls, consular assistants, interpreters, student interpreters, vice consuls, marshals, clerks, messengers and others.[3]

The board of review.—The year following the establishment of the personnel office another valuable practice was developed in the department. A conference of inspectors was called in Washington in the summer of 1922, and a Board of Review composed of five consuls general at large was constituted to examine the background of all individual ratings, based upon the data contained in the files.

The work of the Board of Review was advisory only, and in addition to establishing individual ratings it was charged with the duty of valuing evidence of special qualifications for political, commercial, economic investigational, or executive work, or for performing

---

2General Instruction, Consular, No. 798, Sept. 22, 1921.
3General Instruction, Consular, No. 525, June 27, 1917.

the duties of a consul general, or consul general at large.

Through the operations of the board the relative standing of all officers in the service was given a complete reorientation as a basis of future promotions.

The work of the first board having been highly successful, the practice was perpetuated, and has now become permanent.

Diplomatic personnel.—In the Diplomatic Service there were no inspectors and consequently this chief source of personnel information was lacking. No elaborate system, such as that existing in the Consular Service, having been worked out, diplomatic secretaries in good standing received promotions, as a rule, in the order of seniority of service. With the passage of the reorganization act providing for the amalgamation of the two branches, and giving rise to a system of unified direction, the methods of personnel control have now been consolidated and brought into a single system.

It should be pointed out that through the abolition of the classification of diplomatic secretaries and of consular officers,[4] and the creation of the classified salary title of Foreign Service officer,[5] the competition for promotion becomes a question of winning advancement from class to class on a common basis as Foreign Service officers; not as diplomatic secretaries or as consular officers.

The presidential Executive order.—By way of giving effect to the statute, the President on June 7, 1924, issued an Executive order[6] the effect of which was to strengthen the character of the entire service adjust-

---

[4] Act of May 24, 1924, Sec. 5.
[5] *Ibid.*, Sec. 2.
[6] See Appendix F.

ment by providing means for elevating the standard of personnel to the highest possible degree.

Under the regulations thus established, vacancies in all classes, from one to nine, are to be filled by promotion from the lower classes, based upon ability and efficiency as shown in the service. All admissions to the service are to the grade of Foreign Service officer, unclassified, which comprises a consolidated group of subordinates below class nine.

Officers and employees, after five years of continuous service in the Department of State, are eligible for appointment or transfer to any class in the Foreign Service upon recommendation of the Foreign Service Personnel Board and with the approval of the Secretary of State. This provision is valuable in that it lends an added attraction to positions in the Department of State, through a form of amalgamation with the field.[7] It should appeal strongly to future applicants for positions of this character to whom the salary inducements alone are insufficient.

The foregoing principles lay the foundation for a stable service, well guarded as against the possibility of political or bureaucratic intrusions or meddlings.

The Foreign Service Personnel Board.—By the Executive order the new system of personnel control is vested in a Foreign Service Personnel Board, composed of the following members: The Undersecretary of State, who is the Chairman; an Assistant Secretary of State, to be designated by the Secretary of State; the former Director of the Consular Service, now an Assistant Secretary of State; and the three members of the Executive Committee of the Foreign Service Personnel Board.

---

[7] See page 91.

The Executive Committee, in turn, is composed of a chairman and two other members who are Foreign Service officers of high rank, representing both the diplomatic and the consular branches of the Foreign Service. They are selected by the other members of the Personnel Board with the approval of the Secretary of State.

The duties of the Executive Committee are prescribed by the Secretary of State.[8]

Analysis of the Personnel Board.—Analyzing the composition of this august Board, we find, in its present membership, that the Undersecretary of State, one of the Assistant Secretaries of State and one member of the Executive Committee are diplomatic officials, while the other Assistant Secretary of State has for many years been identified with the Consular Service as its Director, and the two remaining members, consisting of the chairman and the third member of the Executive Committee, are consuls general of high rank. The representation on the Board, therefore, is evenly divided as between the two branches of the service.

Under a change of administration two of these positions would possibly, or even probably, change character; the Undersecretary of State, and one Assistant Secretary. Even were non-service men selected to fill their places, which is more than likely, this would not impart to the Board a political character.

In the first place, the non-partisan nature of the service is now definitely recognized and assured by statute, and secondly, at least two members of the Board will always be service men, while a third member wields the balancing influence of a strongly supported permanent official who is thoroughly devoted to the interests of the

[8]See page 301 for description.

service as a whole and admittedly more highly qualified in that regard than any other public functionary. This reference is to Honorable Wilbur J. Carr, Assistant Secretary of State, formerly Director of the Consular Service, who by the nature of his position and his peculiar personal qualifications may be considered a permanent member of the Personnel Board.

The board elects its secretary from among its own members.

Duties of the Personnel Board.—The reorganization act requires: "That on the date on which this act becomes effective the Secretary of State shall certify to the President, with his recommendation in each case, the record of efficiency of the several secretaries in the Diplomatic Service, consuls general, consuls, vice consuls of career, consular assistants, interpreters, and student interpreters then in office and shall, except in cases of persons found to merit reduction in rank or dismissal from the service, recommend to the President the recommissioning, without further examination, of those then in office." [9]

The first duty of the Board was, therefore:

"To examine into the character, ability, efficiency, experience and general availability of all secretaries in the Diplomatic Service, consuls general, consuls, vice consuls of career, consular assistants, interpreters and student interpreters, and before July 1, 1924, to submit to the Secretary of State such information as he may require regarding the efficiency records of such officers." [10]

In the general reclassification which took place on July 1, 1924, and in fulfilment of this duty, thirty-one

[9] Sec. 7, Act of May 24, 1924.
[10] Sec. 5(a) Executive Order, June 7, 1924.

consular officers and one diplomatic officer were retired on account of age; five officers were dropped from the unassigned list of the Diplomatic Service; eight diplomatic secretaries and thirteen consular officers were demoted, and there were two resignations. All other officers were reclassified as stipulated in the act. This made a general total of thirty-nine removals and twenty-one reductions in rank.

The status of those who were reduced in rank is officially described as follows: "The Secretary of State also submitted to the President the cases of eight diplomatic and thirteen consular officers whose records were not such as to justify recommissioning them in the classes to which they would normally have been assigned and who were therefore recommended for reduction in rank. Under the provisions of Section 7 of the Act it was believed that certain of these officers merited separation from the service, and a recommendation to that effect would have been made except for the fact that separation on July 1, upon such short notice as was then possible, might have proved a serious hardship in some cases. Consequently it was believed that the officers should be reduced in rank and recommissioned, leaving the question of their future disposition to be determined on the basis of the facts. These officers have been notified of the action taken and their cases will shortly be given further consideration by the Board." [11]

Participation of legislative observers.—The proceedings of the Board are strictly confidential, but it is the duty of the chairman, within a reasonable time prior to each meeting of the Board, for the purpose of recommending promotions, demotions or removals, to invite

---

[11] General Instruction, Dip. Serial No. 288, July 29, 1924.

the Chairman of the Senate Committee on Foreign Relations and the Chairman of the House Committee on Foreign Affairs or some Committee Member designated by the Chairman, to sit with the Board through its deliberations, without, however, participating in its decisions.[12]

The object of this innovation is to assure impartiality, and a faithful application of the merit system. All action taken by the Board is strictly non-partisan, based exclusively upon the records of efficiency of the officers concerned. With two distinguished legislative observers watching these operations, it is scarcely conceivable that any suspicions of mismanagement which may at times arise in legislative quarters could long survive against the clarifying explanations of two prominent members of Congress whose familiarity with the processes of the system would enable them to speak with authority.

Recommending promotions.—Resulting from the sifting of personnel data and the digest of relative ratings, the Board is charged with the following continuous duty as a part of its regular work:

"From time to time after the Act of May 24, 1924, becomes effective, and as vacancies arise, to submit to the Secretary of State lists of those Foreign Service officers whose records of efficiency entitle them to advancement in the service, and who are therefore recommended for promotion, and the names of those officers and employees in the Department of State who, after five years of continuous service, and because of special ability and merit are recommended for appointment by transfer to the position of Foreign Service officer. All such lists to be signed by the Chairman and at least

12Sec. 9, Executive Order, June 7, 1924.

three members of the Board, except in the case of a tie vote when the Secretary of State shall decide." [13]

As has been seen, the action of the Board, in these circumstances, will be taken under the vigilant eyes of two legislative observers.

Promotion to the grade of minister.—No single aim of reorganization is of more vital importance to the men in the service, or to the service as a whole, than the facilities which are provided for the appropriate recognition of merit, efficiency and general fitness for promotion to the grade of minister. While the President remains free, with the consent of the Senate, to make any such appointments as he may deem proper, the hope of the entire system and the very future of the service itself depends directly upon the support and encouragement that is given through the advancement of trained men. No service could be expected to develop men of the capacity of strong ambassadors or ministers with those positions substantially closed to them. Recognizing this important fact, the President has made it a duty of the Foreign Service Personnel Board:

"To submit to the Secretary of State the names of those Foreign Service officers who, in the opinion of the Board, have demonstrated special capacity for promotion to the grade of Minister. Each list thus submitted shall enumerate the names of the officers in the order of merit and shall be complete in itself, superseding all previous lists. A list shall be submitted to the Secretary of State whenever there is a vacancy in the grade of Minister or when requested by the President or the Secretary of State and in no case shall it contain more names than there are vacancies to fill. Each such list shall be signed by the Chairman and at least three mem-

[13]Sec. 5(b) Executive Order, June 7, 1924.

bers of the Board, and if approved by the Secretary of State, shall be submitted to the President." [14]

The effect of the foregoing provision should be most salutary. It establishes for the first time an orderly procedure for the recognition of the meritorious claims of service men. In appropriate circumstances the Board determines upon a service nominee whose claims are sufficiently outstanding to warrant the hope that the President will accept him for appointment to the grade of minister as against an untrained man whose candidacy is supported wholly by outside, political endorsements. With this reassuring possibility, officers in the service should not feel tempted to go out of channels to urge their own promotion over the heads of their colleagues. Indeed, the President may conclude that in the case of service men the endorsement of the Board is a prerequisite, and that it outweighs other forms of support.

The designation of counselors.—Under Section 16 of the act, the President may designate and assign any Foreign Service officer as counselor of embassy or legation.

Accordingly, the Foreign Service Personnel Board is charged with the duty of submitting to the Secretary of State the names of those Foreign Service officers who are recommended for such designation.

Assignments and transfers.—Perhaps no phase of Foreign Service administration has elicited a keener interest on the part of the officers in both branches than that which relates to the method of determining assignments and transfers, especially from one branch of the service to the other.

By the Executive order it is made a duty of the Per-

---

[14] Sec. 5(c), Executive Order, June 7, 1924.

sonnel Board "to recommend to the Secretary of State the assignment of Foreign Service officers to posts and the transfer of such officers from one branch of the service to the other, according to the needs of the service." For the purposes of this action, however, the Undersecretary of State and the two Assistant Secretaries of State who are members of the Board are deemed to constitute the full Board, although the Executive Committee is given the power of making recommendations. In other words, assignments and transfers are very naturally left to the determination of the duly constituted administrative officers of the department, aided, but not controlled in their judgment, by the suggestions or recommendations of the three service officers of the Executive Committee, acting collectively.

Policy in transfers and assignments.—In outlining its policy, the Board has adopted the following general line of procedure:

"In regard to the policy to be followed in connection with transfers between the two branches of the Foreign Service, it may be said in general that such transfers will depend upon the needs of the Service and the fitness of individual officers to meet those needs. Aside from experience in both branches which may be found advantageous in the training of young officers in the early years of their service, indiscriminate transfers from one branch to the other clearly would not be in the interest of the Government or of the officers themselves. Whenever it is apparent, however, that an officer in one branch can render better service to the Government with consequent increased advantage to himself, or meet an existing need in the other branch, the Department will feel free to transfer him and it will expect him to accept cheerfully the changed status.

"The general policy with relation to the branch of the Service in which an officer shall make the major portion of his career may be stated as follows: if an officer is particularly adapted to and fitted for one branch of the Service he will be expected to serve in that branch regardless of his own preferences; if on the other hand the qualifications of an officer should appear to render him almost equally valuable for either branch, he will be permitted to remain in the branch of his choice so far as that course may be consistent with the best interests of the Service.

"Without in any sense obscuring the line of distinction between the functions of the two branches of the Foreign Service, a distinction well established by international law and practice, it is desirable for members of both branches to bear in mind that while they may be performing different functions they are all members of one Service with equal rights and responsibilities, entitled to advancement in the several classes of Foreign Service officers upon relative merit, and ultimately, if consistent with their particular qualifications and records of efficiency, to recommendation to the President for appointment to the grade of minister." [15]

Controversies and delinquencies.—In like manner, the consideration of controversies and delinquencies and the corrective action determined upon in such cases is purely an administrative function. Therefore, the same three administrative officials are deemed to constitute a full Board for the discharge of the duty which requires it "to consider controversies and delinquencies among the service personnel and recommend to the Secretary appropriate disciplinary measures where required." In this case, as in the case of assignments and transfers,

[15] General Instruction, Dip. Serial No. 288, July 29, 1924.

the members of the Executive Committee, acting collectively, have the power of recommendation.

The system of elimination.—With a view to the unrelenting enforcement of a high service standard, the machinery of elimination is operative at every point. Original appointments are made contingent upon the demonstration of acceptable qualifications during a period of probation. At the end of a year of probationary instruction and observation, the fitness of the candidate is judged and he is either finally commissioned or dropped.

Having attained to a classified grade, he then falls within the disciplinary jurisdiction of the Personnel Board whenever his rating drops below that of his colleagues. The duty of the Board in this connection is prescribed as follows:

"Whenever it is determined that the efficiency rating of an officer is poor and below the required standard for the Service, the Personnel Board shall so notify the officer, and if after due notification the rating of such officer continues nevertheless to be unsatisfactory, his name shall be reported to the Secretary of State with a full recital of the circumstances and a recommendation of the Board for separation from the Service.

"Whenever such recommendation for separation from the service is made, the Board shall at the same time notify the officer of the action taken." [16]

In commenting upon this feature of the reorganized service, Honorable Wilbur J. Carr has stated:

"The stability of the career and the permanence of its personnel have been assured. All the vulnerable features of the old régime have been replaced by solid barriers against meddling and uncertainty. A young officer

---

[16]Sec. 6, Executive Order, June 7, 1924.

just entering the service will find that he is offered a course of invaluable instruction before entering upon his permanent duties, but that at the same time he will be on probation and his every act and qualification open to the severest scrutiny with respect to his personal fitness. After his definite acceptance, and when he has entered upon the discharge of his regular duties, he will find that the same observing eyes are watching with the same scrutiny all evidences of his success or failure. Throughout his entire career the machinery of elimination, which is set up by the Executive order, will so constantly guard and enforce the high standard of the service that the period of probation through which he entered will, in effect, seem to extend to the very day of his superannuation." [17]

Duties of the Executive Committee.—It has already been shown that the Executive Committee of the Foreign Service Personnel Board is composed of a chairman and two Foreign Service officers of high rank, representing both the diplomatic and consular branches of the Foreign Service. The Executive order which created this committee to operate in conjunction with the Personnel Board authorized the Secretary to prescribe its duties. This has been done by departmental order as follows:

1. "To take into its possession and consolidate immediately all records and material relating to the personnel of the Foreign Service, both diplomatic and consular. The Diplomatic Bureau, the Consular Bureau and the Office of Consular Personnel will promptly surrender all such files and records as may be in their possession.

---

[17] American Consular Bulletin, July, 1924.

2. "To keep the efficiency records of all Foreign Service officers and employees.

3. "To collect, collate, and record pertinent data relating to foreign service personnel.

4. "To submit to the Foreign Service Personnel Board recommendations for the assignment of officers to posts and the transfer of such officers from one branch of the service to the other.

5. "To recommend the granting of leaves of absence.

6. "To interview applicants and prospective applicants for the Foreign Service.

7. "To examine and recommend for appointment applicants for positions as subordinate employees in the Foreign Service.

8. "To maintain contact with Foreign Service officers and employees while on visits to the United States. For this purpose a register of visiting officers and employees shall be kept.

"All personnel records shall be held strictly confidential, and no papers, documents, data or reports relating thereto shall be revealed except to the Secretary of State, the members of the Foreign Service Personnel Board, and the Board of Review." [18]

The Board of Review.—Bringing forward and adopting the former consular practice of an annual board of review for the purpose of examining the background of individual ratings and determining, in an advisory sense, the relative standing of all officers in the service, the Secretary of State has now provided a similar practice for the Foreign Service as follows:

"At least once a year, or whenever the Secretary of State shall so order, all personnel records, ratings and

---

[18]Departmental Order No. 295, June 9, 1924.

accumulated material shall be examined impartially by a Board of Review and a report rendered to the Foreign Service Personnel Board as to the relative standing of officers and employees. The Board of Review shall be composed of five members, of whom the Chairman of the Executive Committee shall be the Chairman, and the remaining four drawn from Foreign Service officers of high rank by the Secretary of State." [19]

The Board of Examiners.—It has been shown that formerly two separate boards of examiners existed for the Diplomatic and Consular Services and that the nature and scope of the examinations, though similar in many respects, were essentially different in other important particulars.[20] Manifestly, in administering the unified service, a single examination, consolidating the previous requirements for the two branches, became necessary. Furthermore, in order to maintain uniformity and consistency in selection requirements, and to provide for the enforcement of a definite service standard, it likewise became necessary to entrust all procedure in connection with entrance examinations to a single board.

The President in his Executive order, therefore, has established the following system:

"There is hereby constituted a Board of Examiners composed of the following members; to wit: The Undersecretary of State, an Assistant Secretary of State to be designated by the Secretary of State, the Director of the Consular Service (on and after July 1, 1924, this title becomes Assistant Secretary of State), the Chairman of the Executive Committee of the Foreign Service Personnel Board, and the Chief Examiner of the Civil

---

[19] *Ibid.*
[20] See pages 22, 26.

Service Commission or such person as may be designated by him to serve in his stead.

"It shall be the duty of the Board of Examiners to formulate rules for and hold examinations of applicants for commission to the Foreign Service and to determine from among the persons designated by the President for examination those who are fitted for appointment.

"The scope and method of the examinations shall be determined by the Board of Examiners, but among the subjects shall be included the following: at least one modern language other than English (French, Spanish, or German by preference), elements of international law, geography, the natural, industrial, and commercial resources and the commerce of the United States; American history, government and institutions; the history since 1850 of Europe, Latin America and the Far East; elements of political economy, commercial and maritime law.

"The examinations shall be both written and oral.

"Examinations shall be rated on a scale of 100, and no person rated at less than 80 shall be eligible for certification.

"No one shall be certified as eligible who is under twenty-one or over thirty-five years of age, or who is not a citizen of the United States, or who is not of good character and habits and physically, mentally, and temperamentally qualified for the proper performance of the duties of the Foreign Service, or who has not been specially designated by the President for appointment subject to examination and to the occurrence of an appropriate vacancy.

"Upon the conclusion of the examinations, the names of the candidates who shall have attained upon the whole examination the required rating will be certified by the

Board to the Secretary of State as eligible for appointment.

The eligible list.—"The names of candidates will remain on the eligible list for two years, except in the case of such candidates as shall within that period be appointed or shall withdraw their names. Names which have been on the eligible list for two years will be dropped therefrom and the candidates concerned will not again be eligible for appointment unless upon fresh application, designation anew for examination, and the successful passing of such examination.

"Applicants for appointment who are designated to take an examination and who fail to report therefor shall not be entitled to take a subsequent examination unless they shall have been specifically designated to take such subsequent examination.

"In designations for appointment subject to examination and in appointments after examination, due regard will be had to the principle that, as between candidates of equal merit, appointments should be made so as to tend to secure proportional representation of all the States and Territories in the Foreign Service; and neither in the designation for examination nor certification nor appointment after examination will the political affiliations of the candidates be considered.

Appointments.—"The Board of Examiners is authorized to issue such notices and to make all such rules as it may deem necessary to accomplish the object of this regulation.

"New appointments to the service shall be to the grade of Foreign Service officer, unclassified, and no promotions to a higher grade shall be made except on the recommendation of the Foreign Service Personnel Board, with the approval of the Secretary of State, after the completion of one full term of instruction, or the equivalent thereof, in the Foreign Service School hereinafter established.

"Those candidates for appointment as diplomatic or consular officers whose names are on the eligible list at the time the Act of May 24, 1924, becomes effective shall be eligible for appointment as Foreign Service officers."

The Foreign Service School.—It has been noted that Section 5 of the reorganization act provides "that hereafter appointments to the position of Foreign Service officer shall be made after examination and a suitable period of probation in an unclassified grade * * *"

The former practice was to admit candidates to the service by giving them a direct appointment without in all cases an opportunity of examining thoroughly into their general fitness for the service. Furthermore, it not infrequently occurred that these men were sent to their posts abroad with insufficient instruction as to the nature of their duties.

Taking advantage of the period of probation now prescribed by the statute, the President has established in the Department of State a Foreign Service School for the instruction of new appointees, covering a period of one year. The direction of the school is entrusted to a Foreign Service School Board, composed of the Undersecretary of State, an Assistant Secretary of State to be designated by the Secretary of State, the former Director of the Consular Service, now an Assistant Secretary of State, the Chairman of the Executive Committee of the Foreign Service Personnel Board, and the Chief Instructor of the Foreign Service School. A full description of this unique institution and of its mode of operation will be found in Chapter XII.

CHAPTER XI

THE RETIREMENT SYSTEM

The corner-stone of reorganization.—For several important reasons the retirement system may be regarded as the corner-stone of the Foreign Service reorganization structure. To build a permanent service—a life career—with no outlet for superannuated officials would be tantamount to stagnation. In the course of a few years the higher grades would become clogged with men of advanced age, thus effectually blocking all prospect of promotion for those in the lower ranks. Indeed, strong symptoms of such a condition had already begun to manifest themselves in the old service, where the maintenance of the prevailing standard of efficiency was rapidly becoming an administrative problem. In seeking the presidential approval of the reorganization plan, Secretary of State Hughes referred to the proposal for a retirement system as follows:

"Owing to the length of time that the Diplomatic and Consular Services have been on a civil service basis, there are a number of positions, especially in the Consular Service, being held by officers advanced in years whose retention impairs the efficiency of the service as a whole. It has become urgently necessary to provide for the retirement of these officers, and in view of the fact that both branches of the service are well established on a civil service basis it appears feasible to bring them under the provisions of the civil service retirement act of May 22, 1920, modified only as to the age of retirement, the rate of contribution, and the rate of annuity. The immediate benefits of such an enactment would be appreciable. In fact, no proposal in connection with the improvement of the Foreign Service commends itself to my judgment with greater force." [1]

In the interest of the service itself there were other commanding reasons why a retirement system had become necessary. No plan of adjustment could be expected to succeed which did not, in an appropriate degree, blend the welfare of the individual officer with that of his service. That the old organization was sadly deficient in this regard has been clearly shown by Secretary Hughes, whose arguments before the Committee on Foreign Affairs are convincing. He said:

"I have said that there should be provided a career as more of an inducement to the right men, who do not happen to have private means, to enter the service. But it is not enough to give them a mere living wage as they go along. Having entered this service as a career, it means that when they get through they are unfitted for anything else. They are down and out. Under no salary scale that this Government will ever give, certainly not under the one that is here suggested, will anybody lay up money. They can not do it.

"What are they going to do when they come to 65 years of age, after thirty-odd years in the service? They can not go into anything else; they are through. There ought to be some provision for retirement allowances. What is the consequence at the present time? It is a consequence which is observed not only in our service, in the Department of State, but throughout the Gov-

---

[1]Letter to the President, Aug. 22, 1922, see Hearings before the Committee on Foreign Affairs, on H. R. 17 and H. R. 6357, 68th Cong., 1st Sess., p. 24.

ernment service, and that is, we train men for other enterprises. They enter young, they are promising, they do good work, and just as they have got the experience which should reinforce their native ability and their acquisition of knowledge, they say, 'Well, what is before me?' They are picked up by private enterprise. You can not absolutely prevent that result, but you can make a man feel that he has the protection of his Government in his career if he serves the Government with fidelity, and that when he gets through with the career, in which the Government has not enabled him to save anything, in his old age the Government will give him reasonable protection." [2]

Retirement a factor of efficiency.—But it must not be imagined that the interests of the men were uppermost in the minds of those who advocated reform. Far from it, these personal interests were secondary to the main thought of building a strong Foreign Service and were only allowed to figure in the plan to a degree which would assure the desired result. Honorable Wilbur J. Carr expressed it clearly when he said to the committee:

"I hope in anything I may say here that I may not be understood as merely advocating doing something for men. The thought that lies back of anything that I may say to the committee is that what we need to concern ourselves with is the building of a service, the building of efficiency in that service, getting into the higher diplomatic posts and higher consular posts the best men we can develop and induce them to remain in the service." [3]

The principle of retirement on account of age has come to be recognized as an essential factor of efficiency.

[2] Hearings before the Committee on Foreign Affairs, on H. R. 17 and H. R. 6357, 68th Cong., 1st Sess., pp. 14, 15.
[3] *Ibid*, p. 110.

The proof of this lies in the fact that it has been widely adopted by important corporations and business organizations which operate for profit, and has long been applied in many of the separate State governments.

Retirement systems in operation.—The following enumeration, which is necessarily incomplete, will serve to illustrate the extent to which various forms of pension, or contributory retirement systems are now being inaugurated:

States enacting legislation in relation to pensions and retirement, 1918-1920: Pennsylvania, Wisconsin, New York, Minnesota, New Jersey, Illinois, Oregon, Kentucky, Massachusetts, Oklahoma, Missouri, Kansas, Utah, Montana, Washington, Connecticut, California, Maryland, Maine, Iowa, and Porto Rico.

Corporations paying the entire cost of pensions granted to their employees: Canadian Pacific Railway; Pennsylvania Railroad Co.; the Pennsylvania lines west of Pittsburgh; the New York Central & Hudson River Railroad; the Boston & Albany Railroad; the Baltimore & Ohio Railroad; the Illinois Central Railroad; the Southern Pacific Railroad Co.; the Delaware, Lackawanna & Western Railroad; the Philadelphia & Reading Railroad; the Midvale Steel Co.; the Cumberland Valley Railroad; the San Antonio & Aransas Pass Railroad; the Champlain Transportation Co.; the Metropolitan Street Railway Co.; the Houston & East Texas Railroad Co.; the Oregon Railroad & Navigation Co.; the Boston Irrigation Co.; the Fourth National Bank of Philadelphia; the First National Bank of Pittsburgh; the Girard National Bank of Philadelphia; the Bank of New York National Banking Association; the Merchants National Bank of Baltimore, Md.; the Old Dominion Steamship Co.

Corporations requiring contributions from employees to the pension: Grand Trunk Railway Co., of Canada, 2½ per cent contribution from the employees and a like amount from the company; the First National Bank of Chicago, 3 per cent contribution based on employees' salary.[4]

Federal retirement systems.—As regards the Federal Government, the policy with respect to retirement may be said to have assumed very definite form. Federal Judges are retired on full pay without contribution; Army and Navy officers are retired on three-quarters pay without contribution; there is a retirement system for the Coast Guard, for the Lighthouse Service, and for the Civil Service, which embraces practically the entire range of Federal employees. The Foreign Service was the last important group to be given a retirement status, although for many reasons it might well have been among the first.

The problem of retaining good men.—Consular training is business training. It not only equips a man for the handling of business problems, but gives him at the same time a rare and intimate knowledge of foreign business methods and of international affairs in general. These are looked upon as important assets, equally valuable in some forms of private business and in the Government service. Nearly all efficient consuls are at some stage of their careers tempted by flattering business offers which many have found it exceedingly difficult to decline.

Honorable Wilbur J. Carr has shown the difficulties of holding efficient officers under such circumstances. Too frequently the decision to resign has been forced

---

[4]Extract from hearings before the Committee on Reform in the Civil Service, House of Representatives, Sixty-sixth Congress, first session, p. 105.

by reason of simple justice to oneself with very little latitude for the exercise of preference or of choice. Mr. Carr stated:

"There is a spirit in the Foreign Service which the man on the outside does not quite appreciate. These men who go out of the service, who are highly useful men and ought to stay in, are often driven out by force of circumstances and not from any wish to go out merely for the sake of larger compensation. * * * What we need to do, and I am sure you will agree with me in this, is all that can be reasonably done to retain as much as possible of the ability that we can accumulate in this Foreign Service of ours. We are coming into a period when experience, technical knowledge, personality, and ability to negotiate are going to be more essential than ever before to the welfare of this Government in connection with its foreign relations.

"Now, I would like to prove what I said to you a moment ago in regard to the desire of our officers to remain in the service by citing an example of a man who has so far resisted the importunities of private business establishments and remained in the service. How much longer he will do so, I do not know. He happens to be unmarried and have a salary of $5,000 and traveling expenses—he is an inspector. When he takes a post as consul-general he will be eligible to $8,000. He is, as I say, unmarried. He has, to my certain knowledge, declined offers beginning at $15,000 and increasing until the last one he declined was $28,000. He said, 'No; I will not leave the service.' Suppose he should marry and want to bring up a family. Force of circumstances are almost certain to make that man leave the service because he will then have to think of making some provision for old age. With legislation such as this, I am practically confident this man would remain with the Government." [5]

Analysis of the Foreign Service retirement system.— The system of retirement adopted for the Foreign Service is the same in principle as that applying to the Civil Service from which it differs by way of adaptation only to the extent made necessary by the peculiar requirements of the foreign career. The administration of the system is placed under the direction of the Secretary of State, the President being authorized to prescribe rules and regulations for its enforcement in accordance with the general framework of principles contained in the act.

The retirement fund.—The system is contributory. There is a special fund, known as the Foreign Service retirement and disability fund, to which all Foreign Service officers eligible to retirement are required to contribute at the rate of five per centum of their basic salaries. The term "basic salary" means the regular statutory salary applying to each class, exclusive of any extra compensation, allowances, or emoluments whatsoever. The amount of the contribution in each case is deducted from salary by the Secretary of the Treasury and transferred on the books to the credit of the Foreign Service retirement and disability fund. It will be noted that the contribution of five per centum is double the rate of contribution required of civil service employees, which is two and one-half per centum of the basic salary.

The age of retirement.—The age of retirement for the Foreign Service is sixty-five years, which applies to all officers who have rendered fifteen years of service. As the age limit for entrance into the service has, since 1906, been fifty years, all officers now in the service who

---

[5] Hearings before Committee on Foreign Affairs on H. R. 17 and H. R. 6357, pp. 110-111.

were appointed after examination will have performed at least fifteen years of duty upon reaching the age of sixty-five.

Retirement at sixty-five is automatic, but the President may, in his discretion, retain an officer on active duty for such period not exceeding five years as he may deem for the interests of the United States; that is, he may retain an officer until the age of seventy, but no longer.[6]

Under the civil service retirement law, the age of automatic retirement is seventy years, although in the case of certain employees who perform work of a particularly active character it ranges as low as sixty-two.

The report of the board of government actuaries makes the following comment on the age of automatic retirement for the Foreign Service: "Age 65 is not itself a comparatively low age for the minimum permissive retirement age; age 60 is more commonly adopted as the minimum age. The change from 70 to 65 for the Foreign Service is, therefore, not a radical reduction and is believed advisable both from the standpoint of the employees and the service."[7]

The scale of annuities.—Annuities are paid to Foreign Service officers under a classification based upon length of service and the amount of the basic salary. The classification is as follows:

Class A—30 years and over		60%
Class B—27 to 30 years		54%
Class C—24 to 27 years		48%
Class D—21 to 24 years		42%
Class E—18 to 21 years		36%
Class F—15 to 18 years		30%

[6]Consul General John G. Foster, who is stationed at Ottawa, Canada, has been thus retained for an additional year by order of the President. This is the only exception made so far. In the general reclassification effective July 1, 1924, there were thirty-two retirements on account of age.

[7]Report of Board of Actuaries on the foreign service retirement and disability plan, January 7, 1924.

Applying this scale to the various classes, the following table shows the amount of annuity due in certain instances:

FOREIGN SERVICE RETIREMENT BENEFITS

RANK		RATE OF ANNUITIES					
Class	Basic Salary	A 30 Years	B 27 to 30 Years	C 24 to 27 Years	D 21 to 24 Years	E 18 to 21 Years	F 15 to 18 Years
1	$9,000	$5,400	$4,860	$4,320	$3,780	$3,240	$2,700
2	8,000	4,800	4,320	3,840	3,360	2,880	2,400
3	7,000	4,200	3,780	3,360	2,940	2,520	2,100
4	6,000	3,600	3,240	2,880	2,520	2,160	1,800
5	5,000	3,000	2,700	2,400	2,100	1,800	1,500
6	4,500	2,700	2,430	2,160	1,890	1,620	1,350
7	4,000	2,400	2,160	1,920	1,680	1,440	1,200
8	3,500	2,100	1,890	1,680	1,470	1,260	1,050
9	3,000	1,800	1,620	1,440	1,260	1,080	900

The factor of accrued liability.—The chief difficulty in instituting a contributory retirement system lies in the fact that no past contributions have been made by the men already in the service. As these men are due to retire before having contributed their proportional share for each year of service they constitute an additional burden of expense on the retirement fund. The past services of present employees thus constitute an accrued liability which must be met in part from the contributions of other men, and in part from appropriations. Not until the present personnel is retired and entirely out of the way will the system have liquidated its accrued liabilities and reached its normal basis.

Comparative cost.—The following table, which shows a comparison between the civil service retirement system under the act of May 22, 1920, and the Foreign Service retirement system under the act of May 24, 1924, gives the estimated cost of operation and the relation which the contributions of the men bear to those of the Government:

| | CIVIL SERVICE | | FOREIGN | SERVICE |
	Rate	Annual Payment	Rate	Annual Payment
Normal	3.26%	$91,511	6.94%	$194,813
Deficiency	1.86	52,212	3.85	108,073
Total	5.12%	$143,723	10.79%	$302,886
Payable by Employees.	2.50	70,178	5.00	140,355
Payable by Government	2.62%	$ 73,545	5.79%	$162,531

It will be observed from these figures that the normal cost of maintaining the Foreign Service retirement and disability fund will be 6.94 per cent of the totality of basic salaries. As 5 per cent is being contributed by the men, this leaves a contribution of only 1.94 per cent from the Government. When the system reaches its normal basis, therefore, the contributions of the men will cover 72 per cent of the total cost and those of the Government 28 per cent. But on account of the accrued liability, and until this is completely discharged, it is estimated that 10.79 per cent of the totality of salaries will be required. As the service will contribute 5 per cent, there remains 5.79 per cent to be contributed by the Government; or in other words, slightly more than one-half.

Limiting the cost to the government.—But the act provides that in no event shall the aggregate total appropriations made by the Government exceed the aggregate total of the contributions of the Foreign Service officers theretofore made and accumulated interest thereon. In order to assure this even break as between the contributions of the men and the cost to the government, three expedients have been adopted with a view to eliminating the small fractional difference of .79 per cent:

(a) It is provided that those officers who retire before having contributed for each year of service shall have withheld from their annuities to the credit of the Foreign Service retirement and disability fund such proportion of five per cent thereof as the number of years in which they did not contribute bears to the total length of service. In other words, such officers, upon retirement, begin to contribute from their annuities and continue such contributions as long as they draw retirement benefits. Those who were retired on July 1, 1924, having made no contributions, are required henceforth to contribute 5 per cent of their annuities.

The formula employed for calculating these deductions from annuities is a simple ratio. To determine its application in a given case let us imagine an officer whose basic salary is $6,000, whose length of service is 30 years and who has contributed for only five years. Thirty years of service would rank him in Class A, entitling him to 60 per cent of his basic salary, or $3,600 per annum. Since he has contributed for five years there would be 25 years in which he has not contributed. Therefore, he would have deducted from his annuity the same proportion of 5 per cent thereof as 25 years bear to 30. In other words, the formula would be $30:25::5\%:(x)$. Solving this equation we get $150 as the amount to be deducted annually from his annuity.

(b) The second expedient is contained in Section 18(1), which provides:

"Whenever a Foreign Service officer becomes separated from the service except for disability before reaching the age of retirement, 75 per centum of the total amount of contribution from his salary without interest shall be returned to him."

This means that in cases to which the provision applies, 25 per centum of the officer's contributions, plus interest, are forfeited to the retirement fund.

(c) The third expedient is less direct. Section 18 (m) provides:

"Whenever any Foreign Service officer, after the date of his retirement, accepts a position of employment the emoluments of which are greater than the annuity received by him from the United States Government by virtue of his retirement under this Act, the amount of the said annuity during the continuance of such employment shall be reduced by an equal amount: Provided, That all retired Foreign Service officers shall notify the Secretary of State once a year of any positions of employment accepted by them stating the amount of compensation received therefrom and whenever any such officer fails to so report it shall be the duty of the Secretary of State to order the payment of the annuity to be suspended until such report is received."

In simple language, a retired Foreign Service officer is allowed to accept a position which pays him as much as his annuity. But in proportion as such salary may exceed the amount of his annuity, the annuity itself becomes curtailed. Thus, if the annuity be $5,000, he may accept a position paying $5,000, making his total income $10,000; but if the position should pay $6,000, his annuity would be reduced to $4,000.

The advantage to an officer in accepting such a position lies in the fact that he may thereby defer for a number of years exhausting the amount of his contributions, plus interest, which is to his credit in the retirement fund. It is reasonable to assume that instances of this character will arise, with corresponding benefit to the fund.

The very conservative figures used in the hearings before the Committee on Foreign Affairs in reckoning the cost of retirement did not take into consideration the above described factors of expediency, which were adopted later. The following table shows the estimated annuities payable to Foreign Service officers up to the year 1945 when the first governmental appropriation will become due:

TABLE OF ANNUITY PAYMENTS

Fiscal Year Ending June 30	Annuities Payable During Year	Available Retirement Fund from Contributions with Interest Compounded at 4 per cent	Balance after Payment of Annuities	Necessary Appropriation
1925	$ 61,176.41	$143,719.85	$ 82,543.44	....
1926	71,791.67	229,405.80	157,614.13	....
1927	80,866.60	307,343.20	226,476.60	....
1928	86,633.43	378,873.36	292,219.93	....
1929	93,260.35	446,654.93	353,394.58	....
1930	97,131.26	510,257.20	413,125.94	....
1931	101,759.00	572,762.10	471,003.10	....
1932	111,163.40	632,812.27	521,648.87	....
1933	116,355.09	685,406.97	569,051.88	....
1934	129,925.29	734,502.58	604,577.28	....
1935	141,951.55	771,268.00	629,316.95	....
1936	149,410.66	796,989.63	647,578.97	....
1937	164,715.13	815,902.13	651,267.00	....
1938	179,978.65	819,817.68	639,839.13	....
1939	199,987.14	807,932.70	607,945.56	....
1940	212,814.00	774,763.38	561,949.38	....
1941	232,009.55	726,927.36	494,827.81	....
1942	248,431.01	657,120.92	408,689.91	....
1943	265,266.43	567,537.51	302,271.08	....
1944	308,209.60	456,861.92	148,652.32	....
1945	346,050.10	297,098.00	....	$48,951.69

It will be seen that the system is self-sustaining from contributions, plus interest, for a period of twenty years, or until 1945, at which time the Government must make an appropriation of approximately $50,000.

Had the Government begun, as was required of the men, by making its proportional share of the contributions annually, the eventual burden of its expense would have been ameliorated through the accumulation of compound interest. But as this plan has not been adopted, the Government must, at the end of twenty years, begin to make up its past contributions. This will entail increasing appropriations from year to year until the peak of approximately $500,000 is reached, about 1960. Having passed the peak, the amount of the governmental contributions will decrease steadily until the normal basis of the system is reached.

The disability feature.—The act provides that any Foreign Service officer who, before reaching the age of retirement, becomes totally disabled for useful and efficient service by reason of disease or injury not due to vicious habits, intemperance, or wilful misconduct on his part, shall, upon his own application, or upon order of the President, be retired on an annuity following the same scale as in the case of retirement on account of age. If the disability is not of a permanent nature, a physical examination will be required each year, and payment of the annuity will cease from the date of the medical examination showing recovery.

At this point the language of the act is deficient, for it fails to state what is to become of the officer; that is, whether he is to be reinstated at his original salary, or dropped from the service. Manifestly, a great injustice would result from the latter course, wherefore it is to be anticipated that in administrative practice such officers will be restored to their original grades without impairment of their rights to further retirement benefits upon reaching the retirement age.

There is also another deficiency in the law in connection with the disability feature. Retirement annuities are earned only after fifteen years of service, whereas an officer is liable to become incapacitated at any time. If he must have served fifteen years before earning the right to disability benefits, cases of disability may arise after shorter terms of service, in which no benefits would accrue.

Service at unhealthful posts.—The President is authorized from time to time to establish by Executive order a list of places in tropical countries which, by reason of climatic or other extreme conditions, are to be classed as unhealthful posts, and each year of duty at such posts, while so classed, inclusive of regular leaves of absence, shall be counted as one year and a half, and so on in like proportion in reckoning the length of service for the purposes of retirement.

This follows the practice of other countries. As the Foreign Service covers the entire world, its officers are exposed to all manner of trying conditions. Manifestly, as regards the climate requirements of Americans, all so-called unhealthful posts are not to be found in the tropics, nor are all tropical posts to be considered as unhealthful. In the main, however, administrative practice has shown that certain localities in tropical countries are likely to impair the health of officers if retained there too long. The President has not yet prescribed the posts to which this provision shall apply.

Retirement of ministers.—One of the most important and essential features of the retirement act is contained in Section 18(o) which provides that:

"Any diplomatic secretary or consular officer who has been or any Foreign Service officer who may hereafter be promoted from the classified service to the grade of ambassador or minister, or appointed to a position in the Department of State, shall be entitled to all the benefits of this section in the same manner and under the same conditions as Foreign Service officers."

Obviously, the effect of the foregoing is to render officers in the classified service eligible for promotion to the grade of minister; for without the retention of their retirement status, they would be in no financial position to separate themselves from the classified service and assume the burdens of a chief of mission. It is not difficult to understand why an officer would be loath to accept promotion under such circumstances. At the age when he may be tendered an appointment as minister, his vested interest in the retirement fund should have assumed an importance of many thousands of dollars. According to insurance tables, the number of years an officer may be expected to live after retirement is about eleven. Considering him to have reached class one after thirty years of service, he would, at the age of 65 years, be entitled to $5,400 per annum for the rest of his life. Based upon the average experience, the total of his retirement benefits should approximate $60,000, whereas, with a prolongation of life beyond the average age this amount would be correspondingly increased. The retirement system, therefore, offers as its maximum reward, at the age of retirement, what is equivalent to the usufruct, or interest, at 5.4 per cent on an estate of $100,000 in gilt-edged government securities.

Under the regulations governing the reorganized service, the entrance age is from twenty-one to thirty-five, hence all future appointees will serve a minimum period of thirty years before reaching the age of retirement. This will entitle them to 60 per cent of their basic salaries.

Comparison with the British system.—It is interesting at this point to draw a comparison between the range of salaries and retirement benefits in the Consular Service of the United States and that of Great Britain. In examining the following table, due note should be taken of the fact that representation allowances and rent allowances under the British system are variable in amount.

RETIREMENT PAY OF BRITISH CONSULAR SERVICE COMPARED WITH RETIREMENT PAY OF UNITED STATES

Grade of Officer	Salary in British Service	Representation in British Service	House and Rent Allowance in British Service	Total Salary and Emoluments	Salary in United States Service	Maximum Pension in British Service	Maximum Pension in United States Service
Consuls general	$7,299 to $5,839	$1,459	$1,216	$9,974 to $8,514	$9,000 to $7,000	$4,987 to $4,257	$5,400 to $4,200
Consuls	4,866 to 3,893	1,216	973	7,055 to 6,082	6,000 to 3,000	3,527 to 3,041	3,600 to 1,800
Vice consuls	2,919 to 1,459	729 to 486	973 to 486	4,621 to 2,431	3,000 to 2,500	2,310 to 1,215	
Interpreters, student interpreters, and consular assistants.....					3,000 to 1,500		

Notes.—There is no contribution required from officers under British pension system. In the British service the pension is based upon salary and emoluments at time of retirement or average for last three years if there has been a change within that period. It begins upon completion of 10 years' service, and increases by an annual increment of one-eighteenth until the completion of 40 years' service, or until retirement. This applies to all officers who have entered service since September 20, 1909. All officers appointed before that date receive ten-sixtieths of their retirement pay for the first 10 years' service and one-sixtieth for each year thereafter until completion of 40 years or until retirement.

In the British service retirement is voluntary at 60 and compulsory at 65 unless the Government wishes to continue an officer in service longer, in which case it may continue him by intervals until he is 70 years of age.

The retention of good men.—An officer in the Foreign Service may be expected to reach his maximum efficiency after fifteen years of active service, or about the age of forty to forty-five years. This is the point at which business interests usually tempt him with flattering offers; but it is also the point at which, in the normal experience, his interest in the retirement fund should have become appreciable.

He should already have earned a half interest in his retirement estate, entitling him to some $1,400 a year for life. To resign the service would mean to surrender this interest. Given the fact that there is no provision for reinstatement except in the case of officers resigning to accept some other government position, there will be no such thing as experimental plunges out of the service into business and back into the service again.

While the system is called contributory, the contributions do not result from a levy on salaries. Quite to the contrary, the horizontal salary increase granted under the reorganization plan amounts to a fraction over 26 per cent. Thus, as the rate of contribution to the retirement fund is only 5 per cent, there remains a net raise in salaries of about 21 per cent. Literally speaking, the Government has not only provided this substantial increase in compensation, but it has also provided the 5 per cent to cover the contributions.

Effect of the retirement provision.—The retirement system effectually relieves the Foreign Service of its chief menace, namely, that of penury and dependency in declining years. It affords an outlet for superannuated officials, thus providing vacant positions in the upper grades for the steady advancement of those who merit promotion. It gives to each officer a vested interest in the service, a reason for staying with it, and an incentive to reach the top. Whatever element of doubt may have remained as to the permanence and the stability of the Foreign Service career, all misgivings are now dispelled by the inauguration of a system in which both the men and the Government undertake to contribute to its maintenance on a life basis.

CHAPTER XII

EDUCATION FOR THE FOREIGN SERVICE

A brief sketch of the movement.—Education for the Foreign Service is an old and a persistent topic of discussion. It has been approached from many angles and has formed the subject of several concrete proposals, all of which have contemplated some form of governmental aid.

In other countries there have been notable achievements of this character, particularly in France, where the diplomatic disasters of 1870 led to the founding of the *École Libre des Sciences Politiques;*[1] in Germany where, "as a result of the diplomatic defeats in this war a scheme for an *Auslands Hoch-Schule* has been revived, and is being realized in Berlin"; and in England where "as a result of our (the British) diplomatic discomfitures in the early part of the war, a movement was started by liberal parliamentarians for a School of Foreign Affairs in London."[2]

---

[1]"The French *École Libre des Sciences Politiques* furnishes an admirable course in preparation for the Foreign Service. Although the candidates who take the Government examinations receive no credit for their attendance at the school, nevertheless it is only exceptionally that a man enters the Service without the preparation which it affords. More recently another school, established in Paris, trains men for these examinations, and the rivalry between the two is stimulating. In the diplomatic section of the *École Libre des Sciences Politiques,* which offers a training for diplomats and consuls, will be found young men from all parts of the world who have come to prepare themselves for the foreign service of their own country. The *École Libre,* presided over by a remarkable group of teachers, has carried French influence to all parts of the world. It would be of great advantage to this country if similar institutions could be established at the capital or in some of our principal cities."—National Civil Service Reform League, "Report on the Foreign Service" (1919), p. 31.

[2]George Young, "Diplomacy Old and New," p. 98.

A National Consular School proposed.—In 1909, when the business interests of the United States were urging the enactment of an adequate consular law, a bill was introduced by Representative Frank O. Lowden, of Illinois, proposing the establishment of a "National Consular School," and providing that all candidates for the Consular Service should be appointed from among its graduates, the President retaining the power to make appointments at large only when no graduates of the school were available.[3]

The National Business League of America, which was then leading the movement for consular reform, undertook an investigation of the educational facilities afforded by the established universities and colleges of the country, as a result of which the following resolution was adopted on February 15, 1909:

"Resolved, That the Board of Directors of the National Business League of America hereby disapproves of all measures for the establishment of a National Consular School, especially as adequate facilities for fitting young men for the American foreign service are abundantly supplied by American universities." [4]

Among the considerations which prompted this action was the allegation that the proposal for a national consular school was discriminatory, and "would practically exclude graduates of the consular and commerce schools of our leading universities, which during the last few years have at great expense provided courses to fit young men for the foreign service." [5] At the same time another point of objection was raised by Charles Willis

---

[3]H. R. 26991, 60th Cong., 2nd Sess.

[4]See booklet entitled "American Universities, American Foreign Service, and an Adequate Consular Law," issued by The National Business League of America (Chicago, 1909), p. 55.

[5]*Ibid.*, p. 54.

Needham, LL. D., President of George Washington University, as follows:

"As things are now, and are likely to be for another generation, a Government School would become either the football of partisan politics or, what is worse, the Annex of the 'Spoils System' as applied to the Consular Service." [6]

The National Council on Foreign Service Training.— With the general awakening of public interest in international affairs following the outbreak of the World War, an educational conference was held at Washington on December 31, 1915, on the invitation of the Commissioner of Education, and under the joint auspices of the Pan American Union, the Consular Service of the Department of State, the Bureau of Foreign and Domestic Commerce, and the United States Bureau of Education, to consider the question of training for Foreign Service. As a result of the work of this conference, the National council on Foreign Service Training came into being, and is still in active operation.[7] Honorable Wilbur J. Carr, then Director of the Consular Service, now Assistant Secretary of State, in an address before the convention, brought out several points of fundamental importance. He stated that since 1906 the average annual number of appointments to the classified Consular Service had been twenty-seven, and that the ac-

---

[6] *Ibid.*, p. 8.

[7] "Through the effort and investigation of the council, the purpose that underlay its appointment has been kept steadily in mind, namely, to plan for and promote a type of training which would not only give to business and to the service of the Government at all times an adequate supply of properly trained personnel, but would aid in building an intelligent and informed public opinion on all matters relating to foreign contacts and relations of our Government and our people."—Report of the National Conference on Foreign Service Training, Washington, December 26, 1923, Bureau of Education Bulletin, 1924, No. 21, prepared by Glen Levin Swiggett, Specialist in Commercial Education.

tual problem was therefore the proper education of twenty-seven men each year. He further stated:

"It is not sufficient to consider mere educational training for the Consular Service, and, I might say, also for the Diplomatic Service. Something more than mere educational training is needed, and that is careful attention to the personality of candidates. Too much emphasis can not be placed upon the importance of personality. A man may come to us with ever so good an education and prove to be utterly useless for our purposes. If I could apportion the weight of education to that of personality, I should almost be inclined to say that the proportion should be about two-thirds personality and one-third education. * * *

"Personally, I am more strongly convinced each year that building up an efficient service requires that admission be restricted to young men with proper educational equipment and that the greater part of the professional training should take place after entrance into the service. Business experience even for a few months is of the greatest value, but it would be a mistake to make it an absolute requirement for admission. * * *

"A careful examination of the records of the personnel of the American Consular Service fails to show that men who have had actual business experience make the best consular officers. Indeed, they do not show that any particular vocation or profession is superior to any other in training men for successful consular careers."[8]

Training for commerce.—Since the conference of 1915 the educational movement for Foreign Service training has very largely taken on the character of preparation

[8]Speech of Honorable Wilbur J. Carr before the Conference on Training for Foreign Service, December 31, 1915, at Washington, Bureau of Education Bulletin, 1917, No. 37, prepared by Glen Levin Swiggett, Organizing Secretary.

for foreign trade, from which it seems to have received its greatest impetus. According to the latest circular of the Bureau of Education, November 1, 1924, there were in 1923-24, seventy-five universities and colleges claiming to give subjects relating to this type of training with an enrollment of 8,602 students. Of this number eighteen universities are said to offer instructions in subjects relating to preparation for the Foreign Service of the United States (diplomatic and consular), although in most instances such claims are modest, as will be seen from the fact that several of them indicate only one subject, while others indicate two or more.

Foreign service pupils proposed.—The original Rogers bill, for the reorganization and improvement of the Foreign Service, contained the following proposal as a means of providing special educational training for candidates:

"That from time to time, as the needs of the service require, the Secretary of State is directed to designate, after their preliminary examination under rules and regulations prescribed by him, Foreign Service pupils, who shall be not less than eighteen nor more than twenty-five years of age, who shall attend such universities as he may prescribe during a period of not less than three years, who shall follow courses of instruction at such universities as shall be prescribed by him, and who, having successfully passed such examinations as may be prescribed at the conclusion of their course of study, may be appointed as Foreign Service officers, unclassified; and such Foreign Service pupils shall be under no expense for subsistence or tuition within a limit of $1,500 per annum while following the prescribed courses of study, but each shall be paid within that limit an amount prescribed for him by the Secretary of State out of funds appropriated by Congress annually for that purpose, and shall enter into a contract in writing that if appointed a Foreign Service officer of the United State of America he will remain in the service during a term of not less than five years from the date of such appointment." [9]

Objection to the plan.—In the revision of the bill the foregoing provision failed to receive the approval of the Department of State and was eliminated. Secretary Hughes, in discussing its merits, and exposing the reasons which actuated him in withholding his endorsement, brought out the following important considerations:

"Adverting to the proposal that a corps of foreign-service pupils be created and the present corps of consular assistants abolished, I do not feel that we are ready at this time for such a change in practice. Under the present system young men who enter the service as consular assistants invigorate the lower ranks by the varied resources which they are able to contribute through the diversified training acquired in our schools and colleges. Their practical education begins by actual contact with the work in the field, and promotion is won after a thorough grounding has been acquired.

"The substitution for this system of a selected corps of foreign-service pupils might have the effect of limiting the scope of selection to young men whose designation would be undertaken at too early an age for their capabilities to be correctly appraised. We can always make appropriate suggestions as to advisable courses of study for young men contemplating a diplomatic career, and further consideration of a plan for foreign-service pupils seems to be advisable." [10]

9Sec. 15, H. R. 17, 1st Sess., 67th Cong.
10Letter from Secretary of State Hughes to Hon. John Jacob Rogers,

Congressional comment.—When the Rogers bill came up for debate in the House of Representatives the absence of an educational provision was noted and commented upon as follows:

"Mr. Fess. Is there any increased facility in educational institutions for the training which the gentleman has mentioned for the Consular Service?

"Mr. Rogers. More and more institutions are giving courses or groups of courses which are adapted to the training of young men for the Foreign Service.

"But to my mind—and important as the academic training is—far beyond what any educational institution can do is the going to school in the consulate. I want to see a man enter the service with thorough knowledge of at least one foreign language, with knowledge of international law, with knowledge of the methods of foreign commerce and intercourse, and so forth, so that he will start as far along on his journey as possible. Then I want him to go to the most practical school in the world —the school in the consular office abroad. * * *

"Mr. Husted. Has the gentleman ever considered the desirability and practicability of maintaining a diplomatic and consular school in the State Department, just as we do for the Army service, just as we do for the Navy service, with instruction in a classroom, practical experience in the consulates and legations and embassies? It is a technical training, and I think it would be a wonderful thing to do.

"Mr. Rogers. I have given a great deal of thought to that question. In an earlier draft of this bill I had a provision for very much the thing the gentleman has in mind. Mr. Hughes, in going over my original proposal,

Oct. 31, 1922, printed in *Hearings before the Committee on Foreign Affairs,* 68th Cong., 1st Sess., on H. R. 17 and H. R. 6357, p. 27.

recommended that for the present at least the school idea be not considered. If the gentleman has the opportunity he will find in a letter to me from the Secretary of State, which appears on page 61 of the hearings, an analysis of the reasons that led him to postpone the recommendation for the present, at least. * * * [11]

"Mr. Husted. I agree with the gentleman that if this bill becomes a law and young men are admitted to the service under its provisions they will in the consulates and legations get the practical experience of the trained men, but I think a great deal would be added if we maintained a school where we could teach the theoretical side as well, where they could get instruction in economic and other technical subjects which they must know both practically and theoretically if they are to function to the best advantage of the Government as consular officers or as diplomatic officers. [12] * * *

"Mr. Husted. * * * The money that we expend for the Army and for the Navy in peace times is largely in the nature of insurance. It is to protect the Government against what may happen, against which we must provide adequate safeguards. The money that we expend for our Foreign Service comes back to us over and over again in direct and indirect benefits. * * * This bill, if it becomes law, will accomplish a great deal, but I believe there is one other thing which we ought to do to enable our Diplomatic and Consular Service to reach the highest point of efficiency. I believe we should have a diplomatic and consular school in the State Department. We maintain at Annapolis a school that we may have efficient naval officers. We maintain a Military

---

[11]*Cong. Record,* Feb. 6, 1923, pp. 3203, 3204.
[12]*Ibid.,* pp. 3209-3210.

Academy at West Point in order that we may have efficient Army officers.

"Mr. Browne of Wisconsin. Will the gentleman
yield?

"Mr. Husted. Yes.

"Mr. Browne of Wisconsin. Does not the gentleman
know that the colleges and universities have courses in
foreign service for that purpose? Georgetown and most
of the universities have courses of that kind.

"Mr. Husted. Some have courses in diplomacy, but
that is also true so far as military instruction is concerned. Nearly all the colleges to-day give instruction
in military subjects, but we would not think of abolishing West Point and we do not consider abolishing
the Naval Academy at Annapolis. I say it is just as
important, and I believe it is far more important, to
maintain a school where we can train men to be consuls
and diplomatic officers as it is to maintain military and
naval academies. The work is highly technical and the
best instruction can be given in the State Department
by our own consuls and diplomats.

"Mr. Moore of Virginia. Will the gentleman yield?

"Mr. Husted. Yes.

"Mr. Moore of Virginia. Does not the gentleman
think that notwithstanding the fact that some of the
universities and colleges have these courses that provision should be made for training these men in the very
business they will have to engage in?

"Mr. Husted. I certainly do think so. Something is
being done in the colleges, but I believe it could be done
much better here at Washington and at very small expense. We have in the State Department the men who
could be the teachers. The classes would be comparatively small. I do not believe there would be more than

25 or 30 men in a class. We would not have to employ additional instructors. The men are right here at the head of the various bureaus and divisions in the State Department. We have the economists and technical experts ready at hand. This is an easy, inexpensive, and practical way to secure a body of highly trained men who are needed in the field to advance the commercial and political interests of the United States. There is no other way, in my opinion, in which the results can be obtained as quickly or as well." [13]

The Foreign Service School.—From the tenor of the foregoing debate it became obvious that an enlightened opinion in Congress supported the idea of special educational training for the Foreign Service, and the State Department was not tardy in taking advantage of this fact. Following out the very practical suggestion of Representative Husted, the bill, before its final passage, was amended to provide for "a suitable period of probation in an unclassified grade" as an entrance requirement.[14] This had the effect of permitting the retention of new appointees in the Department of State for instruction purposes, thus making possible the realization of what is known as the Foreign Service School.

The presidential Executive order, establishing the administrative rules and regulations for the new Foreign Service, carries the following provisions:

"There is hereby established in the Department of State a Foreign Service School for the instruction of new appointees.

"The Foreign Service School shall be under the direction of a Foreign Service School Board, composed of

[13]*Ibid.*, p. 3215.
[14]Sec. 5, Act of May 24, 1924.

the following members; to wit: the Undersecretary of State, an Assistant Secretary of State to be designated by the Secretary of State, the Director of the Consular Service (on and after July 1, 1924, this title becomes Assistant Secretary of State), the Chairman of the Executive Committee of the Foreign Service Personnel Board, and the Chief Instructor of the Foreign Service School. The School Board will act in all matters with the approval of the Secretary of State.

"The Chief Instructor shall be selected by the other members of the School Board from among the officers of the Foreign Service, with the approval of the Secretary of State.

"Other instructors shall be selected from among the qualified officers of the Department of State, the Foreign Service, the other executive departments of the Government, and other available sources in the discretion of the School Board.

"The term of instruction in the Foreign Service School is one year which shall be considered a period of probation during which the new appointees are to be judged as to their qualifications for advancement and assignment to duty. At the end of the term, recommendations shall be made to the Secretary of State by the Personnel Board for the dismissal of any who may have failed to meet the required standard of the Service.

"The Secretary of State is authorized to prescribe rules and regulations for the governance of the Foreign Service School." [15]

The governance of the Foreign Service School.—By departmental order the Secretary of State has prescribed the following rules and regulations for the Foreign Service School:

---

[15] Executive Order, June 7, 1924.

"The President by Executive order of June 7, 1924, having provided for the establishment of a Foreign Service School in the Department of State, the following rules and regulations are hereby made for the governance of the School:

"1. The chief instructor shall be selected from among Foreign Service officers of Class V or over.

"2. He shall have the following duties:

"(a) To prepare and submit to the School Board for approval a complete schedule of work to be covered during the term of instruction.

"(b) To select instructors in the various subjects from among the qualified officers of the Department of State, the Foreign Service, the other Executive Departments of the Government, and other available sources.

"(c) To instruct the School in subjects selected and approved by the Board.

"(d) To maintain the discipline of the School and bear responsibility therefor.

"(e) To keep a record of attendance and an impartial, confidential rating of each pupil with respect to his qualifications for the Foreign Service.

"(f) To act as a member of the School Board.

"(g) To make reports on the work of the School and the individual pupils at the end of the term of instruction or whenever required by the School Board or the Secretary of State.

"3. Each term of instruction shall begin and end on dates to be fixed by the School Board.

"4. Each Foreign Service pupil shall be assigned to one of the divisions or bureaus of the Department of State, where he will report for duty when not attending classes.

"5. The chiefs of the divisions or bureaus shall report to the chief instructor the character of the work done by the pupils assigned to them, together with any delinquencies." [16]

Opportunities for practical instruction.—As no candidates have as yet been admitted to the service under the new system, the Foreign Service School has had no occasion to function or to develop beyond the mere framework of its organization. While the scope and method of instruction are still to be determined, a fair estimate of these may be deduced in part from past practices, and in larger measure from the purpose which the department seems to have had in mind at the time the plan was adopted.

Heretofore new appointees have gone to their posts abroad with very meager knowledge of their duties, many of them largely ignorant of our own governmental institutions, and none of them having an adequate comprehension of how foreign affairs are actually conducted. In this neglected state of mind they are likely to grope about for years uncertain as to how their own labors may be made contributory to the general plan, and how their individual careers may be broadened and strengthened to that end. Such experiences, therefore, suggest three categories of practical instruction as a basis of preparation:

1. *Duties of Foreign Service officers.*—Under this heading it may be assumed that regular instruction will be given in diplomatic and consular regulations and practice and in all related subjects. These may be very briefly summarized as including:—International law, especially as applying to the rights and duties of diplomatic and consular representatives and the rights

---

[16] Departmental Order No. 296, June 9, 1924.

and privileges of American citizens; citizenship, naturalization, expatriation, passports, registration; diplomatic and consular protection of American citizens and interests abroad; maritime laws and regulations governing American shipping and seamen; the protection and promotion of American trade and commerce; economics, especially as regards the interrelation of commercial and political factors in international problems; notarial duties, business and commercial documents; relations with, and services for, the other departments of the government.

2. *Governmental institutions of the United States.*— As Washington affords unparalleled opportunities for a first-hand study of the Government of the United States, it seems probable that each month, in appropriate order, the school may devote a portion of its time to a careful study of one of the executive departments or independent establishments. By way of illustrating how this could be done, let us take for example the Department of Commerce. First there would be an examination into its statutory origin, its scope and purpose, its organization, growth and development; next, daily visits to its various bureaus and divisions, followed by lectures from its principal experts, and concluded by an address from the Secretary of Commerce. The relations of the Department of State with the Department of Commerce could then be studied intelligently, with special reference to their general betterment, and the strengthening of the system of practical cooperation among their respective foreign representatives.

Again, let us consider the legislative branch of the government—the work of Congress—so vital and yet so little understood by the average new appointee. Some important bill might be taken up, especially one relating to foreign affairs or the work of the Foreign Service; for example, the recent immigration bill. Its whole process of development might be followed intimately in the hearings before the committee, on the floor of the House, and in the Senate, where parliamentary tactics and procedure could also be observed. Following the enactment of the measure, its translation into administrative practice would so complete the practical education of a young officer that nowhere in the world would he be inclined to lose from mind the sense of his immediate responsibilities thereunder.

3. *The conduct of foreign relations.*—The third category of subjects affords, perhaps, the greatest opportunity of all. The Department of State is manned by experts who handle currently every phase of foreign intercourse. It is provided that each pupil in the school shall be assigned to one of the geographical divisions or bureaus where he will perform laboratory work, so to speak, in personal contact with its daily operations. The experts themselves, according to the Executive order, are to be instructors in their respective subjects. In this way the class of probationary appointees should have the great privilege of seeing at close range the realities of the foreign service career as reflected in the work of the Department of State.

Aside from such important studies as the history of American foreign relations and policies, the student may be shown the concrete application of these to the actual cases in hand.

Take, for instance, a politico-economic subject like oil; the world struggle for the possession of sources of supply might be shown, the status of American interests explained, and the policy of the administration described in such a way as to provide a clear conception of the duties of our foreign representatives for their guidance in all circumstances.

This brief description has been hazarded only with a view to illustrating some of the obvious possibilities of the Foreign Service School; not with the idea of prejudging, or suggesting either the nature or the scope of its work.

The institution seems to afford, in substance, all the elements of a post-graduate year in which the academical training of the pupils may be blended with the practical demands of the career.

A Foreign Service Academy proposed.—Since the proposal of Representative Lowden for a National Consular School, there have been occasional suggestions that a Foreign Service Academy should be established with a somewhat broader field of application and utility. Of recent date this movement seems to have enlisted substantial support and even to have assumed the character of a definite project.

At the Seventh National Foreign Trade Convention, held in San Francisco in May, 1920, Mr. W. W. Nichols made the following suggestion:

"Assuming that we can offer the required career for life, our first step is to provide the groundwork for such a career by education. We applaud the wisdom of our forefathers in establishing early two institutions at West Point and Annapolis for the intensive training of our youth for war. Let us hope that sometime our Government will have for peace promotion a third educational institution of equal standing for the same high order of training for its Foreign Service." [17]

---

[17] Official Report of the Seventh National Foreign Trade Convention held at San Francisco, California, May 12-15, 1920, p. 311.

Again, in an address before the Academy of Political Science in New York, December 10, 1920, Mr. Nichols stated:

"At San Francisco the hope was expressed that sometime our Federal Government will have for peace promotion a third educational institution, as well qualified to fulfill its destiny as the academies at West Point and Annapolis have been in the intensive training of our youth for war. These academies have long been noted for their preeminence in the educational field and furnish a fine demonstration of the possible efficacy of governmental administration in the development and maintenance of high efficiency in a special service. To profit by this example there should be established, under similar government auspices, a Foreign Service Academy to operate in principle, on behalf of our foreign departments and peace, exactly as West Point and Annapolis do for the army and navy, on behalf of war. Analogously, graduates of the Foreign Service Academy, in return for an extraordinary mental discipline provided by the nation, contract to enter government service for a stipulated term of years, with the ordinary expectation that thus they begin a career for life."

An "Academy of Diplomacy" advocated.—At its annual meeting in June, 1924, the Sulgrave Institution gave consideration to a proposal made by Judge Townsend Scudder for the establishment of an "Academy of Diplomacy" as a feature of the George Washington Bi-Centennial Celebration projected for February 22, 1932. The plan is thus described in a pamphlet issued by the institution:

"It has been suggested by a member of the Sulgrave Institution, Judge Townsend Scudder, and favorably discussed by members of the Board, that another memorial to George Washington, and one which would meet a present need of the Republic, would be to create an Academy of Diplomacy, on precisely the same basis of operation as was devised for the Military Academy at West Point and the Naval Academy at Annapolis; in other words, that scholarship in the Academy of Diplomacy should be by appointment by the members of the Congress, and to a number annually that would meet the needs of the Department of State, Commerce, Labor, etc., etc. For it has long been the contention that because the social state of our people has never produced a class that has regarded self-sacrificing work for the State as a high duty, our diplomatic service has always been conducted too much on a political basis and not sufficiently upon the basis of the merit of education and experience. America needs trained men to represent her abroad; and an Academy of Diplomacy, created as one of the memorials to George Washington, would in every wise meet this present requirement.

"A Bill to this end will be drafted and an effort made to interest the ·Government and the Congress in the project."

With such substantial endorsement as that of the Sulgrave Institution, which numbers among its membership many of the most prominent men in public life, the plan for the founding of an academy of this character becomes so real an issue as to open the way to profitable discussion. As it is understood that the details of the proposal are not all worked out, a brief analysis of the tentative plan as so far exposed may serve to elucidate some of the points involved, and to contribute towards the realization of the general idea.

Analysis of the plan.—In the first place, the designation "Academy of Diplomacy" would seem to visualize only the diplomatic branch of the Foreign Service as an objective. The number of classified officers in this branch on the date of reorganization (July 1, 1924), was 121, while the average turnover, or number of vacancies to be filled annually, is about five. It is noted that the proposal contemplates meeting the needs of the "Department of State, Commerce, Labor, etc., etc." This being the case, the designation "Academy of Diplomacy" becomes a misnomer, as the vast majority of its graduates could not be appointed to diplomatic positions.

There is a magic suggestion about the word "diplomacy" which is as seductive to the youthful mind as a title of nobility. If trained to the belief that he is a diplomat by special dispensation of his Government, a young student in the Academy of Diplomacy would find it difficult indeed to divest himself of this character at the moment of his graduation, and accept willingly the less alluring duties of a more plebeian task. It would seem more in consonance with the spirit of the present amalgamated Foreign Service organization were a broader designation, as for example, "Academy of Foreign Relations," to be adopted. There are other substantial reasons why this change of name might prove desirable.

The element of political patronage.—It is proposed that appointments to the Academy should be made by members of Congress. This would have the effect of reintroducing the same element of political patronage which it has taken a century of hard struggle to eliminate from the Foreign Service. Doubtless the proposal, aside from following the precedent of West

Point and Annapolis, is intended to popularize the idea with Congress, and to influence its favorable consideration at the hands of the legislators.   Congress has by recent action deliberately placed the Foreign Service beyond the reach of spoilsmen of whatever character or influence.   Both the House and the Senate are thoroughly imbued with the desire to have done with the spoils system in that branch of the Government, and the number of Congressmen who would be attracted rather than repelled by the idea of reverting to the annoyances and abuses of the patronage system is believed to be negligible.   Far from influencing votes, it could be counted upon to arouse energetic opposition both in defense of the national interest and as a measure of self-protection to the members of Congress themselves.

There are many organizations and disinterested private citizens who are vigilant in the interest of civil service reform and who would doubtless view with disfavor the reestablishment of a political qualification as a starting point for the Foreign Service career.

The element of discrimination.—As has been shown, there are seventy-five universities and colleges in the United States which claim to afford facilities for Foreign Service training.   These have an enrollment of 8,602 students in the special subjects offered. [18]   Does this not raise again, and even more acutely, the same issue which prompted the National Business League of America to pass its resolution of 1909 condemning the establishment of a National Consular School, namely, discrimination against the students of the established universities? [19]

---

[18]Bureau of Education, Commercial Education Circular No. 23, Nov. 1, 1924. See also page 330.

[19]See page 327.

As now contemplated, the proposed academy would start its course of academical training at an early age, covering practically the same ground as that already covered by the universities. This is duplication, not progress, in educational facilities. In order to succeed, the academy would have to monopolize the field, thus scrapping all competitive university equipment. Would it not be better to utilize this equipment and make it contributory to the general plan? Secretary of State Hughes, in withholding his approval of the proposal to create a corps of Foreign Service pupils, stressed the fact that young men entering the service "invigorate the lower ranks by the varied resources which they are able to contribute through the diversified training acquired in our schools and colleges." He further pointed out that it "might have the effect of limiting the scope of selection to young men whose designation would be undertaken at too early an age for their capabilities to be correctly appraised." [20]

Caste tendencies.—Were appointments to the Foreign Service restricted to graduates trained from youth in a single academy, the tendency would be to produce a stock-model rather than to profit of the broad and varied cultural resources of the United States. The element of competition would be supplanted by that of privilege, which is a tempting atmosphere for the creation of a diplomatic caste. Nothing could endanger our foreign representation more than to have it unrepresentative; to permit it to take on an exclusive or un-American character. The outstanding principle of the recent reorganization was the democratization of the service. This was accomplished by removing the necessity for private incomes and rescuing our diplo-

[20]See page 330.

matic representation from the hands of a privileged class. Unless the career is to be kept open to all Americans on a basis of ability alone, there will be little of the spirit of democracy in its ranks.

As a closed circle it would gravitate, under foreign influences, back in the direction of its aristocratic tradition where secret and mysterious whisperings and other discarded essentials of old-line diplomacy were practiced both as a deception and as a pose.

Foreign Service training a post-graduate task.—Diplomatists are not to be made by academical training. Honorable Wilbur J. Carr has stressed the importance of personality, stating that "something more than mere educational training is needed." [21] The correct method of selecting Foreign Service appointees is, of course, to have them win their way in open competition; to accept only those who are able to demonstrate special fitness. The first requisite of an educational order is breadth; breadth of character, breadth of comprehension, breadth of vision. These are not to be obtained by starting a young man in on special subjects before he has received his general education. The aim, therefore, should be not to substitute a special for a general education, but to superimpose upon the latter a considerable enlargement in a special field. Young students cannot grasp the subjects of international relations; only graduates are equipped for such an undertaking.

Professor Carl Russell Fish, of the University of Illinois,[22] in discussing the teaching of the diplomatic history of the United States as a university subject, has stated:

"It has been my experience that the subject matter

---

[21]See page 329.
[22]Professor of American History, author of "American Diplomacy."

of the course, the handling of legal concepts, long-continued policies, and particularly the fundamentals of human contact in negotiation, make it too advanced for sophomores. Juniors and Seniors succeed according to their ability. On the other hand, maturity is relatively more important than special training, and I have not found that students without historical background are under any greater disadvantage than they are in any advanced course." [23]

At present there seems to be a wide gap between the educational curriculum of our universities and the demands of the Foreign Service career.

The real need is for an institution that will bridge this gap. This cannot be done by applying technical instruction in the lower grades; it requires an extension of the curriculum beyond anything that is now attempted. It demands a central institution of the most advanced order in which the graduates from our universities and colleges may enroll themselves for diplomatic, or Foreign Service training. That is the field of greatest promise; it is one which would afford our foreign representatives at least an equal start in educational equipment with those of any other nation.

A National Academy of Foregn Relations.—This brings us to the recommendation that instead of an academy of diplomacy for youthful students, there should be established in Washington a National Academy of Foreign Relations which would coordinate and supplement the work of the universities. Governmental scholarships could then be offered in necessary number and distributed among the various universities in proportion to the

---

[23]Quoted in Bureau of Education Bulletin, 1921, No. 27, entitled "Training for Foreign Service," p. 104.

facilities offered by them in the character of training required.

Such scholarships, to be won on merit in open competition, should not in any sense assure an ultimate appointment to a position in the Foreign Service. On the contrary, the academy should be open to any student who might wish to pay his own way. With the same end in view, the examination for appointment to the Foreign Service should be left open and unrestricted.[24] The field of usefulness of such an academy would not be limited to the needs of the Foreign Service. Equally essential is the educational enlightenment of the nation in matters of foreign affairs. Honorable Elihu Root has appropriately said: "A democracy which undertakes to control its own foreign relations ought to know something about the subject."[25] He has also said:

"When foreign affairs were ruled by autocracies or oligarchies the danger of war was in sinister purpose. When foreign affairs are ruled by democracies the danger of war will be in mistaken beliefs. The world will be the gainer by the change, for, while there is no human way to prevent a king from having a bad heart, there is a human way to prevent a people from having an erroneous opinion."[26]

Journalists and independent writers, lawyers, business men, financiers, economists, are as much in need of educational training in foreign relations as are our pros-

---

[24] The French system as practiced in connection with the *École Libre des Sciences Politiques* applies this competitive principle successfully. See note, page 326.

[25] Quoted by John H. Latané, Johns Hopkins University, in an article entitled "The Foreign Relations of the United States," Bureau of Education Bulletin, 1921, No. 27.

Professor Latané holds that: "Questions of foreign policy will undoubtedly be among the most vital issues of the future, and the study of our foreign relations must be given a place in the curriculum of every American college and university." *Ibid.*, p. 105.

[26] Elihu Root, in *Foreign Affairs*, Sept., 1922.

pective diplomatists. The whole of the educational movement along this line in the United States requires coordination. A National Academy of Foreign Relations with governmental scholarships as its nucleus and public funds as its basis would seem to offer the most effective medium for the purpose. There is little doubt that Congress is alive to the need, and would be receptive to the proposal if properly presented and sponsored.[27]

Bibliography.

Bureau of Education: "Training for Foreign Service"; Bulletin No. 27, 1921, and Commercial Education, *Circular No. 23,* November 1, 1924.

Barnes, Julius: "Foreign Affairs; a Neglected Study"; *New York Times,* January 21, 1923.

Carey, Edward: "Journalism and International Affairs"; *International Conciliation No. 21,* August, 1909.

National Civil Service Reform League: "Report on the Foreign Service"; New York, 1919.

National Business League of America: "American Universities, American Foreign Service, and an Adequate Consular Law"; Chicago, 1909.

National Conference on Foreign Service Training, Report of December 26, 1923, Bureau of Education Bulletin, 1924, No. 21.

---

[27]There is a substantial movement now under way for the endowment at Johns Hopkins University, Baltimore, Maryland, of a graduate institute for the study of international relations as a memorial to the late Walter Hines Page, Ambassador to Great Britain. According to a prospectus recently issued, The Walter Hines Page School of International Relations "will be something new in education. It will meet a long-felt need. Research into the underlying facts and conditions of international life—including international law, international trade, economic relations, racial psychology, all the technique of international intercourse and diplomatic customs—will be systematically carried forward."

The conference of eminent educators, publicists, and business men, which recommended the project, reached the conclusion "that a graduate school of international relations will be a practical addition to the field of education and a decisive step forward toward progress in international right and understanding."

Nichols, W. W.: "Reorganization of the Foreign Service of our Government"; Address before the Seventh National Foreign Trade Convention, San Francisco, May 13, 1920.

Recouly, Raymond: "Journalism and International Politics"; *Harper's Magazine,* December, 1922.

Root, Elihu: "The Need for a Popular Understanding of International Law"; *American Journal of International Law,* 1:1, 1905.

Chapter XIII

HOMES FOR OUR DIPLOMATS

The chief defect of the Foreign Service.—The Foreign Service is not yet democratized. In spite of all that has been accomplished through the passage of the Rogers act, the grades of ambassador and minister are still and almost exclusively the spoils of the rich. It is true that representation allowances have been authorized to supplement the salaries of our principal diplomatic representatives to a degree which promises to lighten the burden on their private incomes, but even when liberal appropriations are obtained for this purpose complete democratization will not have been achieved. From the beginning of the government the inadequacy of the compensation paid our foreign representatives has been a source of national humiliation and scandal.[1]

The experience of Thomas Jefferson.—On June 17, 1785, Thomas Jefferson, then on diplomatic mission to Paris, wrote to Colonel Monroe as follows:

"I find that, by a rigid economy, bordering, however, on meanness, I can save, perhaps, five hundred livres a month, at least in the summer. The residue goes for expenses, so much of course and of necessity, that I cannot avoid them, without abandoning all respect for my public character. Yet I will pray you to touch this string, which I know to be a tender one, with Congress, with the utmost delicacy. I had rather be ruined in my fortune than in their esteem. If they allow me half a

---

[1]See Chapter IX.

year's salary as an outfit, I can get through my debts
in time. If they raise the salary to what it was (2,500
pounds), or even pay our house rent and taxes, I can
live with more decency." [2]

A Senate resolution.—Many years later, in 1851, the
Senate became interested in the better adjustment of
diplomatic compensation, and on January 31 of that
year adopted a resolution reading as follows:

"Resolved, that the Secretary of State be requested to
communicate to the Senate any information which he
may possess touching the expediency of adopting a
graduated scale of diplomatic salaries, based upon the
combined considerations of the importance of the mission and the expenses of residence."

When analyzed, both the letter of Thomas Jefferson
and the resolution of the Senate will be found to recognize the principle that the Government should pay the
rent on its official establishments abroad instead of requiring the ambassador to do so, or in other words, that
for purposes of economy, and many additional reasons,
it should own its embassy, legation and consular buildings. But this principle is too well established in the
practice of other nations to admit of any question as to
its advisability, or rather of its necessity. There is no
other important nation which fails to provide appropriate housing accommodations for its diplomats.

The views of Honorable Nicholas Longworth.—In
order to bring the situation promptly to its modern
focus, it is instructive to examine the views of Honorable Nicholas Longworth, as expressed in the House of
Representatives May 23, 1906. He said:

"No one but a very rich man, even as riches are

---

[2] House Doc. No. 94, 22nd Cong., 2nd Sess., vol. 5, Foreign Relations,
p. 11.

counted nowadays, can be an ambassador of the United States in any European capital, and no man who is not at least comparatively wealthy, as we speak of comparative wealth in these days, can be a minister of the United States at any important diplomatic post. In other words, these offices, among the most dignified and important in the gift of the American people, are for rich men and rich men alone. This republic, the greatest, the most democratic republic which has ever existed, has to-day an office-holding aristocracy, an aristocracy more repugnant to our ideals of free institutions than any aristocracy even in Russia, an aristocracy purely and solely of the dollar. The office of ambassador, with the sole exception of the President, is the public official who is the representative of all the American people, can not be filled and never will be filled under our present system by any except a very rich man. I care not how able a man may be, how learned in international law, how experienced in diplomacy, how celebrated in statesmanship, if with all these qualifications he does not possess the one absolutely necessary qualification of great wealth, he is not eligible for appointment to any great diplomatic post. So well has this fact become recognized that there have been of late many instances of men whose sole claim, frankly stated, was that of great wealth, who were serious applicants for appointment as ambassadors. * * *

"Every day we hear on both sides of this chamber that the most serious menace to this country is an aristocracy of wealth. The people are determined that the great public utilities, the great industries of this country, shall not become concentrated in the hands of a few men. Is it not more offensive to our ideals that the high offices should become so concentrated? This being

the spirit of the people, shall we continue to support
an office-holding class, a dollar class, the very ideal of
the aristocracy of wealth? Shall the Congress continue
to tie the hands of the President and circumscribe his
choice in filling great diplomatic positions to men whose
only qualification, absolutely necessary qualification, is
that 'they have the price'?''

All former protests still valid.—The situation thus described has not altered appreciably since the words were
uttered, notwithstanding that the United States has
become the wealthiest nation on earth and its international interests have assumed an entirely new importance. The mode of living of American ambassadors
and ministers continues to be as obtruding upon the
public attention as at any previous epoch. At one moment there will be an ostentatious display of personal
wealth, accompanied by a meager degree of diplomatic
fitness or ability, and a year or two later a successor in
office will reverse the compromising display by lament-
able efforts to economize and noticeable discomfiture in
the task. Between these two extremes lies the formula
of good taste, and American ideals will continue to be
falsified to the world until we adopt it. To say that a
foreign representative of the United States should not be
appropriately housed, like all representative establishments in this country, is a penurious species of national
hypocrisy; to say that he should be allowed, in the name
of Uncle Sam, to wallow in his own wealth in other
lands, and before strangers, is shocking to our sense of
national dignity and pride. Too long it has been believed
in foreign countries that the United States lays chief
stress upon wealth. Such impressions stigmatize the nation with the damaging charge of materialism and dol-
lar-worship, neglecting altogether the higher qualities

of altruism which should inspire our relations with the foreign world. The basis of our diplomacy is thus drawn under suspicion even before negotiations begin.

Furthermore, the opinion has become prevalent at home that none but the rich may represent this country creditably in other lands. The rich, on the other hand, so long as they provide their own residences, very naturally conclude that the embassy is a private home; that the power and prestige of their positions are the perquisites of wealth, and that they themselves may assume towards other Americans and their affairs any attitude which it may suit their pleasure to adopt.

The American Embassy Association.—On April 30, 1909, there was organized in New York an American Embassy Association, the purpose of which was to promote and encourage the acquisition by the United States of permanent homes for its ambassadors in foreign capitals. An elaborate publication was issued and widely circulated throughout the country with the result that hundreds of the most prominent citizens and influential organizations lent their endorsement and active support to the movement. As a decade and a half have now elapsed since the campaign began, it seems fitting at this time, when the subject is about to be revived, that the gist of its arguments should be summoned to our aid and given their current application in a renewal of the quest.

Foreword of the American Embassy Association.— The salient features of the appeal made by the Association were condensed into an admirable foreword for its publication, reading as follows:

"This is a democratic movement. The idea existing in some quarters that this association advocates the purchase of palaces abroad is erroneous; it opposes either the rental or ownership of palaces; it stands purely for the acquisition by our government of suitable buildings that will combine the office and the residence that an ambassador can maintain on his pay, and in which all ambassadors must reside, whether worth millions or dependent on their salaries.

"We believe that 'all ambassadors should look alike.' This will help the poor man, will tend to restrict the extravagances of the rich, and will create a 'standard of appearances' that will be creditable to the nation.

"The experiences of this association show that in democratic sections of this country the sentiment in favor of this is very strong; it is recognized as 'democratic doctrine,' and both William Jennings Bryan and Samuel Gompers have made public addresses to assist our cause.

"We believe it is undemocratic, and that it also reflects on the dignity of the nation, for one ambassador to live in a palace and for his successor to live in a flat.

"We believe that embassies creditable to our nation and strictly American in design can be acquired at an average of not over Three Hundred Thousand Dollars each—a total of only Three Million Dollars for all the countries to which we send an ambassador, and that they will enhance in value.

"As we appropriate annually over Two Hundred Million Dollars in making preparations to keep on a hostile footing with other nations, we can well afford to expend Three Million Dollars to promote friendship with them.

"We conceive an ambassador's duty to be the cultivation of friendship among the people of the country to which he is accredited, so that he may be prepared to speedily smooth over any rough places, thereby averting possible war, and, through being on friendly terms with the government and the people, get everything possible in the way of commercial advantages for our country.

"We do not believe that it is any part of his duty to create a snobbish court circle by entertaining certain traveling Americans. This may aid him, but it brings no benefit to the people of our country. 'It butters no commercial parsnips.' His duty toward Americans abroad lies in throwing the arm of the government around them and protecting them whenever they are in trouble.

"We believe that the President should not be limited in his choice of ambassadors for important posts to men of great wealth.

"Our association believes that our countrymen would point with pride to a place in which they feel they have citizens' rights, and where they may come and go with the same freedom as that existing at the White House at Washington.

"So long as our representatives abroad are compelled to expend large sums from their private fortunes, just so long will our citizens feel that their rights in such residences are uncertain, and that such expenditures on the part of our representatives tends to give them too much independence towards their compatriots and thereby renders them less useful to American citizens.

"We believe that no representative of our government abroad should be called upon to make expenditures from his private fortune, or that it should be necessary for him to have one in order to enable him to accept the appointment and to maintain our dignity in foreign countries.

"Refusal to provide residences for our representatives

precludes the nation from obtaining the services of many eminent citizens.

"The American democratic spirit and the American national pride demand that such a condition of affairs be terminated.

"The American Embassy Association appeals to this democratic spirit and national pride to secure action by Congress to favor the acquisition by the United States of American embassies in foreign countries."

The Lowden Act.—As a result of this vigorous campaign, public interest was aroused and on February 17, 1911, Congress enacted an important measure known by the name of its author as the "Lowden Act." The provisions of this law are as follows:

"Be it enacted by the Senate and House of Representatives of the United States of America in Congress assembled, That the Secretary of State be, and he is hereby, authorized to acquire in foreign countries such sites and buildings as may be appropriated for by Congress for the use of the diplomatic and consular establishments of the United States, and to alter, repair, and furnish the said buildings; suitable buildings for this purpose to be either purchased or erected, as to the Secretary of State may seem best, and all buildings so acquired for the diplomatic service shall be used both as the residences of diplomatic officials and for the offices of the diplomatic establishment: *Provided, however,* That not more than the sum of five hundred thousand dollars shall be expended in any fiscal year under the authorization herein made: *And provided further,* That in submitting estimates of appropriation to the Secretary of the Treasury for transmission to the House of Representatives the Secretary of State shall set forth a limit of cost for the acquisition of sites and buildings

and for the construction, alteration, repair, and furnishing of buildings at each place in which the expenditure is proposed (which limit of cost shall not exceed the sum of one hundred and fifty thousand dollars at any one place) and which limit shall not thereafter be exceeded in any case, except by new and express authorization of Congress." [3]

Views of Honorable Frank O. Lowden.—In explaining the purposes of his bill Representative Frank O. Lowden of Illinois gave expression to several important principles which serve admirably the cause of Foreign Service reform towards which his mind was directed. It has been seen that the keynote of the recent reorganization act was to democratize the service by rendering it possible for trained men to rise on merit to the grades of minister and ambassador. On this point Representative Lowden left no doubt as to his sentiments. He stated:

"But to my mind even more important than either of these is the fact, if we would do justice to our country, that we must so establish facilities for our diplomatic service that the poorest man may look to the highest rewards in diplomacy, provided only he has ability, experience, and industry. By successive executive orders our entire foreign service below the rank of ambassador and minister has been taken out of politics. We thus have the beginning of a profession of diplomacy. It ought to be possible for the lowest man in the foreign service to feel that it is within his power, if his service justifies it, to reach the highest posts. This is impossible under existing conditions. Rents are so high in foreign capitals that only the rich can afford to take the highest places. What would gentlemen think if our practice

[3] 36 Stat., 917,

were such that only the very rich could become Presidents of the United States? What would gentlemen say of this democracy if our policy were such that no man could go upon the federal bench or come to Congress unless he were a millionaire? * * *

"We have boasted through all our history that this is a country of homes. Shall the nation alone be homeless? Shall America's flag be a tramp in the capitals of the world, protecting not a nation's home but only the temporary abiding place of America's representatives? Shall we arise to the nation's needs, imposed upon her by the last dozen years of our history?

"I would not say one word in criticism of the great body of the men who have represented us in foreign lands. Beginning with Benjamin Franklin and coming down to the present, they have served us faithfully and well. Now, let this nation do its part. Let us either withdraw from the capitals of the earth, or let us enable our foreign representatives to serve their country abroad on something like equal terms with the rest of the world." [4]

Views of Honorable William Jennings Bryan.—The democratic principle involved in the ownership of homes for our ambassadors and ministers has made a telling, if somewhat fruitless, appeal. It has enlisted the ardent support of men whose public careers have generally aligned them with the interests of the masses; Honorable William Jennings Bryan, for example, who, when Secretary of State, made the following statement to Congress:

"The first trip I made to Europe was ten years ago and I had not been there long before I became a firm believer in the purchase of embassies. I put it on two

---

[4] *Congressional Record*, March 2, 1910.

grounds, and they are both democratic in the broad sense. In the first place, I think it is undemocratic to have a branch of the service from which men are excluded because they are not rich. It limits selection to too small a number, because diplomatic ability does not always go with the power to accumulate money. So that the first proposition is that every branch of the service ought to be open to men upon merit, and not be entered through the possession of a certain amount of money. But that is only one. The other reason is just as democratic. You will find that in the past men who have been appointed differed in their wealth, and not only in their wealth, but in their disposition to spend it, and one man who is very wealthy and willing to spend it will set a pace that will embarrass the next man who goes there, and I think it is very important that the Government shall fix within certain limits the expenditures of its representatives, that they may represent real America and not a spurious America. And I am very anxious that we shall carry out this policy as rapidly as possible, and that in the selection of these places we shall select places or build buildings that will represent the solid, substantial American ideal; that we will not attempt to enter into rivalry with other nations in the matter of elegance, but that we shall fix that which shall be fairly representative of our Nation, so that there will be no noticeable change when an ambassador leaves and another takes his place.

"For those two reasons I am strongly in favor of purchasing buildings as rapidly as we can. Of course it would not be wise to ask that money be appropriated at one time for all of these things, but we commence here with three. If I were going to change it, I would increase it rather than decrease it, for I think the sooner we get upon a sound democratic basis the better." [5]

Before the Lowden Act.—At the time the Lowden Act was passed the United States owned embassy or legation buildings in four foreign capitals as follows:

1. *Bangkok, Siam.*—This building was presented by the King of Siam in 1884, subject to an annual ground rent of $84.00. In 1889 the United States Minister, Jacob S. Child, reported that it was a "wreck dangerous for occupation, shaking in strong wind." [6]

In 1890 it was again reported as an "old barn" [7] and an additional sum of $2,000 was appropriated for improvements. [8]

2. *Pekin, China.*—A very suitable and appropriate legation building was purchased at Pekin, China, by virtue of an appropriation of $60,000 granted by Congress in the act of March 22, 1902.

3. *Constantinople, Turkey.*—This was said to be our only ambassadorial building which did the nation credit. It was purchased at a cost of $150,000, provided by Congress in the diplomatic and consular appropriation act of June 16, 1906.

4. *Tokyo, Japan.*—By act of February 26, 1906, Congress appropriated $16,000 for the purchase from the Japanese Government of the building and site then occupied by the United States Legation at Tokyo, subject to an annual ground rent not exceeding $200.

The building acquired proved unsuitable for embassy purposes. By act of June 30, 1914, Congress appro-

---

[5]Statement before Committee on Foreign Affairs, House of Representatives, Diplomatic and Consular Appropriation Bill Hearings, Dec. 17, 1913, pp. 63-64.

[6]Senate Doc. 29, 51st Cong., 1st Sess.

[7]Senate Doc. 251, 56th Cong., 1st Sess.

[8]See "American Embassies, Legations and Consulates Mean Better Foreign Business," p. 8, published by the American Embassy Association, 505 Fifth Avenue, New York.

priated $100,000 for the construction of a new building to be used "both as a residence of the diplomatic offi-cers and for the offices of the embassy, and for furnish-ing the same."

As this sum was wholly inadequate for the purposes mentioned it was not expended. The old building was demolished in the earthquake of 1923, leaving the mis-sion homeless.

The situation in the Consular Service.—Turning to the Consular Service, we find a still worse condition, as may be seen from the following facts which are taken from the publication of the American Embassy Association:

1. *Amoy, China.*—May 14, 1871, the Chinese govern-ment granted the land to the American consul, a Mr. Legendre, conditioned that a hospital for sick and dis-abled seamen should be erected there.

Mr. Legendre leased the building to a Mr. Manson, who established a hospital.

In 1891 the American consul took possession of the ground because conditions were not being fulfilled.

In 1893 the consulate was moved into the building, since which time the Government has paid an annual ground rent of $25.50.

The building is subject to floods and damp, and was reported by Mr. Huntington Wilson, Assistant Secretary of State, as "in danger of being washed away by the annual typhoon, leaky when it rains and un-healthful." It has been reported by others as "a disgrace to the Government."

Since the building was "reconstructed" in 1904, there has been expended from time to time on repairs, about $2,000, so that its total cost as it stands to-day repre-sents an expenditure on the part of the American gov-ernment of only about $5,000.

The mortar for the building was mixed with salt water, making it impossible to paint the walls and present a decent appearance.

Every few years white ants destroy a considerable amount of the timber.

The building is described in one report as an "unsubstantial shell."

2. *Tangier, Morocco.* — The Sultan of Morocco granted this property to John Mullowney, American Consul from 1820 to 1830. He, deeming it his personal property, sold one-half, and in 1841, one of his successors, a Mr. Carr, sold another part to Shiriqui Essouri, whose heirs claimed it.

On May 24, 1891, Consul Mathews obtained from the pasha of the province, a title showing the property to be transferred to the United States. The cost of obtaining title was about $65. As a piece of government property it does not reflect credit upon us.

3. *Tahiti, Society Islands—French.*—In 1832 Queen Pomare granted ground for an American consulate, which grant was confirmed in 1848 by the French governor. A building was erected at the expense of the American consul and each subsequent consul purchased the property from his predecessor. Mr. Salmon, consul in 1860, purchased it for $320, but did not, it is said, turn it over to his successor. Mrs. Salmon, it is reported, began suit for the collection of rent in 1868, and Consul Perkins was forced to purchase the house for about $300, but as the Government did not reimburse him, the title to the building remained in him. The building was later destroyed by a cyclone. In 1906 Congress appropriated $5,171.27 for the erection of the present consulate.

4. *Seoul, Korea.*—A home was purchased here in 1887 for $4,400, under congressional appropriation of July 1, 1886, of $5,000. The grounds are spacious, but the living rooms are built so close to the ground as to be damp and unhealthful. The building is of poor character and in bad repair.

5. *Yokohama, Japan.*—Consul-General Van Buren leased the ground subject to an annual ground rent of $87.35, on condition that if it ceased to be used by our Government it reverted to the Japanese Government. Mr. Van Buren subsequently erected a building at his own expense and rented it to his successors, Congress having failed to appropriate money for its purchase. When E. C. Bellous was consul, the Van Buren heirs offered it for public sale and Bellous bought it in personally rather than have the ground revert to the Japanese Government. No appropriation being made by the United States to reimburse him, he sold the building to his successor. The value of the building when offered for sale was reported as less than $5,000. It was completely destroyed in the great earthquake of 1923.

Acquisitions under the Lowden Act.—The following appropriations have been made since 1911 for the acquisition of embassy, legation and consular buildings and grounds, and furnishing, improving, altering and repairing such properties:

City	Amount Appropriated	Date of Appropriation	Object
Tokyo, Japan	$100,000	June 30, 1914	Embassy (unexpended)
Mexico City, Mexico	150,000	June 30, 1914	Embassy
Yokohama, Japan	2,275	March 4, 1915	Consular building
Shanghai, China	355,000	July 1, 1916	Consulate General and U. S. Court
Habana, Cuba	100,000	July 1, 1916	Legation
San Jose, Costa Rica	40,000	March 3, 1917	Legation
Pekin, China	2,000	April 15, 1918	Repairs to Legation

City	Amount Appropriated	Date of Appropriation		Object
San Salvador, Salvador	{ 50,000 { 11,000	April March	15, 1918 2, 1921	Legation
Santiago, Chile	{ 130,000 { 20,000	June March	4, 1918 20, 1922	Embassy
Christiania, Norway ..	125,000	March	2, 1921	Legation
Paris, France	{ 150,000 { 150,000	March April	2, 1921 2, 1924	Embassy
London, England	150,000	June	1, 1922	Alteration, repairs, furnishings
Tangier, Morocco	14,435	June	1, 1922	Repairs to Agency and Con. Gen.
Rio de Janeiro, Brazil	50,000	March	4, 1923	Additional land, alteration and furnishings
Bangkok, Siam	14,000	Jan.	3, 1923	Repairs to Legation
Mukden, China	3,000	Jan.	3, 1923	Plot of land for consulate

Unsatisfactory results.—As will be seen from the foregoing tabulation, since the passage of the Lowden Act, fourteen years ago, only eight embassy and legation buildings have been acquired by the United States, one of those being a gift. In the meantime, the old embassy at Tokyo has been destroyed, while the $100,-000 appropriated for a new building in 1914 remains unexpended. The total of appropriations made to cover these seven purchases was $926,000. In addition to this, appropriations amounting to $230,435 have been made for furnishings, alterations and repairs. During the same period $355,000 was appropriated for the consulate general and the United States Court at Shanghai, China, $2,275 for the purchase of a small consular building at Yokohama which has since been destroyed, and $3,000 for a plot of ground for consular purposes at Mukden, China.[9] The total of appropriations for these purposes since 1911 is $1,616,710.

---

[9] Acting Secretary Polk in his letter to Chairman Flood, Jan. 16, 1919, says: "One of the prominent members of the American missionary community in China recently said: 'When traveling in the Far East I pick out, on arriving at a port, the poorest and most disreputable looking business

At this rate of acquiring new properties it would require about ninety years to house our Diplomatic Service alone, and when even a few necessary consulates are taken into account, we find that the fulfillment of the program contemplated by the law would cover a period of almost a century and a half, or approximately as long as our Government has existed. Surely this is not the American way of proceeding to the attainment of a desirable end!

And what is the cause of the delay—of the seeming indifference to a great national policy which has been deliberately adopted for the purification of our institutions and the better transaction of our international business?

Defects in the present system.—There are three main defects in the present system:

1. The limit of $150,000 to be expended at any one place is too low. This amount will not purchase a suitable property—except in the rare case of an accidental bargain—in any of the principal capitals of the world.

2. Even when a desirable property is found, special legislative authorization must be obtained from Congress, and a specific appropriation granted. Experience has shown this method to be unwieldy and in some several instances, unworkable. Before Congress has time to act, the opportunity for advantageous purchase is lost.

3. There is no adequate administrative machinery in the Department of State for dealing with the acquisition, maintenance, and care of embassy, legation and

building to be seen, and invariably find it to be the American consulate—a marked contrast to the German consulate, which is just as invariably the best building in the port.' "—Diplomatic and Consular Appropriation Bill for 1920, Additional Data, p. 3, quoted in the Report of the National Civil Service Reform League on "The Foreign Service" (1919), p. 318.

consular properties. Manifestly the subject requires special study in the gathering of data and the formulation of plans. Now that the diplomatic branch of the Foreign Service is to be inspected regularly, the time is appropriate for the situation at each foreign capital to be examined and reported upon. It should be a part of the regular duties of each inspector to gather and transmit all necessary information for the guidance of the department and of Congress. Were there no other duties attaching to his office the single task of ascertaining the best manner of bettering the housing conditions of our diplomatic missions would more than justify the expense of travel and the cost of inspection.

The New Embassy in Paris.—As a glaring and timely example of the present mode of operation, the following article recently appeared in the American Foreign Service Journal:

"On April 11, 1924, the American Ambassador in Paris took title, in the name of the United States Government, to the property situated at No. 2 Avenue d'Iéna. This property will be used as a residence and office for the Ambassador. As Ambassador Herrick says in his telegram announcing the purchase: 'In acquiring this building I am justifying 107 years later the statement of Albert Gallatin (then American Minister to France): 'I fully expect to be housed in a Legation owned by my Government within a year.'

"The first appropriation for $150,000 under the provisions of the so-called Lowden Act of February 17, 1911, was approved March 2, 1921. Instructions were sent to the Ambassador in Paris to canvass carefully the situation and report on such houses for sale as were available and appropriate. In all some fifteen houses were inspected but in spite of the fairly favorable rate of exchange none were found that came within the limit of the appropriation.

"In the summer of 1922, the Honorable Benjamin L. Fairchild, Congressman from the Twenty-fourth District of New York State, was in Europe and while in Paris became intensely interested in the Embassy situation. On his return to Washington he introduced legislation authorizing an expenditure of $300,000 for the Paris Embassy which, thanks to his efforts, finally passed on March 4, 1923.

"Again the hunt began! Even with $300,000 available it was difficult to find a suitable house. At last the Ambassador recommended the purchase of No. 2 Avenue d'Iéna, the residence of former President Grevy and belonging to the family of Jules Ferry, a former Prime Minister of France.

"Mr. Herrick was authorized to obtain an option in dollars, if possible, as only $150,000 had been appropriated, the balance being merely authorized. The owners refused to give an option in dollars but eventually the Ambassador on his own responsibility took one in francs for a month. Time dragged on. Congress did not get to the appropriation bill. The option was about to expire. Heroic measures were necessary. At this moment the franc which had been going down steadily reached the extraordinary low level of twenty-seven to the dollar.

"But Myron T. Herrick had more faith in France and sold $200,000 of his own money and purchased the house on his own account. However, before exercising his option he offered to release the owner from it, in view of the fall of the franc, but the latter preferred to sell.

"On March 11, the Ambassador cabled 'I have personally bought the property at No. 2 Avenue d'Iéna.

. . . I shall hold this property for the Government at cost price.'

"The bill appropriating the necessary funds was finally approved on April 2, 1924, and as stated above the title passed to this Government on April 11. The franc in the meantime had largely recovered and the purchase price at the rate of exchange on April 11 would have been $318,000. Mr. Herrick by his foresight had saved the Government $118,000.

"The new Embassy is a dignified stone building in French style, admirably situated on the east side of the Trocadéro gardens. The entrance is on the broad Avenue d'Iéna. On the west side is a small garden stretching from the house to the rue de Magdebourg and overlooking the Trocadéro. To the south is the rue Frésnel.

"The main floor has a large entrance hall, small and large reception rooms, large dining room, offices for the Ambassador and a library. All of these rooms are being redecorated and refinished and will be used for official entertaining.

"The next floor has six bed rooms and baths and a sitting room. On the third floor are four guest rooms and rooms for servants.

"While the new house is in no sense palatial, it is amply large for most occasions and entirely appropriate as a residence for the American Ambassador. The Government is to be congratulated on the acquisition of No. 2 Avenue d'Iéna, and it owes Ambassador Herrick a debt of gratitude for his timely assistance in consummating the transaction."

A constructive step.—Realizing that something must be done to improve this deplorable and almost ludicrous state of affairs, Congress, in the diplomatic and consular appropriation act of March 2, 1921, appropriated the sum of $300,000 for the acquisition of embassy, legation and consular buildings and grounds at any of the following places: Rome, Brussels, Berlin, Christiania, Athens, Belgrade, Bucharest, Prague, Monrovia, Vienna, Budapest, Canton, Hankow, and Amoy, subject to the approval of a commission composed of important legislators and cabinet officials as follows:

"There is hereby constituted a commission composed of the chairman and the ranking majority member of the Committee on Foreign Relations of the Senate, the chairman and the ranking minority member of the Committee on Foreign Affairs of the House of Representatives, the Secretary of State, and the Secretary of the Treasury, of which the chairman of the Committee on Foreign Relations of the Senate shall be the chairman, whose duty it shall be to consider and formulate plans or proposals for the purchase of embassy, legation, and consular buildings and grounds under the authority contained in this Act." [10]

The same act also authorized the purchase of buildings and grounds from foreign governments indebted to the United States, the cost thereof to be credited to their accounts. Nothing, however, came of this provision.

It likewise authorized the acceptance by the President of the J. Pierpont Morgan property at 13-14 Prince's Gate, London, as a gift from the owner, and added a further provision as follows: "That the President is hereby authorized in his discretion to accept on behalf of the United States unconditional gifts of land, buildings, furniture, and furnishings, or any of them, for the use of diplomatic and consular offices and residences." [11]

---

[10] 41 Stat., 1214.
[11] Act of March 2, 1921.

The following year, on June 1, 1922, an appropriation of $150,000 was granted for the furnishing, alteration and repair of the Morgan property, but as this appropriation was not expended, it has now lapsed, and the American Embassy in London is still homeless.

The work of the commission.—The commission above named has taken action in only one instance, namely, that of authorizing the purchase of the legation property at Christiania, Norway. The idea, however, is far more valuable as a guide to a future system than are the achievements of the commission to date, as these have been hampered by the limitations of the law with respect to appropriations.

There are many evidences that the mind of Congress is fully made up on this subject, but it is dealing with a cumbersome arrangement which does not afford that ease of operation so essential to the success of a business transaction. A business basis is the first requisite if satisfactory results are to be expected within this generation. Perhaps at no previous period have foreign conditions been more favorable to the acquisition of properties of the character required. Exchange conditions, the burdens of taxation on real property, the shifting of fortunes, and the menace of radicalism have in many countries contributed to the general lowering of real estate values. These conditions, though, may prove to be short-lived. Action at this time would not only procure for the United States all such immediate advantages, but would strengthen our entire foreign situation, and greatly improve both our international relations and our trade.

The new Rogers bill.—Honorable John Jacob Rogers, a strong advocate of Foreign Service improvement, and a student of its needs, has recently introduced a bill in

Congress which takes into account the chief defects in the present system and provides a practical means of overcoming them. If the popular campaign of 1909, 1910, and 1911 has amply justified itself through the enactment of the Lowden Act, there is equal reason why at this time the same forces should renew their energies for the passage of the new Rogers Bill, or some measure of similar import. The text of the new Rogers Bill is as follows:

"Be it enacted by the Senate and House of Representatives of the United States of America in Congress assembled, That the commission created by the Act entitled 'An Act making appropriations for the Diplomatic and Consular Service for the fiscal year ending June 30, 1922,' approved March 2, 1921, and composed of the chairman and the ranking minority member of the Committee on Foreign Relations of the Senate, the chairman and the ranking minority member of the Committee on Foreign Affairs of the House of Representatives, the Secretary of State, and the Secretary of the Treasury, of which the chairman of the Committee on Foreign Relations of the Senate is the chairman, shall consider, formulate, and approve plans and proposals for the acquisition of embassy, legation, and consular buildings and grounds and for the alteration, repair, and furnishing of such buildings, under the Act of February 17, 1911: *Provided,* That the limit of cost is hereby increased to $500,000 in each of the following foreign capitals: Buenos Aires, Argentina; Paris, France; Berlin, Germany; Rome, Italy; Tokyo, Japan; and Madrid, Spain; and to $300,000 in each of the following cities: Vienna, Austria; Brussels, Belgium; Lima, Peru; Hankow, Tientsin, and Canton, China.

"Sec. 2. The approval by the commission shall constitute full authority for the Secretary of State to conclude all necessary transactions relating thereto within the limit of the amounts provided by law as if specifically authorized by law in each case.

"Sec. 3. The chairman of the commission shall report to the Secretary of State and the Secretary of the Treasury all plans adopted by the commission.

"Sec. 4. Appropriations in an amount not exceeding $5,000,000 are hereby authorized, and when made shall constitute a standing fund which the Secretary of the Treasury is directed to set aside to cover expenditures under the authority of this Act.

"Sec. 5. All appropriations now available for the acquisition of embassy, legation, and consular buildings and grounds, and for the alteration, repair, and furnishing of such buildings, shall be credited to and form a part of the standing fund herein authorized.

"Sec. 6. The limit of $500,000 to be expended in any one year, as provided in the Act of February 17, 1911, is hereby increased to the full amount of appropriations remaining unexpended in the standing fund.

"Sec. 7. The Secretary of State is directed to collect information and to formulate plans for the use of the commission and to supervise and preserve the diplomatic and consular properties of the United States."

The experiences of Honorable Walter Hines Page.—It would be difficult indeed to find more fitting material for closing a chapter on homes for our diplomats than is contained in the humiliating experiences of our late lamented ambassador to Great Britain, Honorable Walter Hines Page. His writings are rich with intimate and shocking passages such as these:

"That residence at the Coburg Hotel for three months was a crowded and uncomfortable nightmare. The indignity and inconvenience—even the humiliation —of an ambassador beginning his career in an hotel, especially during the Court season, and a green ambassador at that! I hope I may not die before our Government does the conventional duty to provide ambassadors' residences.

"The next morning I went to the Chancery (123 Victoria Street) and my heart sank. I had never in my life been in an American Embassy. I had had no business with them in Paris or in London on my previous visits. In fact I had never been in any embassy except the British Embassy at Washington. But the moment I entered that dark and dingy hall at 123 Victoria Street, between two cheap stores—the same entrance that the dwellers in the cheap flats above used—I knew that Uncle Sam had no fit dwelling there. And the Ambassador's room greatly depressed me—dingy with twenty-nine years of dirt and darkness, and utterly undignified. And the rooms for the secretaries and attachés were the little bedrooms, kitchen, etc., of that cheap flat; that's all it was. For the place we paid $1,500 a year. I did not understand then and I do not understand yet how Lowell, Bayard, Phelps, Hay, Choate, and Reid endured that cheap hole. Of course they stayed there only about an hour a day; but they sometimes saw important people there. And, whether they ever saw anybody there or not, the offices of the United States Government in London ought at least to be as good as a common lawyer's office in a country town in a rural state of our Union. Nobody asked for anything for an embassy: nobody got anything for an embassy. I made up my mind in ten minutes that I'd get out of this place." [12]

An important episode.—A further tit-bit is given us by Ambassador Page as follows:

---

[12]Hendrick, "Life and Letters of Walter H. Page," vol. I, pp. 133, 134.

"But very early after my arrival, I was of course summoned by the King. * * * He shook my hand, and I spoke my little piece of three or four sentences.

"He replied, welcoming me, and immediately proceeded to express his surprise and regret that a great and rich country like the United States had not provided a residence for its ambassadors. 'It is not fair to an ambassador,' said he; and he spoke most earnestly.

"I reminded him that, although the lack of a home was an inconvenience, the trouble or discomfort that fell on an ambassador was not so bad as the wrong impression which I feared was produced about the United States and its Government, and I explained that we had had so many absorbing domestic tasks and, in general, so few absorbing foreign relations, that we had only begun to develop what might be called an international consciousness." [13]

Although all his American readers are grateful to Dr. Page for this subtle defense, can it really be said that the Lowden act of 1911 and the fixed national policy of providing homes for our diplomats were adopted by semi-conscious action? Fourteen years have passed since the nation became all of one mind on this subject. Present tendencies therefore would seem to indicate that the next ambassador who undertakes to defend our shortcomings in this regard may find it difficult indeed to overlook the factor of inertia.

Bibliography.

American Embassy Association: "American Embassies, Legations and Consulates Mean Better Foreign Business"; 505 Fifth Ave., New York, 1909.

Hendrick, Burton J.: "Life and Letters of Walter H. Page"; Doubleday, Page & Co., New York, 1922.

---

[13]*Ibid.*, pp. 135, 136.

CHAPTER XIV

THE NEED FOR A STRONG FOREIGN SERVICE

General considerations.—Eminent authorities have held, with extraordinary unanimity, that a democracy, as contrasted with a monarchial government, is virtually impotent in the practice of diplomacy; that it is quite incapable of giving enlightened direction to the conduct of its foreign relations, or consistency to its adopted policies. Without attempting to rehearse their arguments or to give validity to their conclusions, certain it is that popular opinion, especially in the United States, is indifferent to international issues and, as in all other countries, is largely ignorant of their true significance. Only in moments of great international stress does the average citizen awaken to the fact that both our national security, and the every-day prosperity of the individual are inextricably bound up in what others think of us and how they act toward us.[1]

There is no loyal American who will not admit the desirability of fostering cordial and friendly relations with other nations, not for selfish but for altruistic rea-

---

[1]"Despite the fact that the murder of an Austrian Archduke was the occasion of our (the British) being involved in a world-war; and although there is an obvious connection between unemployment at home and the condition of Continental Europe, the general public seems hardly to consider the vital importance to its daily life of Foreign Affairs. Unskilled conduct of our Foreign Policy—not merely at moments of crisis, but from month to month—may bring ultimate unavoidable disaster: its skilful conduct brings respect, prosperity, and peace."—A. L. Kennedy, "Old Diplomacy and New," p. 1 of Preface.

sons; there is no practical American who cannot see the importance of the same attitude, not for altruistic but for selfish reasons. Both our idealism and our practical judgment are involved in the formula of neighborly esteem and good-will.

But what are we to do with ignorance and indifference—with national incapacity in foreign affairs? It would be absurd to imagine that a vast population by some sudden burst of enlightenment can or will change its preoccupations from things near and personal to things remote and obscure. Yet ignorance is at the bottom of practically all international misunderstanding; it is frequently the only tyrant where tyranny is proclaimed. Even when we believe confidently in the correctness of our own motives, how are we to reflect them to others in their true light so that they may be understood by peoples who reason from altogether different angles and reach conclusions by what seems to us the reverse process of logic?

Mr. Elihu Root has said: "If the instinctive occidental reformer and the instinctive oriental fatalist are to work together they must make biological studies of each other." [2]

Obviously, as our vital interests are involved, somebody in this country must be trained and equipped to understand foreign affairs. Was there ever a case more plainly requiring an efficient Foreign Service, so trained, organized, and directed as to command the full confidence of the public?

Economic considerations.—The world is now an economic unit. "Everything that affects industry and commerce in one country affects it in every other, and affects it instantaneously, so widespread and so swift have

---

[2] *Foreign Affairs,* September issue, 1922.

communications become." [3] It would be trite to argue this point, but let us use again the words of Mr. Elihu Root by way of finding a conclusion:

"Our people have been taught by events to realize that with the increased intercommunication and interdependence of civilized states all our production is a part of the world's production, and all our trade is a part of the world's trade, and a large part of the influences which make for prosperity or disaster within our own country consist of forces and movements which may arise anywhere in the world beyond our direct and immediate control." [4]

The stake of the United States in this economic interdependency is greater than that of any other country.

We are a creditor nation. Some twelve billion dollars are involved in our foreign loans, while private capital is going into loans and investments abroad at the rate of hundreds of millions per annum.

We are an industrial nation. Already production has so far surpassed our domestic consumptive capacity as to render us largely dependent upon exports for the essential margin of prosperity. What is to be our industrial future if not in export trade?

We are an agricultural nation. The annual yield of agricultural products far exceeds the domestic demand. The surplus which is sold abroad comprises in value about one-half our total exports. Roughly, sixty per cent of our raw cotton, a half of our tobacco, a third of our wheat, and nearly a fourth of our dressed meats are sold in foreign lands. It is largely the foreign demand that fixes the prices of these keystone agricultural prod-

---

[3] Bryce, "International Relations," p. 257.
[4] *Foreign Affairs*, September issue, 1922.

ucts and determines the prosperity of the farmer as well as those who serve him.

We are an importing nation. To keep our industries running and to maintain our standards of prosperity and comfort, we buy from other nations essential materials amounting in value to some four billions of dollars annually, which is almost as great as our export sales.

We are a traveling nation. It is a national characteristic of Americans to want to visit foreign lands for business, educational, and pleasurable purposes. No nation in the world travels to a like degree. This characteristic demands foreign rights, international courtesy, hospitality in every land. There is no present prospect that any of these factors of international dependency will diminish in importance; quite the contrary, if all goes well, they should increase by giant leaps until their proportions become staggering. As the manner in which our foreign relations are conducted will largely decide how the nation is to fare in the competitive field, surely there would be little defense for entrusting their management to unskilled hands, and none at all for doing less than our best to improve them.[5]

Political considerations.—The institutions of the world are now largely democratized, except for the medium of intercourse—diplomacy. Books have been written and statesmen have harangued the public about the democratization of foreign affairs, but it is not yet ac-

---

[5]"Foreign affairs, if you examine the matter, are really domestic affairs —the most domestic of all our affairs, for this reason: they touch the life, the interest, and the pocket of every member of the community. It is in relation to our foreign affairs that every man and woman in this country secures immunity from war, relief from the heavy burden of taxation, prosperity of trade and industry."—Marquis Curzon, November 11, 1922.

complished.[6] The United States has a keen interest in this subject. Given the extent of her foreign relations, there must either be constant negotiation or conflict. Manifestly this country cannot adopt the practices of old line diplomacy, nor can it cope or cooperate with them successfully and dependably, as has been observed. In ordinary matters this fact might not be overly alarming, but it immediately becomes so when we consider the astounding objectives of diplomacy.

It is a fallacy to imagine that the diplomatic arm is always outstretched in defense of peace, or that diplomacy has failed when war is declared. According to traditional conceptions, the authority and force of diplomacy are derived from the power of a nation to inflict injury upon another. War, or the use of force, is as much a part of diplomatic action as is the despatching of courteous notes or an ultimatum. When a nation feels that its "place in the sun" lies beyond the trenches, it is diplomacy which prepares the ground for trench-digging. Armaments are an effect; not a cause. Armies and navies move under sealed orders written by diplomacy; they cease firing when diplomacy gives the command. In varying circumstances and degrees, war and peace become diplomatic objectives in faithful accordance with the national requirements.[7] Manifestly the

---

[6]In writing of the social, economic and political changes wrought by the World War, Sir Valentine Chirol has said: "That diplomacy itself should have been profoundly affected by them was inevitable, but whether the changes which it has undergone suffice to justify the distinction which he (Mr. A. L. Kennedy) draws between an 'old' and a 'new' diplomacy may perhaps be doubted."—Introduction to "Old Diplomacy and New," by A. L. Kennedy.

[7]"Foreign policy supposes two elements which it is as impossible to separate in practice as it is in a theoretical study: diplomacy and war. A people makes diplomacy with its military power, the army constitutes the assets on which the operations of foreign policy lean; war is the continuance of diplomacy; moreover, diplomacy is never more active than during a war; the two must go together. In 1870 'the strategists counted upon

United States is in no position to engage in a secret, no-limit game of this character, and yet, what is the alternative? The world looks to this country more than to any other for a workable substitute; for a formula of democratic diplomacy. The United States is the oldest and the most powerful democracy. It understands democratic principles and practices better than any other nation and its opinions and judgments are therefore highly prized in determining what would be practicable and acceptable as a general reform.

The true peacemaker is he who achieves an improvement in the processes of diplomacy. This can be America's greatest gift to the world. The moral force of enlightened public opinion is the only effective substitute for armed and accoutered coercion.[8] But to shift diplomacy to another basis—to a democratic basis—is not a task for amateurs; it presupposes and demands trained men; it requires a Foreign Service skilled enough to

---

alliances to organize victory; the diplomatists counted upon victory to organize alliances.' In the course of the present war one might cite a number of victories or defeats on the diplomatic terrain which have had more importance than strictly military events."—Joseph-Barthélemy, *"Démocratie et Poiltique Étrangère,"* p. 4.

8"But beyond diplomatists and beyond governments there rests the public opinion of the civilized world, and the public opinion of the world can punish. It can bring its sanction to the support of a prohibition with as terrible consequences as any criminal statute of Congress or of Parliament.

"We may grant that in matters which are complicated and difficult, where the facts are disputed and the argument is sophistic, public opinion may be confused and ineffective; yet when a rule of action, clear and simple, is based upon the fundamental ideas of humanity and right conduct, and the public opinion of the world has reached a decisive judgment upon it, that rule will be enforced by the greatest power known to human history, the power that is the hope of the world, and will be a hope justified. That power was the object of all the vast propaganda of the late war; that power was the means of determining the conflict in the late war; and the power, the clear opinion of the civilized world, stigmatizing as a violation of the fundamental rules of humanity and right a specific course of conduct, will visit a nation that violates its conclusion with a punishment that means national ruin."—Elihu Root, at the Fifth Plenary Session of the Conference on the Limitation of Armament.

devise the means and strong enough to enforce them. This argumentation is not advanced with a crusading motive or even in the spirit of mild altruism; it is a practical necessity if the United States is to look to her interests in her every-day and most commonplace affairs.

Bibliography.

Atlantic Monthly: "Democratic Control of Foreign Policy"; August, 1916.

Barnes, Julius: "Foreign Affairs; a Neglected Study"; *New York Times,* January 21, 1923.

Barthélemy, Joseph: *"Démocratie et Politique Étrangère";* Felix Alcan, Paris, 1917.

Blennerhasset, Sir Rowland: "Foreign Policy"; *Fortnightly Review,* 91 (N. S. 85): 625, April, 1909.

Brooks, Sydney: "American Foreign Policy"; *English Review,* 9:682, November, 1911.

Brown, Philip Marshall: "International Society"; Macmillan, New York, 1923.

Brown, Philip Marshall: "International Realities"; Scribner's Sons, New York, 1917.

Coolidge, Archibald Cary: "The United States as a World Power"; Macmillan, New York, 1912.

Gibbons, Herbert Adams: "America's Place in the World"; Century Co., New York, 1924.

Hankey, Sir Maurice: "Diplomacy by Conference."

Kennedy, A. L.: "Old Diplomacy and New"; Appleton, New York, 1923.

Lippmann, Walter: "The Stakes of Diplomacy," Henry Holt, New York, 1915.

Lowell, Abbott Lawrence: "Public Opinion and Popular Government"; Longmans Green, New York, 1913.

Moore, John Bassett: "Four Phases of American Development: Federalism, Democracy, Imperialism, Expansion"; Johns Hopkins Press, Baltimore, 1912.

Mowrer, Paul Scott: "Our Foreign Affairs"; Dutton & Co., New York, 1924.

Mahan, A. T.: "Some Neglected Aspects of War"; Little, Brown & Co., Boston, 1907.

Mahan, A. T.: "The Interest of America in Sea Power, Present and Future"; Little, Brown & Co., Boston, 1910.

Ponsonby, Arthur: "Democracy and Diplomacy"; Methuen & Co., Ltd., 36 Essex St., London.

Reinsch, Paul S.: "Secret Diplomacy: How Far Can It Be Eliminated?"; Harcourt, Brace & Co., 1922.

Root, Elihu: "A Requisite for the Success of Popular Diplomacy"; *Foreign Affairs*, September, 1922.

APPENDICES

Appendix A

REORGANIZATION OF THE CONSULAR SERVICE

(Act of April 5, 1906)

Be it enacted by the Senate and House of Representatives of the United States of America in Congress assembled, That the consular system of the United States be reorganized in the manner hereinafter provided in this Act.

Sec. 2. That the consuls-general and the consuls of the United States shall hereafter be classified and graded as hereinafter specified, with the salaries of each class herein affixed thereto.

Consuls-General.

Class one, twelve thousand dollars.—London, Paris.

Class two, eight thousand dollars.—Berlin, Habana, Hongkong, Hamburg, Rio de Janeiro, Shanghai.

Class three, six thousand dollars.—Calcutta, Cape Town, Constantinople, Mexico City, Montreal, Ottawa, Vienna, Yokohama.

Class four, five thousand five hundred dollars.—Antwerp, Barcelona, Brussels, Canton, Frankfort, Marseilles, Melbourne, Panama, Saint Petersburg, Seoul, Tientsin.

Class five, four thousand five hundred dollars.—Auckland, Beirut, Buenos Ayres, Callao, Chefoo, Coburg, Dresden, Guayaquil, Halifax, Hankau, Mukden, Munich, Niuchwang, Rome, Rotterdam, Saint Gall, Singapore.

Class six, three thousand five hundred dollars.—Adis Ababa, Bogota, Budapest, Guatemala, Lisbon, Monterey, San Salvador, Stockholm, Tangier.

Class seven, three thousand dollars.—Athens, Christiania, Copenhagen.

Consuls.

Class one, eight thousand dollars.—Liverpool.

Class two, six thousand dollars.—Manchester.

Class three, five thousand dollars.—Bremen, Dawson, Belfast, Havre, Kobe, Lourenco Marquez, Lyon, Pretoria.

Class four, four thousand five hundred dollars.—Amoy, Amsterdam, Birmingham, Cienfuegos, Fuchau, Glasgow, Kingston (Jamaica), Nottingham, Santiago, Southampton, Veracruz, Valparaiso.

Class five, four thousand dollars.—Bahia, Bombay, Bordeaux, Colon, Dublin, Dundee, Harbin, Leipzig, Nanking, Naples, Nuremberg, Para, Pernambuco, Plauen, Reichenberg, Santos, Stuttgart, Toronto, Tsingtau, Vancouver, Victoria.

Class six, three thousand five hundred dollars.—Apia, Barmen, Barranquilla, Basel, Berne, Bradford, Chemnitz, Chungking, Cologne, Dalny, Durban, Edinburgh, Geneva, Genoa, Georgetown, Lucerne, Mannheim, Montevideo, Nagasaki, Odessa, Palermo, Port Elizabeth, Prague, Quebec, Rimouski, San Juan del Norte, Sherbrooke, Smyrna, Three Rivers (Quebec), Vladivostok, Winnipeg, Zurich.

Class seven, three thousand dollars.—Aix la Chapelle, Annaberg, Barbados, Batavia, Burslem, Calais, Carlsbad, Colombo, Dunfermline, Dusseldorf, Florence, Freiburg, Ghent, Hamilton (Ontario), Hanover, Harput, Huddersfield, Iquitos, Jerusalem, Kehl, La Guaira, Leghorn, Liege, Mainz, Malaga, Managua, Nantes, Nassau, Newcastle (New South Wales), Newcastle (England), Port Antonio, Port au Prince, Sandakan, Seville, Saint John (New Brunswick), Saint Michaels, Saint Thomas (West Indies), San Jose, Sheffield, Swansea, Sydney (Nova Scotia), Sydney (New South Wales), Tabriz, Tampico, Tamsui, Trieste, Trinidad.

Class eight, two thousand five hundred dollars.—Acapulco, Aden, Algiers, Alexandretta, Bamberg, Batum, Belize, Bergen, Breslau, Brunswick, Cardiff, Chihuahua, Ciudad Juarez, Ciudad Porfirio Diaz, Collingwood, Cork, Crefeld, Curacao, Eibenstock, Gothenburg, Hamilton (Bermuda), Hull, Jerez de la Frontera, La Rochelle, Leeds, Madrid, Magdeburg, Malta, Maracaibo, Martinique, Matamoros, Mazatlan, Milan, Moscow, Nice, Nogales, Nuevo Laredo, Orillia, Plymouth, Port Hope, Port Limon, Prescott, Puerto Cortez, Rheims, Rosario, Roubaix, Saint Johns (Newfoundland), Saint Etienne, Sarnia, Sault Sainte Marie, Stettin, Tamative, Tegucigalpa, Teneriffe, Trebizond, Valencia, Weimar, Windsor (Ontario), Yarmouth, Zanzibar, Zittau.

Class nine, two thousand dollars.—Aguascalientes, Antigua, Asuncion, Bagdad, Belleville, Belgrade, Bristol, Campbellton, Cape Gracias, Cape Haitien, Cartagena, Castellamare di Stabia, Catania, Ceiba, Charlottetown, Coaticook, Cornwall, Durango, Ensenada, Fort Erie, Funchal, Gaspe, Gibraltar, Glauchau, Goree-Dakar, Grenoble, Guadeloupe, Hermosillo, Hobart, Iquique, Jalapa, Jamestown, Kingston (Ontario), La Paz, Limoges, Manzanillo, Maskat, Messina, Moncton, Niagara Falls, Patras, Port Louis, Port Rowan, Port Stanley, Progreso, Puerto Cabello, Puerto Plata, Riga, Rouen, Saigon, Saint Christopher, Saint Hyacinthe, Saint Johns (Quebec), Saint Pierre, Saint Stephen, Saltillo, Sierra Leone, Sivas, Stavenger, Suva, Tahiti, Turin, Turks Island, Tuxpam, Utilla, Venice, Warsaw, Windsor (Nova Scotia), Woodstock.

Sec. 3.   That the offices of vice-consuls-general, deputy consuls-general, vice-consuls, and deputy consuls shall be filled by appointment, as heretofore, except that whenever, in his judgment, the good of the service requires it, consuls may be designated by the President without thereby changing their classification to act for a period not to exceed one year as vice-consuls-general, deputy consuls-general, vice-consuls, and deputy consuls; and when so acting they shall not be deemed to have vacated their offices as consuls.   Consular agents may be appointed, when necessary, as heretofore.   The grade of commercial agent is abolished.

Sec. 4.   That there shall be five inspectors of consulates to be designated and commissioned as consuls-general at large, who shall receive an annual salary of five thousand dollars each, and shall be paid their actual and necessary traveling and subsistence expenses while traveling and inspecting under instructions from the Secretary of State.   They shall be appointed by the President, with the advice and consent of the Senate, from the members of the consular force possessing the requisite qualifications of experience and ability.   They shall make such inspections of consular offices as the Secretary of State shall direct, and shall report to him.   Each consular office shall be inspected at least once in every two years.   Whenever the President has reason to believe that the business of a consulate or a consulate-general is not being properly conducted and that it is necessary for the public interest, he may authorize any consul-general at large to suspend the consul or consul-general, and administer the office in his stead for a period not exceeding ninety days. In such case the consul-general at large so authorized shall have power to suspend any vice or deputy consular officer or clerk in said office during the period aforesaid. The provisions of law relating to the official bonds of consuls-general, and the provisions of sections seventeen hundred and thirty-four, seventeen hundred and thirty-five, and seventeen hundred and thirty-six, Revised Statutes of the United States, shall apply to consuls-general at large.

Sec. 5. No person who is not an American citizen shall be appointed hereafter in any consulate-general or consulate to any clerical position the salary of which is one thousand dollars a year or more.

Sec. 6. Sections sixteen hundred and ninety-nine and seventeen hundred of the Revised Statutes of the United States are hereby amended to read as follows:

"Sec. 1699. No consul-general, consul, or consular agent receiving a salary of more than one thousand dollars a year shall, while he holds his office, be interested in or transact any business as a merchant, factor, broker, or other trader, or as a clerk or other agent for any such person to, from, or within the port, place, or limits of his jurisdiction, directly or indirectly, either in his own name or in the name or through the agency of any other person; nor shall he practice as a lawyer for compensation or be interested in the fees or compensation of any lawyer; and he shall in his official bond stipulate as a condition thereof not to violate this prohibition.

"Sec. 1700. All consular officers whose respective salaries exceed one thousand dollars a year shall be subject to the prohibition against transacting business, practicing as a lawyer, or being interested in the fees or compensation of any lawyer contained in the preceding section. And the President may extend the prohibition to any consul-general, consul, or consular agent whose salary does not exceed one thousand dollars a year or who may be compensated by fees, and to any vice or deputy consular officer or consular agent, and may require such officer to give a bond not to violate the prohibition."

Sec. 7. That every consular officer of the United States is hereby required, whenever application is made to him therefor, within the limits of his consulate, to administer to or take from any person any oath, affirmation, affidavit, or deposition, and to perform any other notarial act which any notary public is required or authorized by law to do within the United States; and for every such notarial act performed he shall charge in each instance the appropriate fee prescribed by the President under section seventeen hundred and forty-five, Revised Statutes.

Sec. 8. That all fees, official or unofficial, received by any officer in the consular service for services rendered in connection with the duties of his office or as a consular officer, including fees for notarial services, and fees for taking depositions, executing commissions or letters rogatory, settling estates, receiving or paying out moneys, caring for or disposing of property, shall be accounted for and paid into the Treasury of the United States, and the sole and only compensation of such officers shall be by salaries fixed by law but this shall not apply to consular agents, who shall be paid by one half of the fees received in their offices, up to a maximum sum of one thousand dollars in any one year, the other half being accounted for and paid into the Treasury of the United States. And vice-consuls-general, deputy consuls-general, vice-consuls, and deputy consuls, in addition to such compensation as they may be entitled to receive as consuls or clerks, may receive such portion of the salaries of the consul-general or consuls for whom they act as shall be provided by regulation.

Sec. 9. That fees for the consular certification of invoices shall be, and they hereby are, included with the fees for official services for which the President is authorized by section seventeen hundred and forty-five of the Revised Statutes to prescribe rates or tariffs; and sections twenty-eight hundred and fifty-one and seventeen hundred and twenty-one of the Revised Statutes are hereby repealed.

Sec. 10. That every consular officer shall be provided and kept supplied with adhesive official stamps, on which shall be printed the equivalent money value of denominations and to amounts to be determined by the Department of State, and shall account quarterly to the Department of State for the use of such stamps and for such of them as shall remain in his hands.

Whenever a consular officer is required or finds it necessary to perform any consular or notarial act he shall prepare and deliver to the party or parties at whose instance such act is performed a suitable and appropriate document as prescribed in the consular regulations and affix thereto and duly cancel an adhesive stamp or stamps of the denomination or denominations equivalent to the fee prescribed for such consular or notarial act, and no such act shall be legally valid within the jurisdiction of the Government of the United States unless such stamp or stamps is or are affixed and canceled.

Sec. 11. That this Act shall take effect on the thirtieth day of June, nineteen hundred and six.

Sec. 12. That all Acts or parts of Acts inconsistent with this Act are hereby repealed.

Approved, April 5, 1906.

(34 Stat., 99)

EXECUTIVE ORDER

(JUNE 27, 1906)

Consular Service—Regulations Governing Appointments and Promotions.

Whereas, The Congress, by Section 1753 of the Revised Statutes of the United States, has provided as follows:—

"The President is authorized to prescribe such regulations for the admission of persons into the civil service of the United States as may best promote the efficiency thereof, and ascertain the fitness of each candidate in respect to age, health, character, knowledge, and ability for the branch of service into which he seeks to enter and for this purpose he may employ suitable persons to conduct such inquiries, and may prescribe their duties, and establish regulations for the conduct of persons who may receive appointments in the civil service."

And, whereas, the Congress has classified and graded the consuls-general and consuls of the United States by the act entitled "An act to provide for the reorganization of the consular service of the United States," approved April 5, 1906, and has thereby made it practicable to extend to that branch of the civil service the aforesaid provisions of the Revised Statutes and the principles embodied in the Civil Service Act of January 16, 1883.

Now, therefore, in the exercise of the powers conferred upon him by the Constitution and laws of the United States, the President makes the following regulations to govern the selection of consuls general and consuls in the civil service of the United States, subject always to the advice and consent of the Senate:—

1. Vacancies in the office of consul-general and in the office of consul above class 8 shall be filled by promotion from the lower

grades of the consular service, based upon ability and efficiency as shown in the service.

2. Vacancies in the office of consul of class 8 and of consul of class 9 shall be filled:

(a) By promotion on the basis of ability and efficiency as shown in the service, of consular clerks, and of vice consuls, deputy consuls, and consular agents who shall have been appointed to such offices upon examination.

(b) By new appointments of candidates who have passed a satisfactory examination for appointment as consul as hereafter provided.

3. Persons in the service of the Department of State with salaries of two thousand dollars or upwards shall be eligible for promotion, on the basis of ability and efficiency as shown in the service, to any grade of the consular service above class 8 of consuls.

4. The Secretary of State, or such officer of the Department of State as the President shall designate, the Chief of the Consular Bureau, and the Chief Examiner of the Civil Service Commission, or some person whom said Commission shall designate, shall constitute a Board of Examiners for admission to the consular service.

5. It shall be the duty of the Board of Examiners to formulate rules for and hold examinations of applicants for admission to the consular service.

6. The scope and method of the examinations shall be determined by the Board of Examiners, but among the subjects shall be included at least one modern language other than English; the natural, industrial and commercial resources and the commerce of the United States, especially with reference to the possibilities of increasing and extending the trade of the United States with foreign countries; political economy; elements of international, commercial and maritime law.

7. Examination papers shall be rated on a scale of 100, and no person rated at less than 80 shall be eligible for certification.

8. No one shall be examined who is under twenty-one or over fifty years of age, or who is not a citizen of the United States, or who is not of good character and habits and physically and mentally qualified for the proper performance of consular work, or who has not been specially designated by the President for appointment to the consular service subject to examination.

9. Whenever a vacancy shall occur in the eighth or ninth class of consuls which the President may deem it expedient to fill, the

Secretary of State shall inform the Board of Examiners, who shall certify to him the list of those persons eligible for appointment, accompanying the certificate with a detailed report showing the qualifications, as revealed by examination, of the persons so certified. If it be desired to fill a vacancy in a consulate in a country in which the United States exercises extra-territorial jurisdiction, the Secretary of State shall so inform the Board of Examiners, who shall include in the list of names certified by it only such persons as have passed the examination provided for in this order, and who also have passed an examination in the fundamental principles of the common law, the rules of evidence and the trial of civil and criminal cases. The list of names which the Board of Examiners shall certify shall be sent to the President for his information.

10. No promotion shall be made except for efficiency, as shown by the work that the officer has accomplished, the ability, promptness and diligence displayed by him in the performance of all his official duties, his conduct and his fitness for the consular service.

11. It shall be the duty of the Board of Examiners to formulate rules for and hold examinations of persons designated for appointment as consular clerk, and of such persons designated for appointment as vice consul, deputy consul and consular agent, as shall desire to become eligible for promotion. The scope and method of such examination shall be determined by the Board of Examiners, but it shall include the same subjects hereinbefore prescribed for the examination of consuls. Any vice consul, deputy consul or consular agent now in the service, upon passing such an examination shall become eligible for promotion, as if appointed upon such examination.

12. In designations for appointment subject to examination and in appointments after examination, due regard will be had to the rule that as between candidates of equal merit, appointments should be so made as to secure proportional representation of all the States and Territories in the consular service; and neither in the designation for examination or certification or appointment will the political affiliations of the candidate be considered.

THEODORE ROOSEVELT.

THE WHITE HOUSE,
  June 27th, 1906.
      [No. 469.]

EXECUTIVE ORDER

(NOVEMBER 26, 1909)

Regulations Governing Appointments and Promotions in the Diplomatic Service and for the Improvement of the Personnel of the Department of State.

Whereas, The Congress, by Section 1753 of the Revised Statutes of the United States, has provided as follows:—

"The President is authorized to prescribe such regulations for the admission of persons into the civil service of the United States as may best promote the efficiency thereof, and ascertain the fitness of each candidate in respect to age, health, character, knowledge, and ability for the branch of service into which he seeks to enter; and for this purpose he may employ suitable persons to conduct such inquiries, and may prescribe their duties, and establish regulations for the conduct of persons who may receive appointments in the civil service."

And, Whereas, it is deemed best for the public interest to extend to the diplomatic service the aforesaid provision of the Revised Statutes and the general principles embodied in the Civil Service Act of January 16th, 1883;—

The Secretary of State is hereby directed to report from time to time to the President, along with his recommendations, the names of those secretaries of the higher grades in the diplomatic service who by reason of efficient service have demonstrated special capacity for promotion to be chiefs of mission.

There shall be kept a careful efficiency record of every officer of the diplomatic service, in order that there may be no promotion except upon well established efficiency as shown in the service,

398

and that retention in the service may be conditioned upon the officers' maintaining a degree of efficiency well up to the average high standard which the interests of the service demand.

Initial appointments from outside the service to secretaryships in the diplomatic service shall be only to the Classes of Third Secretary of Embassy, or, in case of higher existent vacancies, of Second Secretary of Legation, or of Secretary of Legation at such post as has assigned to it but one secretary. Vacancies in secretaryships of higher classes shall be filled by promotion from the lower grades of the service, based upon efficiency and ability as shown in the service.

To make it more practicable to extend to the appointment, promotion, transfer, or retention of secretaries in the diplomatic service the civil service principle of promotion on the basis of efficiency as shown in the service, and in order that the action of the Department may be understood by the officers concerned, all secretaryships in the diplomatic service shall be graded according to the importance, volume, difficulty, or other aspects of the work done by each mission in proportion to the number of men allotted to it, and this classification shall be made known to the members of the service.

A person separated from a secretaryship in the diplomatic service without delinquency or misconduct at his own request in writing may, within a period of one year from the date of such separation, be reinstated in the grade from which he was separated, provided he shall have been originally appointed after the prescribed examination for that grade. In the event, however, that such separation shall be for the purpose of undertaking other work under the Department of State, the limitation of one year for eligibility for reinstatement shall not hold. This rule shall be applicable as regards reinstatements to the consular service and also to the Department of State when transfer shall have been to another branch of the foreign service.

The Assistant Secretary of State, the Solicitor for the Department of State, the Chief of the Diplomatic Bureau, and the Chief of the Bureau of Appointments, and the Chief Examiner of the Civil Service Commission or some person whom the Commission shall designate, or such persons as may be designated to serve in their stead, are hereby constituted a Board whose duty it shall be to determine the qualifications of persons designated by the President for examination to determine their fitness for possible appointment as secretaries of embassy or legation.

The examination herein provided for shall be held in Washington at such times as the needs of the service require. Candidates will be given reasonable notice to attend, and no person shall be designated to take the examination within thirty days of the time set therefor.

The examinations shall be both oral and in writing and shall include the following subjects:—international law, diplomatic usage, and a knowledge of at least one modern language other than English, to wit, French, Spanish, or German; also the natural, industrial and commercial resources and the commerce of the United States, especially with reference to the possibilities of increasing and extending the trade of the United States with foreign countries; American history, government and institutions; and the modern history since 1850 of Europe, Latin America and the Far East. The object of the oral examination shall also be to determine the candidate's alertness, general contemporary information, and natural fitness for the service, including mental, moral, and physical qualifications, character, address, and general education and good command of English. In this part of the examination the applications previously filed will be given due weight by the Board of Examiners. In the determination of the final rating, the written and oral ratings shall be of equal weight. A physical examination shall also be included as supplemental.

Examination papers shall be rated on a scale of 100, and no person with a general rating of less than 80 shall be certified as eligible.

No person shall be certified as eligible who is under twenty-one or over fifty years of age, or who is not a citizen of the United States, or who is not of good character and habits and physically, mentally, and temperamentally qualified for the proper performance of diplomatic work, or who has not been specially designated by the President for appointment to the diplomatic service subject to examination and subject to the occurrence of an appropriate vacancy.

Upon the conclusion of the examinations, the names of the candidates who shall have attained upon the whole examination the required mark will be certified by the Board to the Secretary of State as eligible for appointment.

The names of candidates will remain on the eligible list for two years, except in the case of such candidates as shall within that period be appointed or shall withdraw their names. Names which have been on the eligible list for two years will be dropped therefrom and the candidates concerned will not again be eligible for appointment unless upon fresh application, designation anew for examination, and the successful passing of such second examination.

Applicants for appointment who are designated to take an examination and who fail to report therefor shall not be entitled to take a subsequent examination unless they shall have been specifically designated to take such subsequent examination.

In designations for appointment subject to examination and in appointments after examination, due regard will be had to the rule, that as between candidates of equal merit, appointments should be made so as to tend to secure proportional representation of all the States and Territories in the diplomatic service; and neither in the designation for examination or certification or appointment after examination will the political affiliations of the candidates be considered.

The Board of Examiners is authorized to issue such notices and to make all such rules as it may deem necessary to accomplish the object of this regulation.

Transfers from one branch of the foreign service to another shall not occur except upon designation by the President for examination and the successful passing of the examination prescribed for the service to which such transfer is made. Unless the exigencies of the service imperatively demand it, such person to be transferred shall not have preference in designation for the taking of the examination or in appointment from the eligible list, but shall follow the course of procedure prescribed for all applicants for appointment to the service which he desires to enter. To persons employed in the Department of State at salaries of eighteen hundred dollars or more, the preceding rule shall not apply and they may be appointed, on the basis of ability and efficiency, to any grade of the diplomatic service.

The Secretary of State may, as provided by Rule III of the present Civil Service Rules, request the Civil Service Commission to hold special examinations for the position of clerk of class two or above in the Department of State, such examination to follow generally and so far as the Secretary of State shall deem practicable, the lines of the present foreign service examinations.

In the case of promotions in the Department of State to the grades of clerk of class two or above, the Secretary of State may require the passing of an examination in the general nature of the present diplomatic or consular service examinations.

With further reference to the matter of promotions in the Department of State, the Secretary of State is directed to cause to be kept, as a guide in determining the promotion or retention of the personnel, a careful record of the efficiency of each clerk in the Department.

WM. H. TAFT

THE WHITE HOUSE,
November 26, 1919.
[No. 1143.]

Amendments to Executive Order of November 26, 1909.

Clause 1 of paragraph 2 of section 9 of the Order of November 26, 1909, prescribing regulations for appointments and promotions in the diplomatic service and for the improvement of the personnel of the Department of State, is hereby amended to read "No person shall be certified as eligible who is under twenty-one or over thirty-five years of age."

WOODROW WILSON

THE WHITE HOUSE,
21 April, 1915.
[No. 2173.]

The Executive Orders of November 26, 1909, and April 21, 1915, concerning examinations for the diplomatic service, are hereby amended so as to permit persons not over 40 years of age to be designated for the next regular examination to be held for the purpose of obtaining eligibles for secretaryships in the diplomatic service.

WOODROW WILSON

THE WHITE HOUSE,
March 15, 1919.
[No. 3065.]

REORGANIZATION OF THE DIPLOMATIC AND CONSULAR SERVICE

(ACT OF FEBRUARY 5, 1915)

Be it enacted by the Senate and House of Representatives of the United States of America in Congress assembled, That hereafter all appointments of secretaries in the Diplomatic Service and of consuls general and consuls shall be by commission to the offices of secretary of embassy or legation, consul general, or consul, and not by commission to any particular post, and that such officers shall be assigned to posts and transferred from one post to another by order of the President as the interests of the service may require: *Provided,* That any such officer may be assigned for duty in the Department of State without loss of grade, class, or salary, such assignment to be for a period of not more than three years, unless the public interests demand further service, when such assignment may be extended for a period not to exceed one year, and no longer: *Provided further,* That no secretary, consul general, or consul shall be promoted to a higher class except upon the nomination of the President, with the advice and consent of the Senate.

Sec. 2. That secretaries in the Diplomatic Service and consuls general and consuls shall hereafter be graded and classified as follows, with the salaries of each class herein affixed thereto.

Secretaries.

Secretary of class one ....$ 3,000
Secretary of class two 2,625
Secretary of class three 2,000
Secretary of class four 1,500
Secretary of class five 1,200

Consuls-General.

Consul general of class one $12,000
Consul general of class two ... 8,000
Consul general of class three .. 6,000
Consul general of class four ... 5,500
Consul general of class five 4,500

Consuls.

Consul of class one $8,000
Consul of class two 6,000
Consul of class three 5,000
Consul of class four 4,500
Consul of class five 4,000
Consul of class six 3,500
Consul of class seven 3,000
Consul of class eight 2,500
Consul of class nine 2,000

Sec. 3. That section sixteen hundred and eighty-five of the Revised Statutes is hereby amended to read as follows:

"Sec. 1685. That for such time as any secretary of embassy or legation shall be lawfully authorized to act as chargé d'affaires ad interim at the post to which he shall have been appointed or assigned, he shall be entitled to receive, in addition to his salary as secretary of embassy or legation, compensation equal to the difference between such salary and fifty per centum of the salary provided by law for the ambassador or minister at such post; and for such time as any vice consul shall be lawfully authorized to assume charge of a consulate general or consulate during the absence of the principal officer at the post to which he shall have been appointed or assigned, he shall be entitled to receive, in addition to his regular salary or compensation as a subordinate consular officer or employee, compensation equal to the difference between such salary or compensation and fifty per centum of the salary provided by law for the principal consular officer at such post."

Sec. 4. That a secretary, consul general, or consul of whatever class detailed for special duty outside of the city of Washington shall be paid his actual and necessary expenses for subsistence during such special detail not exceeding $5 per day:

Provided, That such special duty shall not continue for more than sixty days unless in the case of international gatherings, congresses, or conferences, when such subsistence expenses shall run only during the life of the international gathering, congress, or conference, as the case may be.

Sec. 5. That the Secretary of State is directed to report from time to time to the President, along with his recommendations for promotion or for transfer between the department and the foreign service, the names of those secretaries in the Diplomatic Service and the names of those consular officers or departmental officers or employees who by reason of efficient service, an accurate record of which shall be kept in the Department of State, have demonstrated special efficiency, and also the names of persons found upon examination to have fitness for appointment to the lower grades of the service.

Sec. 6. That section sixteen hundred and seventy-four of the Revised Statutes is hereby amended to read as follows:

"Sec. 1674. That the official designations employed throughout this title shall be deemed to have the following meanings, respectively:

"First. 'Consul general' and 'consul' shall be deemed to denote full, principal, and permanent consular officers as distinguished from subordinates and substitutes.

"Second. 'Consular agent' shall be deemed to denote consular officers subordinate to such principals exercising the powers vested in them and performing the duties prescribed for them by regulation of the President at posts or places different from those at which such principals are located, respectively.

"Third. 'Vice consuls' shall be deemed to denote consular officers subordinate to such principals exercising and performing the duties within the limits of their consulates at the same or at different points and places from those at which the principals are located, except that when vice consuls take charge of consulates general or consulates when the principal officers shall be temporarily absent or relieved from duty they shall be deemed to denote consular officers who shall be substituted, temporarily, to fill the places of said consuls general or consuls.

"Fourth. 'Consular officer' shall be deemed to include consuls general, consuls, vice consuls, interpreters in consular offices, student interpreters, and consular agents, and none others.

"Fifth. 'Diplomatic officer' shall be deemed to include ambassadors, envoys extraordinary, ministers plenipotentiary, ministers resident, commissioners, chargé d'affaires, agents, secretaries of embassy and legation, and secretaries in the Diplomatic Service, and none others."

The offices of vice consul general, deputy consul general, and deputy consul are abolished.

Sec. 7. That no ambassador, minister, minister resident, diplomatic agent, or secretary in the Diplomatic Service of any grade or class shall, while he holds his office, be interested in or transact any business as a merchant, factor, broker, or other trader, or as an agent for any such person to, from, or within the country or countries to which he or the chief of his mission, as the case may be, is accredited, either in his own name or in the name or through the agency of any other person, nor shall he, in such country or countries, practice as a lawyer for compensation or be interested in the fees or compensation of any lawyer so practicing.

Sec. 8. That this Act shall take effect on the day of its approval by the President, when all Acts or parts of Acts inconsistent with this Act are repealed.

Approved, February 5, 1915.

(38 Stat., 805)

Amendments to Act of February 5, 1915.

That the President may, whenever he considers it advisable so to do, designate and assign any secretary of class one as counselor of embassy or legation: *And provided further,* That section sixteen hundred and seventy-four of the Revised Statutes, fifth paragraph, as amended by section six of the Act approved February fifth, nineteen hundred and fifteen, entitled "An Act for the improvement of the foreign service" is hereby amended to include after the words "chargé d'affaires" the word "counselors."

Act of July 1, 1916, 39 Stat., 252.

That secretaries in the Diplomatic Service shall hereafter be graded and classified as follows: Secretaries of class one, $4,000 per annum; secretaries of class two, $3,625 per annum; secretaries of class three, $3,000 per annum; secretaries of class four, $2,500 per annum.

Act of June 4, 1920, 41 Stat., 740.

REORGANIZATION OF THE FOREIGN SERVICE

(ACT OF MAY 24, 1924)

Be it enacted by the Senate and House of Representatives of the United States of America in Congress assembled, That hereafter the Diplomatic and Consular Service of the United States shall be known as the Foreign Service of the United States.

Sec. 2. That the official designation "Foreign Service officer" as employed throughout this Act shall be deemed to denote permanent officers in the Foreign Service below the grade of minister, all of whom are subject to promotion on merit, and who may be assigned to duty in either the diplomatic or the consular branch of the Foreign Service at the discretion of the President.

Sec. 3. That the officers in the Foreign Service shall hereafter be graded and classified as follows, with the salaries of each class herein affixed thereto, but not exceeding in number for each class a proportion to the total number of officers in the service represented in the following percentage limitations: Ambassadors and ministers as now or hereafter provided; Foreign Service officers as follows: Class 1, 6 per centum, $9,000; class 2, 7 per centum, $8,000; class 3, 8 per centum, $7,000; class 4, 9 per centum, $6,000; class 5, 10 per centum, $5,000; class 6, 14 per centum, $4,500; class 7, $4,000; class 8, $3,500; class 9, $3,000; unclassified, $3,000 to $1,500; *Provided,* That as many Foreign Service officers above class 6 as may be required for the purpose of inspection may be detailed by the Secretary of State for that purpose.

Sec. 4. That Foreign Service officers may be appointed as secretaries in the Diplomatic Service or as consular officers or both; *Provided,* That all such appointments shall be made by and with the advice and consent of the Senate; *Provided further,* That all official acts of such officers while on duty in either the diplomatic or the consular branch of the Foreign Service shall be performed under their respective commissions as secretaries or as consular officers.

Sec. 5. That hereafter appointments to the position of Foreign Service officer shall be made after examination and a suitable period of probation in an unclassified grade or, after five years of continuous service in the Department of State, by transfer therefrom under such rules and regulations as the President may prescribe: *Provided,* That no candidate shall be eligible for examination for Foreign Service officer who is not an American citizen: *Provided further,* That reinstatement of Foreign Service officers separated from the classified service by reason of appointment to some other position in the Government service may be made by Executive order of the President under such rules and regulations as he may prescribe.

All appointments of Foreign Service officers shall be by commission to a class and not by commission to any particular post, and such officers shall be assigned to posts and may be transferred from one post to another by order of the President as the interests of the service may require: *Provided,* That the classification of secretaries in the Diplomatic Service and of consular officers is hereby abolished, without, however, in any wise impairing the validity of the present commissions of secretaries and consular officers.

Sec. 6. That section 5 of the Act of February 5, 1915 (Public, 242), is hereby amended to read as follows:

"Sec. 5. That the Secretary of State is directed to report from time to time to the President, along with his recommendations, the names of those Foreign Service officers who by reason of efficient service have demonstrated special capacity for promotion to the grade of minister, and the names of those Foreign Service officers and employees and officers and employees in the Department of State who by reason of efficient service, an accurate record of which shall be kept in the Department of State, have demonstrated special efficiency, and also the names of persons found upon taking the prescribed examination to have fitness for appointment to the lower grades of service."

Sec. 7. That on the date on which this Act becomes effective the Secretary of State shall certify to the President, with his recommendation in each case, the record of efficiency of the several secretaries in the Diplomatic Service, consuls general, consuls, vice consuls of career, consular assistants, interpreters, and student interpreters then in office and shall, except in cases of persons found to merit reduction in rank or dismissal from the service, recommend to the President the recommissioning, without further examination, of those then in office as follows:

Secretaries of class one designated as counselors of embassy, and consuls general of classes one and two as Foreign Service officers of class one.

Secretaries of class one designated as counselors of legation and consuls general of class three as Foreign Service officers of class two.

Secretaries of class one not designated as counselors, consuls general of class four, and consuls general at large as Foreign Service officers of class three.

Secretaries of class two, consuls general of class five, consuls of classes one, two, and three, and Chinese, Japanese and Turkish secretaries as Foreign Service officers of class four.

Consuls of class four as Foreign Service officers of class five.

Secretaries of class three, consuls of class five, and Chinese, Japanese, and Turkish assistant secretaries as Foreign Service officers of class six.

Consuls of class six as Foreign Service officers of class seven.

Secretaries of class four and consuls of class seven as Foreign Service officers of class eight.

Consuls of classes eight and nine as Foreign Service officers of class nine.

Vice consuls of career, consular assistants, interpreters, and student interpreters as Foreign Service officers, unclassified.

Sec. 8. That consuls general of class one and consuls of class one holding office at the time this Act takes effect shall not, as a result of their recommissioning or reclassification, suffer a reduction in salary below that which they are then receiving: *Provided, however,* That this provision shall apply only to the incumbents of the offices mentioned at the time this Act becomes effective.

That the grade of consular assistant is hereby abolished, and that all consular assistants now in the service shall be recommissioned as Foreign Service officers, unclassified.

Sec. 9. That sections 1697 and 1698 of the Revised Statutes are hereby amended to read as follows:

"Every secretary, consul general, consul, vice consul of career.

or Foreign Service officer, before he receives his commission or enters upon the duties of his office, shall give to the United States a bond, in such form as the President shall prescribe, with such sureties, who shall be permanent residents of the United States, as the Secretary of State shall approve, in a penal sum not less than the annual compensation allowed to such officer, conditioned for the true and faithful accounting for, paying over, and delivering up of all fees, moneys, goods, effects, books, records, papers, and other property which shall come to his hands or to the hands of any other person to his use as such officer under any law now or hereafter enacted, and for the true and faithful performance of all other duties now or hereafter lawfully imposed upon him as such officer: *Provided,* That the operation of no existing bond shall in any wise be impaired by the provisions of this Act: *Provided further,* That such bond shall cover by its stipulations all official acts of such officer, whether as Foreign Service officer or as secretary in the Diplomatic Service, consul general, consul, or vice consul of career. The bonds herein mentioned shall be deposited with the Secretary of the Treasury."

Sec. 10. That the provisions of section 4 of the Act of April 5, 1906, relative to the powers, duties, and prerogatives of consuls general at large are hereby made applicable to Foreign Service officers detailed for the purpose of inspection, who shall, under the direction of the Secretary of State, inspect the work of offices in the Foreign Service, both in the diplomatic and the consular branches.

Sec. 11. That the provisions of sections 8 and 10 of the Act of April 5, 1906, relative to official fees and the method of accounting therefor shall include both branches of the Foreign Service.

Sec. 12. That the President is hereby authorized to grant to diplomatic missions and to consular offices at capitals of countries where there is no diplomatic mission of the United States representation allowances out of any money which may be appropriated for such purpose from time to time by Congress, the expenditure of such representation allowance to be accounted for in detail to the Department of State quarterly under such rules and regulations as the President may prescribe.

Sec. 13. Appropriations are authorized for the salary of a private secretary to each ambassador who shall be appointed by the ambassador and hold office at his pleasure.

Sec. 14.   That any Foreign Service officer may be assigned for duty in the Department of State without loss of class or salary, such assignment to be for a period of not more than three years, unless the public interests demand further service, when such assignment may be extended for a period not to exceed one year. Any Foreign Service officer of whatever class detailed for special duty not at his post or in the Department of State shall be paid his actual and necessary expenses for travel and not exceeding an average of $8 per day for subsistence during such special detail: *Provided,* That such special duty shall not continue for more than sixty days, unless in the case of trade conferences or international gatherings, congresses, or conferences, when such subsistence expenses shall run only during the period thereof and the necessary period of transit to and from the place of gathering: *Provided further,* That the Secretary of State is authorized to prescribe a per diem allowance not exceeding $6, in lieu of subsistence for Foreign Service officers on special duty or Foreign Service inspectors.

Sec. 15.   That the Secretary of State is authorized, whenever he deems it to be in the public interest, to order to the United States on his statutory leave of absence any Foreign Service officer who has performed three years or more of continuous service abroad: *Provided,* That the expenses of transportation and subsistence of such officers and their immediate families, in traveling from their posts to their homes in the United States and return, shall be paid under the same rules and regulations applicable in the case of officers going to and returning from their posts under orders of the Secretary of State when not on leave: *Provided further,* That while in the United States the services of such officers shall be available for trade conference work or for such duties in the Department of State as the Secretary of State may prescribe.

Sec. 16.   That the part of the Act of July 1, 1916 (Public, Numbered 131), which authorizes the President to designate and assign any secretary of class one as counselor of embassy or legation, is hereby amended to read as follows:

"*Provided,* That the President may, whenever he considers it advisable so to do, designate and assign any Foreign Service officer as counselor of embassy or legation."

Sec. 17.   That within the discretion of the President, any Foreign Service officer may be appointed to act as commissioner, chargé d'affaires, minister resident, or diplomatic agent for such period as the public interests may require without loss of grade, class, or salary: *Provided, however,* That no such officer shall receive more than one salary.

That section 1685 of the Revised Statutes as amended by the Act entitled "An Act for the improvement of the Foreign Service, approved February 5, 1915," is hereby amended to read as follows:

"Sec. 1685. That for such time as any Foreign Service officer shall be lawfully authorized to act as chargé d'affaires ad interim or to assume charge of a consulate general or consulate during the absence of the principal officer at the post to which he shall have been assigned, he shall, if his salary is less than one-half that of such principal officer, receive in addition to his salary as Foreign Service officer compensation equal to the difference between such salary and one-half of the salary provided by law for the ambassador, minister, or principal consular officer, as the case may be."

Sec. 18. The President is authorized to prescribe rules and regulations for the establishment of a Foreign Service retirement and disability system to be administered under the direction of the Secretary of State and in accordance with the following principles, to wit:

(a) The Secretary of State shall submit annually a comparative report showing all receipts and disbursements on account of refunds, allowances, and annuities, together with the total number of persons receiving annuities and the amounts paid them, and shall submit annually estimates of appropriations necessary to continue this section in full force and such appropriations are hereby authorized: *Provided,* That in no event shall the aggregate total appropriation exceed the aggregate total of the contributions of the Foreign Service officers theretofore made, and accumulated interest thereon.

(b) There is hereby created a special fund to be known as the Foreign Service retirement and disability fund.

(c) Five per centum of the basic salary of all Foreign Service officers eligible to retirement shall be contributed to the Foreign Service retirement and disability fund and the Secretary of the Treasury is directed on the date on which this Act takes effect to cause such deductions to be made and the sums transferred on the books of the Treasury Department to the credit of the Foreign

Service retirement and disability fund for the payment of annuities, refunds, and allowances: *Provided,* That all basic salaries in excess of $9,000 per annum shall be treated as $9,000.

(d)   When any Foreign Service officer has reached the age of sixty-five years and rendered at least fifteen years of service he shall be retired: *Provided,* That the President may in his discretion retain any such officer on active duty for such period not exceeding five years as he may deem for the interest of the United States.

(e)   Annuities shall be paid to retired Foreign Service officers under the following classification, based upon length of service and at the following percentages of the average annual basic salary for the ten years next preceding the date of retirement: Class A, thirty years or more, 60 per centum; class B, from twenty-seven to thirty years, 54 per centum; class C, from twenty-four to twenty-seven years, 48 per centum; class D, from twenty-one to twenty-four years, 42 per centum; class E, from eighteen to twenty-one years, 36 per centum; class F, from fifteen to eighteen years, 30 per centum.

(f)   Those officers who retire before having contributed for each year of service shall have withheld from their annuities to the credit of the Foreign Service retirement and disability fund such proportion of 5 per centum as the number of years in which they did not contribute bears to the total length of service.

(g)   The Secretary of the Treasury is directed to invest from time to time in interest-bearing securities of the United States such portions of the Foreign Service retirement and disability fund as in his judgment may not be immediately required for the payment of annuities, refunds, and allowances, and the income derived from such investments shall constitute a part of said fund.

(h)   None of the moneys mentioned in this section shall be assignable, either in law or equity, or be subject to execution, levy, or attachment, garnishment, or other legal process.

(i)   In case an annuitant dies without having received in annuities an amount equal to the total amount of his contributions from salary with interest thereon at 4 per centum per annum compounded annually up to the time of his death, the excess of the said accumulated contributions over the said annuity payments shall be paid to his or her legal representatives; and in case a Foreign Service officer shall die without having reached the retirement age the total amount of his contributions with accrued interest shall be paid to his legal representatives.

(j) That any Foreign Service officer who before reaching the age of retirement becomes totally disabled for useful and efficient service by reason of disease or injury not due to vicious habits, intemperance, or willful misconduct on his part, shall, upon his own application or upon order of the President, be retired on an annuity under paragraph (e) of this section: *Provided, however,* That in each case such disability shall be determined by the report of a duly qualified physician or surgeon designated by the Secretary of State to conduct the examination: *Provided further,* That unless the disability be permanent, a like examination shall be made annually in order to determine the degree of disability, and the payment of annuity shall cease from the date of the medical examination showing recovery.

Fees for examinations under this provision, together with reasonable traveling and other expenses incurred in order to submit to examination, shall be paid out of the Foreign Service retirement and disability fund.

When the annuity is discontinued under this provision, before the annuitant has received a sum equal to the total amount of his contributions with accrued interest, the difference shall be paid to him or to his legal representatives.

(k) The President is authorized from time to time to establish, by Executive order, a list of places in tropical countries which by reason of climatic or other extreme conditions are to be classed as unhealthful posts, and each year of duty at such posts, while so classed, inclusive of regular leaves of absence, shall be counted as one year and a half, and so on in like proportion in reckoning the length of service for the purposes of retirement.

(l) Whenever a Foreign Service officer becomes separated from the service except for disability before reaching the age of retirement, 75 per centum of the total amount of contribution from his salary without interest shall be returned to him.

(m) Whenever any Foreign Service officer, after the date of his retirement, accepts a position of employment the emoluments of which are greater than the annuity received by him from the United States Government by virtue of his retirement under this Act, the amount of the said annuity during the continuance of such employment shall be reduced by an equal amount: *Provided,* That all retired Foreign Service officers shall notify the Secretary of State once a year of any positions of employment accepted by them stating the amount of compensation received therefrom and whenever any such officer fails to so report it shall be the duty of the Secretary of State to order the payment of the annuity to be suspended until such report is received.

(n) The Secretary of State is authorized to expend from surplus money to the credit of the Foreign Service retirement and disability fund an amount not exceeding $5,000 for the expenses necessary in carrying out the provisions of this section, including actuarial advice.

(o) Any diplomatic secretary or consular officer who has been or any Foreign Service officer who may hereafter be promoted from the classified service to the grade of ambassador or minister, or appointed to a position in the Department of State shall be entitled to all the benefits of this section in the same manner and under the same conditions as Foreign Service officers.

(p) For the purposes of this Act the period of service shall be computed from the date of original oath of office as secretary in the Diplomatic Service, consul general, consul, vice consul, deputy consul, consular assistant, consular agent, commercial agent, interpreter, or student interpreter, and shall include periods of service at different times in either the Diplomatic or Consular Service, or while on assignment to the Department of State, or on special duty, but all periods of separation from the service and so much of any period of leave of absence as may exceed six months shall be excluded: *Provided,* That service in the Department of State prior to appointment as a Foreign Service officer may be included in the period of service, in which case the officer shall pay into the Foreign Service retirement and disability fund a special contribution equal to 5 per centum of his annual salary for each year of such employment, with interest thereon to date of payment compounded annually at 4 per centum.

Sec. 19. In the event of public emergency any retired Foreign Service officer may be recalled temporarily to active service by the President and while so serving he shall be entitled in lieu of his retirement allowance to the full pay of the class in which he is temporarily serving.

Sec. 20. That all provisions of law heretofore enacted relating to secretaries in the Diplomatic Service and to consular officers, which are not inconsistent with the provisions of this Act, are hereby made applicable to Foreign Service officers when they are designated for service as diplomatic or as consular officers, and that all Acts or parts of Acts inconsistent with this Act are hereby repealed.

Sec. 21.   That the appropriations contained in Title I of the Act entitled "An Act making appropriations for the Departments of State and Justice and for the Judiciary and for the Departments of Commerce and Labor for the fiscal year ending June 30, 1925, and for other purposes," for such compensation and expenses as are affected by the provisions of this Act are made available and may be applied toward the payment of the compensation and expenses herein provided for, except that no part of such appropriation shall be available for the payment of annuities to retired Foreign Service officers.

Sec. 22.   The titles "Second Assistant Secretary of State" and "Third Assistant Secretary of State" shall hereafter be known as "Assistant Secretary of State" without numerical distinction of rank; but the change of title shall in no way impair the commissions, salaries, and duties of the present incumbents.

There is hereby established in the Department of State an additional "Assistant Secretary of State," who shall be appointed by the President, by and with the advice and consent of the Senate, and shall be entitled to compensation at the rate of $7,500 per annum.

The position of Director of the Consular Service is abolished and the salary provided for that office is hereby made available for the salary of the additional Assistant Secretary of State herein authorized.

Sec. 23.   That this Act shall take effect on July 1, 1924.

Approved, May 24, 1924.

EXECUTIVE ORDER

(June 7, 1924)

Regulations Governing the Reorganized Foreign Service.

Whereas, The Congress, by the Act of May 24, 1924, has confirmed and given statutory recognition to the civil service status of the Foreign Service established by the Presidential Executive Orders of June 27, 1906, for the Consular Service, and November 26, 1909, for the Diplomatic Service,

And, whereas, under the provisions of the said Act of May 24, 1924, the President is authorized to prescribe certain rules and regulations for administering the Foreign Service on an interchangeable basis.

Now, therefore, the President, in the exercise of the powers conferred upon him by the Constitution and laws of the United States, makes the following regulations:

1. Vacancies in all classes from 1 to 9 shall be filled by promotion from lower classes, based upon ability and efficiency as shown in the service.

2. All admissions to the service shall be to the grade of Foreign Service Officer, unclassified.

3. Officers and employees, after five years of continuous service in the Department of State, are eligible for appointment by transfer to any class in the Foreign Service upon the recommendation of the Foreign Service Personnel Board and with the approval of the Secretary of State as hereinafter provided.

The Foreign Service Personnel Board.

4. There is hereby constituted a Foreign Service Personnel Board composed as follows:

The Under Secretary of State, who shall be the Chairman, an Assistant Secretary of State to be designated by the Secretary of State, the Director of the Consular Service (on and after July 1, 1924, this title becomes Assistant Secretary of State), and the members of the Executive Committee of the Foreign Service Personnel Board.

5. It shall be the duty of the Board:

(a) To examine into the character, ability, efficiency, experience and general availability of all secretaries in the diplomatic service, consuls general, consuls, vice consuls of career, consular assistants, interpreters and student interpreters, and before July 1, 1924, to submit to the Secretary of State such information as he may require regarding the efficiency records of such officers.

(b) From time to time after the Act of May 24, 1924, becomes effective, and as vacancies arise, to submit to the Secretary of State lists of those Foreign Service Officers whose records of efficiency entitle them to advancement in the service, and who are therefore recommended for promotion, and the names of those officers and employees in the Department of State who, after five years of continuous service, and because of special ability and merit are recommended for appointment by transfer to the position of Foreign Service Officer. All such lists to be signed by the Chairman and at least three members of the Board, except in the case of a tie vote when the Secretary of State shall decide.

(c) To submit to the Secretary of State the names of those Foreign Service Officers who, in the opinion of the Board, have demonstrated special capacity for promotion to the grade of Minister. Each list thus submitted shall enumerate the names of the officers in the order of merit and shall be complete in itself, superseding all previous lists. A list shall be submitted to the Secretary of State whenever there is a vacancy in the grade of Minister or when requested by the President or the Secretary of State and in no case shall it contain more names than there are vacancies to fill. Each such list shall be signed by the Chairman and at least three members of the Board, and if approved by the Secretary of State, shall be submitted to the President.

(d) To submit to the Secretary of State the names of those Foreign Service officers who are recommended for designation as counselors of embassy or legation.

(e) To recommend to the Secretary of State the assignment of Foreign Service Officers to posts and the transfer of such officers from one branch of the service to the other according to the needs of the service.

(f) To consider controversies and delinquencies among the service personnel and recommend to the Secretary appropriate disciplinary measures where required.

For the purposes stated in paragraphs (e) and (f), the Under Secretary of State, the Assistant Secretary of State and the Director of the Consular Service (on and after July 1, 1924, this title becomes Assistant Secretary of State) shall be deemed to constitute the full Board, but the Executive Committee shall have the power of recommendation.

6. Whenever it is determined that the efficiency rating of an officer is poor and below the required standard for the Service, the Personnel Board shall so notify the officer, and if after due notification the rating of such officer continues nevertheless to be unsatisfactory, his name shall be reported to the Secretary of State with a full recital of the circumstances and a recommendation of the Board for separation from the service.

Whenever such recommendation for separation from the service is made, the Board shall at the same time notify the officer of the action taken.

7. The members of the Board, individually and collectively, shall have authority to examine all records and data relating to the personnel of the service.

8. All action taken by the Board shall be strictly nonpartisan, and based exclusively upon the record of efficiency of the officers concerned.

9. The proceedings of the Board shall be strictly confidential, but the Chairman may, and it is hereby made a part of his duty, within a reasonable time prior to each meeting of the Board for recommending promotions, demotions or removals, to invite the Chairman of the Senate Committee on Foreign Relations and the Chairman of the House Committee on Foreign Affairs or some Committee member designated by the Chairman, to sit with the Board through its deliberations without, however, participating in its decisions.

10. The Board shall elect its Secretary from among its members.

The Executive Committee.

11.   There is hereby constituted an Executive Committee of the Foreign Service Personnel Board to be composed of a Chairman, and two other members who shall be Foreign Service officers of high rank representing both the diplomatic and the consular branches of the Foreign Service, to be selected by the other members of the Personnel Board with the approval of the Secretary of State.

The Secretary of State is authorized to prescribe the duties of the Executive Committee.

The Board of Examiners.

12.   There is hereby constituted a Board of Examiners composed of the following members; to wit: The Under Secretary of State, an Assistant Secretary of State to be designated by the Secretary of State, the Director of the Consular Service (on and after July 1, 1924, this title becomes Assistant Secretary of State), the Chairman of the Executive Committee of the Foreign Service Personnel Board, and the Chief Examiner of the Civil Service Commission or such person as may be designated by him to serve in his stead.

13.   It shall be the duty of the Board of Examiners to formulate rules for and hold examinations of applicants for commission to the Foreign Service and to determine from among the persons designated by the President for examination those who are fitted for appointment.

14.   The scope and method of the examinations shall be determined by the Board of Examiners, but among the subjects shall be included the following: at least one modern language other than English (French, Spanish, or German by preference), elements of international law, geography, the natural, industrial, and commercial resources and the commerce of the United States; American history, government and institutions; the history since 1850 of Europe, Latin America and the Far East; elements of political economy, commercial and maritime law.

15.   The examinations shall be both written and oral.

16.   Examinations shall be rated on a scale of 100, and no person rated at less than 80 shall be eligible for certification.

17.   No one shall be certified as eligible who is under twenty-one or over thirty-five years of age, or who is not a citizen of the

United States, or who is not of good character and habits and physically, mentally, and temperamentally qualified for the proper performance of the duties of the Foreign Service, or who has not been specially designated by the President for appointment subject to examination and to the occurrence of an appropriate vacancy.

18. Upon the conclusion of the examinations, the names of the candidates who shall have attained upon the whole examination the required rating will be certified by the Board to the Secretary of State as eligible for appointment.

19. The names of candidates will remain on the eligible list for two years, except in the case of such candidates as shall within that period be appointed or shall withdraw their names. Names which have been on the eligible list for two years will be dropped therefrom and the candidates concerned will not again be eligible for appointment unless upon fresh application, designation anew for examination, and the successful passing of such examination.

20. Applicants for appointment who are designated to take an examination and who fail to report therefor shall not be entitled to take a subsequent examination unless they shall have been specifically designated to take such subsequent examination.

21. In designations for appointment subject to examination and in appointments after examination, due regard will be had to the principle that as between candidates of equal merit, appointments should be made so as to tend to secure proportional representation of all the States and Territories in the foreign service; and neither in the designation for examination nor certification nor appointment after examination will the political affiliations of the candidates be considered.

22. The Board of Examiners is authorized to issue such notices and to make all such rules as it may deem necessary to accomplish the object of this regulation.

23. New appointments to the service shall be to the grade of Foreign Service Officer, unclassified, and no promotions to a higher grade shall be made except on the recommendation of the Foreign Service Personnel Board, with the approval of the Secretary of State, after the completion of one full term of instruction, or the equivalent thereof in the Foreign Service School hereinafter established.

24. Those candidates for appointment as diplomatic or consular officers whose names are on the eligible list at the time the Act of

May 24, 1924, becomes effective shall be eligible for appointment as Foreign Service Officers.

The Foreign Service School.

25. There is hereby established in the Department of State a Foreign Service School for the instruction of new appointees.

26. The Foreign Service School shall be under the direction of a Foreign Service School Board, composed of the following members; to wit: the Under Secretary of State, an Assistant Secretary of State to be designated by the Secretary of State, the Director of the Consular Service (on and after July 1, 1924, this title becomes Assistant Secretary of State), the Chairman of the Executive Committee of the Foreign Service Personnel Board, and the Chief Instructor of the Foreign Service School. The School Board will act in all matters with the approval of the Secretary of State.

27. The Chief Instructor shall be selected by the other members of the School Board from among the officers of the Foreign Service, with the approval of the Secretary of State.

28. Other instructors shall be selected from among the qualified officers of the Department of State, the Foreign Service, the other executive departments of the Government, and other available sources in the discretion of the School Board.

29. The term of instruction in the Foreign Service School is one year which shall be considered a period of probation during which the new appointees are to be judged as to their qualifications for advancement and assignment to duty. At the end of the term, recommendations shall be made to the Secretary of State by the Personnel Board for the dismissal of any who may have failed to meet the required standard of the Service.

30. The Secretary of State is authorized to prescribe rules and regulations for the governance of the Foreign Service School.

CALVIN COOLIDGE

THE WHITE HOUSE,
    June 7, 1924.

[No. 4022.]

Appendix G

DEPARTMENTAL ORDER

(No. 295)

Executive Committee of the Foreign Service Personnel Board.

With a view to strengthening and improving the personnel of the Foreign Service and securing uniform and impartial ratings for all officers and employees, the following duties are hereby prescribed for the Executive Committee of the Foreign Service Personnel Board under the authority contained in the Executive Order of the President, dated June 7, 1924.

1. To take into its possession and consolidate immediately all records and material relating to the personnel of the foreign service, both diplomatic and consular. The Diplomatic Bureau, the Consular Bureau and the Office of Consular Personnel will promptly surrender all such files and records as may be in their possession.

2. To keep the efficiency records of all Foreign Service Officers and employees.

3. To collect, collate, and record pertinent data relating to foreign service personnel.

4. To submit to the Foreign Service Personnel Board recommendations for the assignment of officers to posts and the transfer of such officers from one branch of the service to the other.

5. To recommend the granting of leaves of absence.

6. To interview applicants and prospective applicants for the Foreign Service.

7. To examine and recommend for appointment applicants for positions as subordinate employees in the Foreign Service.

8.   To maintain contact with Foreign Service Officers and employees while on visits to the United States. For this purpose a register of visiting officers and employees shall be kept.

All personnel records shall be held strictly confidential, and no papers, documents, data or reports relating thereto shall be revealed except to the Secretary of State, the members of the Foreign Service Personnel Board, and the Board of Review.

At least once a year, or whenever the Secretary of State shall so order, all personnel records, ratings and accumulated material shall be examined impartially by a Board of Review and a report rendered to the Foreign Service Personnel Board as to the relative standing of officers and employees. The Board of Review shall be composed of five members, of whom the Chairman of the Executive Committee shall be the Chairman, and the remaining four drawn from Foreign Service Officers of high rank by the Secretary of State.

CHARLES E. HUGHES

DEPARTMENT OF STATE,
    June 9, 1924.

DEPARTMENTAL ORDER

(No. 296)

The Foreign Service School.

The President by Executive Order of June 7, 1924, having provided for the establishment of a Foreign Service School in the Department of State, the following rules and regulations are hereby made for the governance of the School:

1. The Chief Instructor shall be selected from among Foreign Service Officers of class five or over.
2. He shall have the following duties:

   (a) To prepare and submit to the School Board for approval a complete schedule of work to be covered during the term of instruction.

   (b) To select instructors in the various subjects from among the qualified officers of the Department of State, the Foreign Service, the other Executive Departments of the Government, and other available sources.

   (c) To instruct the School in subjects selected and approved by the Board.

   (d) To maintain the discipline of the School and bear responsibility therefor.

   (e) To keep a record of attendance and an impartial, confidential rating of each pupil with respect to his qualifications for the Foreign Service.

   (f) To act as a member of the School Board.

   (g) To make reports on the work of the School and the individual pupils at the end of the term of instruction or whenever required by the School Board or the Secretary of State.

3. Each term of instruction shall begin and end on dates to be fixed by the School Board.

4. Each foreign service pupil shall be assigned to one of the divisions or bureaus of the Department of State, where he will report for duty when not attending classes.

5. The Chiefs of the divisions or bureaus shall report to the Chief Instructor the character of the work done by the pupils assigned to them, together with any delinquencies.

CHARLES E. HUGHES

DEPARTMENT OF STATE,
  June 9, 1924.

EXECUTIVE ORDER
(April 4, 1924)

Establishing a System of Cooperation Abroad.

The following regulations are hereby prescribed for the guidance of the representatives of the Government of the United States in foreign countries with a view to giving unified direction to their activities in behalf of the promotion and protection of the commercial and other interests of the United States, insuring effective cooperation, and encouraging economy in administration.

Whenever representatives of the Department of State and other Departments of the Government of the United States are stationed in the same city in a foreign country they will meet in conference at least fortnightly under such arrangements as may be made by the chief diplomatic officer or, at posts where there is no diplomatic officer, by the ranking consular or other officer.

It shall be the purpose of such conferences to secure a free interchange of all information bearing upon the promotion and protection of American interests.

It shall be the duty of all officers to furnish in the most expeditious manner, without further reference, all economic and trade information requested by the ranking officers in the service of other Departments of the Government assigned to the same territory; Provided, That where such compliance would be incompatible with the public interest or where the collection of such information requires research of such exhaustive character that the question of interference with regular duties arises, decision as to compliance shall be referred to the chief diplomatic officer or to his designated representative or, in the absence of such officers, to the supervising consular officer in the said jurisdiction. All failures to provide information requested as hereinbefore set forth shall be reported immediately by cable to the Departments having jurisdiction over the officers concerned.

With a view to eliminating unnecessary duplication of work officers in the same jurisdiction shall exchange at least fortnightly a complete inventory of all economic and trade reports in preparation or in contemplation.

Copies of all economic and trade reports prepared by consular or other foreign representatives shall be filed in the appropriate embassy or legation of the United States or, where no such office exists, in the consulate general and shall be available to the ranking foreign representatives of all Departments of the Government. Extra copies shall be supplied upon request by the officer making the report.

The customary channel of communication between consular officers and officers of other Departments in the foreign field shall be through the supervising consul general but in urgent cases or those involving minor transactions such communications may be made direct; Provided, That copies of all written communications thereof are simultaneously furnished to the consul general for his information. It shall be the duty of supervising consuls general to expedite intercommunication and exchange of material between the consular service and all other foreign representatives of the United States.

Upon the arrival of a representative of any Department of the Government of the United States in any foreign territory in which there is an embassy, legation or consulate general, for the purpose of special investigation, he shall at once notify the head of the diplomatic mission of his arrival and the purpose of his visit and it shall be the duty of said officer or of his designated representative, or in the absence of such officer, then the supervising consular officer, to notify, when not incompatible with the public interest, all other representatives of the Government of the United States in that territory of the arrival and the purpose of the visit, and to take such steps as may be appropriate to assist in the accomplishment of the object of the visit without needless duplication of work.

In all cases of collaboration, or where material supplied by one officer is utilized by another, full credit therefor shall be given.

CALVIN COOLIDGE

The White House,
    April 4, 1924.

[No. 3987.]

INDEX

INDEX

A

Academy of Diplomacy advocated, 342

Academy of Foreign Relations proposed, 348

Academy, Foreign Service, proposed, 341

"A-4-C," Administrative unit of the Department of State, 202

Acts of:
  July 1, 1790, Diplomatic, 6
  April 14, 1792, Consular, 10
  February 28, 1803, Consular, 10
  February 13, 1806, Diplomatic, 8
  March 1, 1855, Diplomatic and Consular, 14, 59
  August 18, 1856, Diplomatic and Consular, 15
  March 1, 1893, creating ambassadors, 19, 60
  April 5, 1906, Consular, 21, 61
  March 2, 1909, restricting appointment of ambasadors, 61
  February 5, 1915, Diplomatic and Consular, 29, 61
  May 24, 1924, Foreign Service Reorganization, 62, 255

Adams, John, letters to John Jay, 263, 268

Adams, John Quincy, letter to Secretary of State, 269

Adams, John Quincy, Memoirs, quotation from, 51

Agents:
  consular, 130
  diplomatic, 104, 282
  secret, the use of, 45

Agricultural agents, 161, 216

Agricultural Economics, Bureau of, 162, 218

Agriculture, Department of, 161
  consular cooperation with, 217
  consular functions of, 191
  International Institute of, 178, 217

Ambassadors, 102
  appointment of, 60
  appointment from Career Service, 242
  grade established, 18

Appointment of Foreign Service officers, 258, 259

Appointments and promotions, consular, 23, 30, 45, 51, 58, 130

Appointments and promotions, diplomatic, 26, 30, 45, 51, 58

Arbitration of outstanding pecuniary claims between the United States and Great Britain, 172
  Permanent Court of, 176

Articles of Confederation, 5

Assignments to Department of State, 31, 90, 281

Assignments and transfers, 297

Assistant Secretaries of State selected from the career service, 244

Attachés, 152
  commercial, 155, 159, 203
  military, 152, 154
  naval, 154

B

Bonds of Foreign Service officers, 282

Boundary, Alaska and Canada, and the United States and Canada, 170

British retirement system compared, 323

Bureau of Agricultural Economics, 162

Bureau of Foreign and Domestic Commerce, 156, 160, 202

Bureau of Manufactures, 202

Bureau of Statistics, 201

Bureau of Trade Relations, 202

Business, engaging in, prohibited, 15, 21, 31, 114

Business interests support merit system, 24, 25

431